Interpretive Theories of Religion

Religion and Reason 20

Method and Theory
in the Study and Interpretation of Religion

MOUTON PUBLISHERS · THE HAGUE · PARIS · NEW YORK

Interpretive Theories of Religion

DONALD A. CROSBY

Colorado State University

MOUTON PUBLISHERS · THE HAGUE · PARIS · NEW YORK

ISBN: 90-279-3039-2

Printed in Great Britain

To William A. Christian

Preface

The subject of this book is a particular, but very basic problem in the philosophy of religion, that of trying to arrive at an adequate theory of the nature of religion. I have approached this problem in three main ways; methodologically, by laying out the task of what I call 'interpretive' theories of religion and identifying some possible types of such theories; historically, by presenting, comparing, and criticizing four important theories of religion from the past; and constructively, by developing a theory of my own, exploring its relations to the other four theories, and discussing certain advantages I believe it to have over the other theories. By combining these three approaches, the book should serve as a useful overview of this problem in the philosophy of religion, and of the relations of this problem to other aspects of the discipline. It should also contribute to an understanding of the nature of religion itself, a contribution that is of obvious importance in its own right and has implications for areas of study other than the philosophy of religion.

I began writing this book during a year's sabbatical leave at Yale University which extended from the Fall of 1971 through the Spring of 1972. Yale graciously accorded me the privilege of being a Postdoctoral Research Fellow in the Department of Religious Studies, where I worked primarily with William A. Christian, who was then a member of the faculty of that department and whose writings and general outlook on the philosophy of religion have influenced me greatly. Professor Christian has read this book in various stages of its development and has offered many insightful suggestions and criticisms. Also, several of my past or present colleagues in the Department of Philosophy at Colorado State University have read parts of the manuscript and made valuable comments: Winston King, Richard Kitchener, and Patrick McKee. And three other colleagues, James Boyd, Bernard Rollin, and Holmes Rolston III, have read and criticized the book in its entirety. I am grateful to all of these friends for their interest in this project and for their very able assistance in helping me to bring it to completion. Lastly, I wish to express my thanks to Colorado State University for its grant of a sabbatical leave.

Donald A. Crosby
Fort Collins, Colorado

Contents

Part One

Methodological

The Task of an Interpretive Theory of Religion

1. SCOPE AND AIM OF THIS BOOK

There are many paths to the study of religion. Some of them are intent upon professing, defending, or criticizing whole religions, or upon assessing or arguing the plausibility of specific religious claims. This is true, for example, of theology and religious philosophy. Others work to contribute to our understanding of the religious side of human history and experience but make no attempt to settle religious questions one way or another. Examples of this approach are history of religions, phenomenology of religions, and (usually) psychology of religion and anthropological studies of religion. As an essay in analytical philosophy of religion, this book falls into the second category.

'Analytical' philosophy of religion, as I will use the term, inquires into the meaning of religious statements and into the patterns of reasoning by which they are linked together in religious systems, without trying to decide on their truth or falsity.[1] And as part of this enterprise, it seeks to clarify the sort of basic interest to which religious statements and systems give expression. The latter is the main concern of this book.

Accordingly, this book differs from most other studies of religion in its degree of generality. Its focus is not upon any given religion or set of religious practices and teachings, nor upon a comparison of particular religions with one another. Instead, it addresses itself to the single (though certainly not simple) question: What can be said about the nature of religion as such, not in its manifold concrete detail, but in its generic character as a fundamental type of human interest? My aim in reflecting on this question is fivefold: to delineate the task of what I shall call interpretive theories of religion; to decide which of the possible types of interpretive theories of religion seems best suited to the purposes of analytical philosophy of religion; to consider and exemplify some of the problems raised by the search for such a theory; to survey and criticize some representative past theories of religion; and to develop and defend a new theory of religion. In pursuing this last aim I will of course draw upon the history and literature of religions, and, in fact, that will be the background of the discussions throughout the book.

2. THEORIES AND DEFINITIONS OF RELIGION

The task of constructing theories of religion needs to be distinguished from that of trying to arrive at definitions of 'religion'. It might be thought that the two tasks come down to the same thing, but there are several reasons for concluding that they do not. For one thing, among the usual goals of a definition is that of terseness, an economy and brevity of expression typified by this definition of an Euclidian triangle: 'a three-sided, closed figure in a single plane, the sum of whose angles is one-hundred and eighty degrees'. But the concept of religion is far more complex than that of an

Euclidian triangle, and it is not likely that it will admit of satisfactory characterization by a few well-chosen words. Also, a concise definition will tend to be so abstract that it will gloss over important nuances and ramifications of religious concerns. A theoretical treatment, by contrast, is under no such obligation to be terse and thus permits elaboration of the subleties of its subject at whatever length seems to be required.

A second difference is also important. Definitions center on terms, and the question for a descriptive definition of religion is how the term 'religion' is used and how to take account of its various uses in a brief formula. But the question for a theory of religion is how to unfold the structure of an entire line of inquiry, a whole way of interpreting experience and looking at the world. Consideration of the uses of the term 'religion' might enter into this process of theorizing as one of its phases, but it could only be a phase, only one of many problems to be dealt with.

This second point might be disputed as follows. The type of definition spoken of is a descriptive definition, which states the accepted meaning or meanings of a term in use. But what we are really after in talking about a definition of relgion is a theoretical definition, because the term 'religion' is too vague and ambiguous in use to be reduced to a descriptive definition. But this objection helps to make the third point I wish to develop in distinguishing between definitions of religion and theories of religion. The kind of definition required would be, I agree, a theoretical one. But theoretical definitions cannot stand alone. They are dependent on theories, since they make use of theoretical terms and acquire their overtones of meaning from the context of theories. So the point is that, while one outcome of deliberating on the nature of religion might be a theoretical definition, it would be a mistake to conceive of this as its primary goal. For the primary goal is the construction of the theory itself, for which the definition can serve only as a convenient summary or short-hand designation. Thus a definition like, 'Religion is that which grows out of, and gives expression to, experience of the holy in its various aspects' might prove to be useful as a handy way of referring to Rudolf Otto's theory of religion (as set forth in Otto, 1958) but it would have little specific meaning in isolation from that theory.

3. INTERPRETIVE AND NORMATIVE THEORIES OF RELIGION

The task of an interpretive theory of religion is different from that of a normative theory of religion. A normative theory tells us what, in the theorist's view, religion <u>ought</u> to be, rather than offering a neutral interpretation of what is is. Or it implies some conclusion about the value of religion in general or the truth or falsity of religions or religious claims in particular. This kind of theory is not appropriate for analytical philosophy of religion, which concerns itself with the meaning and systematic relations of religious statements, including the conditions for making and assessing religious truth-claims, but not with the task of actually trying to settle questions of the truth or falsity, value or disvalue, of such statements or of the systems of thought in which they may be contained.

Of course, a certain type of norm is implied in the very activity of searching for an adequate interpretive theory of religion, namely, norms for distinguishing an adequate from an inadequate theory. I will offer a list of such norms or criteria in the course of this and the following chapter. But these are methodological norms, suited to that kind of activity, not norms of religious value or truth. It is also evident that I value the endeavor to understand the nature of religion, else I would not have bothered to write this book. But this is different from trying to set forth a theory of religion which itself tries to distinguish between good and bad, true and false, religion.

An example might help to clarify the concept of a normative theory of religion and of its difference from an interpretive theory. As part of his theory of religion, which centers religion in 'the feeling of absolute dependence', Friedrich Schleiermacher presented the norm that the highest religion will be the one in which this feeling appears 'in its complete unity and indifference to all that the sensible self-consciousness may contain'. And he used this norm for the apologetic purpose of arguing that monotheistic religions are higher in the scale of truth than polytheistic ones, and that Christianity is superior to other monotheistic religions such as Judaism and Islam (Schleiermacher 1928:35-38). An important part of the task of an interpretive theory of religion is to avoid, so far as is possible, such normative features. Such a theory should help us to understand the differences between religious interest and other kinds of cultural interests, and to distinguish religion from nonreligion, but it should not contain judgments about the superiority or inferiority of particular expressions of religious interest.

4.   INTERPRETIVE THEORIES OF RELIGION, DESCRIPTIONS, AND DESCRIPTIVE GENERALIZATIONS

The task of an interpretive theory of religion can be further explained by distinguishing theories as such from descriptions and descriptive generalizations. The goal of a pure description is to recount or specify as precisely as possible the distinct details of various kinds of events, processes, or situations. Ideally, no interpretation or explanation of these details is attempted in a description, although some interpretation will creep in of necessity in the very process of selecting and emphasizing certain details over others, and in the kinds of linkage among facts which are suggested by our way of recounting them. And of course, nothing can be described in words without the use of some kind of nomenclature for the facts being talked about, so any verbal description will inevitably involve elemental kinds of classification and generalization. To state that this is a 'dog', for example, is to assign it to a particular class of animals, which, in its turn, is a particular class of beings.

But a descriptive account should remain as close to the particularities of a phenomenon as possible, and a person intent upon providing a pure description must be continually on guard lest conventional or unconsciously assumed schemes of classification or interpretation blind him to the richness of concrete detail exhibited in the phenomenon. This is an ideal to be striven for, although it can never be completely attained, since language, acculturation, and past experience make all encounters with phenomena to some extent theory-laden.

While preoccupation with particularity is characteristic of pure descriptions (to the extent that they can be attained), it is natural that at some point one would wish to order the descriptive data and fit them into some more manageable and comprehensive scheme of classification and generalization. It might also be desirable to coordinate a number of descriptive accounts in this way. When this happens, the phase of what I shall call descriptive generalization is entered, i.e., generalizing from the descriptive accounts. The task is now that of describing classes of phenomena instead of the phenomena themselves.

Ideally, this phase is entered only when the descriptive phase is well under way, so as to avoid premature generalization. And again ideally, the classifications and generalizations should be allowed to grow as directly out of the data themselves as is possible, and not be superimposed upon those data. Another way to put this to say that the generalizations should be arrived at through correct inductive inferences. And if the descriptive generalizations are inductively derived, it should be possible to move back and forth from the descriptive accounts to the generalizations, the latter being reducible to the former.

Now it might be thought that a theory of religion could be inductively derived in just this fashion, that through exhaustive comparisons of the religious facts in a variety of cultures, systems, and times we should at last arrive at the traits of religion itself, in a kind of crowning generalization.

Such a theory of religion could then be spoken of as a 'descriptive' theory in the sense of its being a high-level descriptive generalization.

I have avoided the term 'descriptive' theory of religion because it suggests this notion of the task of a theory of religion, which I take to be misconceived on several counts. First, the concept of what are to count as the religious data in culture or human experience is itself a highly theoretical concept. As one noted student of religion has remarked, the very selection of such data for analysis requires 'a concealed or openly operative concept of the essence of religion' (Tillich 1969b: 55). So developing a theory of religion is not a matter of simply generalizing from a base of perfectly obvious, indisputable facts. Second, there is an element of arbitrariness in all schemes of classification that becomes more pronounced as we increase their scope, and this fact militates against the notion that something with the extremely large scope of a theory of religion could be arrived at through a strictly inductive method. Third, and most important, even if we could arrive at a set of traits characteristic of each and every religion by a process of simple description and descriptive generalization, we still would not have a theory of religion. To see why this is so, we need to consider the nature of theories and the ways in which they differ from generalizations.

The first thing to notice about theories is that they are constructed, posited, or invented. They are not generalizations from the facts. Instead, they are bold imaginative constructions, stimulated and informed by reflections upon putative facts and generalizations, but not to be thought of as either derived from them in a straightforward logical manner or as reducible to them. Another way to put this is to say that generalizations pose theoretical problems rather than providing theoretical answers. Reliable generalizations will be of many different sorts, each of more limited scope than is possible for a theory. It is the task of the theory to coordinate these generalizations by bringing them into the unity of a common perspective or general scheme of interpretation.

This brings us to a second characteristic of theories. Their purpose is interpretive or explanatory, not merely descriptive. C. J. Bleeker makes this observation about his own field of study, phenomenology of religions: 'From the studies of its adherents it appears that nobody is any longer content with a pure description of the religious facts. People want to understand their significance and structure' (Bleeker 1963:5-6). This concern for the 'significance and structure' of religious phenomena cannot be satisfied merely by the amassing of descriptive data or generalizations, for it is a theoretical concern. It calls for insightful and lucid interpretation of the facts rather than for a recounting of them or elaborate classifications of them. And different sorts of theories, including theories of religion, can provide contexts for such interpretation.

Theories gain their interpretive power by providing speculative structures which can serve to order data into coherent patterns of meaning. This is a third characteristic of theories. Its importance is brought out forcefully in an article by John Findlay in which he discusses critically a study of mysticism by Walter Stace and then goes on to give his own account of 'the logic of mysticism'. Findlay takes Stace to task for having arrived merely at an enumeration of common traits of a variety of cases commonly recognized as instances of mysticism, his allegation being that the outcome of Stace's study 'is a rag-bag of empirical features, having no plain philosophical significance'. What he means by 'philosophical significance' is spelled out in the following passage (Findlay 1966:152):[2]

I do not regard any mere decanting and classification of empirical fact as genuine philosophical investigation. Philosophy is to me the bringing forth, not the mere registration or discovery, of conceptions which are what I should call intelligible unities, whose various components hang together necessarily, or with some approach to rational necessity, and which alone can illuminate the complex windings of fact.... If mysticism or the mystical is to be a worthwhile theme for philosophical study, it must be a coherent, notional unit, and a coherent notional unit which is necessary for the understanding of man and the world, and so rightly reckoned as fundamental.

Clearly, what Findlay is after is a theory of mysticism, for it is characteristic of theories that they do not merely catalogue or describe but interpret or explain facts and generalizations by means of some kind of intelligible structure or scheme which explores the rational connections of theoretical categories. Similarly, any account of religion which disclosed no illuminating interplay, tensions, or connections among theoretical categories, but simply listed generalized traits and held them up to view, could not be said to be a theory of religion.

A final feature of theories is their deployment as heuristic devices. Their main contribution, as one writer aptly phrases it, 'is the heuristic one of furnishing new conceptual insight, of allowing one to view the old from an intellectually unaccustomed vantage point, and in terms of novel explanatory principles' (Swanson 1967:247). The construction of a theory is not the terminus of a process of investigation but a way of putting it on a new footing. A good theory will pose intriguing new questions, kindle new insights, and give a fresh focus to our thinking, as we continue our inquiries into the 'structure and significance' of descriptive data.

Since they do function as heuristic devices, a variety of theories on the same subject is not as unwelcome as divergent descriptive results would be. Different theories of religion might prove heuristically fruitful in different ways, and each that did would be valuable in its own right, although each might not be equally valuable. It would be a mistake, certainly, to dream of finding the theory of religion which would make all the rest obsolete or render unnecessary any further investigations into the problem of explicating religion's generic structure. The possibility, and even the desirability, of a variety of theories of religion, each with its different illuminating interpretation of the nature of religion, is another reason for my preferring to speak of 'interpretive' rather than 'descriptive' theories of religion.

Even though no finally adequate theory of religion is likely to be found, this does not mean that there can be no progress in the development of such theories. A new theory of religion can incorporate or build upon the insights made available

in previous theories which have come to be regarded
as illuminating and valuable. At the very least it
can complement these 'established' theories, high-
lighting aspects of religion which, despite their
theoretical significance as demonstrated by the new
theory, have been neglected or insufficiently
emphasized by them. I have tried to encompass
aspects of some previous theories in the development
of my own theory of religion, to be presented later
on. But I would not want to claim that it can substitute entirely for those theories, because each
well-devised theory is a conceptual whole whose
heuristic value is in some respects unique and
resists capture by the piecemeal appropriations of
another theory.

5. INTERPRETIVE AND EXPLANATORY THEORIES OF RELIGION

Still another way to demarcate the task of an
interpretive theory of religion is to contrast it with
the task of an explanatory theory of religion. An
explanatory theory of religion will provide some
model or hypothesis designed to explain why religion
first came into being, or why religious institutions,
systems, and practices have loomed so large in
human history, or why new religions arise at certain
points in time. The main interest of an explanatory
theory is in the causes of religion, so it could also
be termed a causal theory of religion. But it may
also try to say something about the nature of
religion based on an analysis of its causes. Such a
theory will also contain or imply some predictive
statements to the effect that, in the presence or
absence of specified causal conditions, religion (or

perhaps a certain type of religion) will or will not be present in individual or social life.

Two examples of explanatory theories of religion can be mentioned, one from the field of psychology, and the other from anthropology. Sigmund Freud (1957, 1970)[3] developed a psychological theory of religion on the model of obsessional neuroses observed clinically in children. Religion is a 'collective neurosis' to which humanity succumbed at an early stage of its development when it was not yet able to deal rationally with the powers of nature or its own instinctive drives. As such, it is an 'illusion' resulting from the sense of helplessness, bewilderment, and frustration in the face of these forces—or more fundamentally, from human ignorance. If this hypothesis is correct, then it can be predicted that, with a growing capacity for reason and the acquisition of sophisticated knowledge about the natural world and the dynamics of the psyche, the hold of religion over human life will be broken. And this was Freud's expectation. Note that there are explicit normative features of this theory as well.

An anthropological example would be a theoretical development of Anthony F. C. Wallace's suggestion (1956:267-268, also 1966:30-39) that the historical origin of a great proportion of religious phenomena has been in 'revitalization' movements. Such movements might be taken as a model of religions in general, so far as their earliest phase of development is concerned. And by constructing a theory which built upon Wallace's description of revitalization movements and his specification of the conditions attendant upon their emergence, we might be able to predict the rise of new religions or the demise of old ones.

To the extent that predictions based on either of these two models turned out to be successful, it would be contended that we have gained insight into the causes (and perhaps into the nature)[4] of religion. Of course, theories of this type can have genuine explanatory value only if they make a sound case for our thinking that the explanatory causes they appeal to are necessary and sufficient to account for the occurrence of the predicted result, so as to avoid the fallacy of affirming the consequent.

To take the example of Freud's theory, should there be a sharp decline of interest in religion in technological societies (as many would argue there has already been), this might be due to a dulling of the finer sensibilities following upon a general dehumanizing and trivializing of life, and not merely to the vanishing of an illusion. Or it might be a sign of the breakup of old religious traditions as a prelude to the emergence of new ones. The long span of time involved and the absence of easy repeatability is a problem with theories of such sweeping historical scope. Freud's theory might be tested in terms of what happens when primitive cultures come into contact with technological societies, but a problem here is that the entire primitive culture usually undergoes drastic change, and not just its religious aspect. In the case of individuals who might become less interested in traditional forms of religion after psychoanalysis, we would have to inquire into the degree of manipulation involved in psychoanalysis, the extent to which the psychoanalytic worldview can itself be termed 'religious', and so on.

As I am defining its task, an interpretive theory of religion will not concern itself, except incidentally, with the causes of religion. An investigation of these comes much more under the competence and concerns of the sciences, especially the social sciences, than of philosophy. The problem of an interpretive theory of religion is not that of explaining why religion is present in human life, but what it means to say that some aspect of human life is religious. Its task is conceptual clarification rather than causal explanation. To the extent that claims about the nature of religion are made on the basis of an investigation of its causes, an analysis of the logic of these claims might be of philosophical interest, but the causal route to a theory of the nature of religion is not the route taken by an interpretive theory of religion. The presence of religious interest, and of systems of thought and practice growing out of that interest, will be taken as given rather than problematic by this sort of theory. I might add that there is a certain priority of interpretive to explanatory theories of religion. For in order to explain why religion exists or to predict its occurrences we must first have some notion of what it is that we are trying to explain, i.e., some notion of what religion itself is.

6. INTERPRETIVE THEORIES OF RELIGION AND THEORIES IN PHYSICS

Much of the current connotative aura of the word 'theory' results from its use in the natural sciences, especially physics. What has been said so far about the nature of theories applies both to interpretive theories of religion and to theories in physics. Both are posited rather than logically derived from descriptive data. Both interpret descriptive data through some sort of speculative scheme which can explicate conceptual relations among theoretical categories. And both function as heuristic devices, implementing further investigations and discoveries. But there are also some important differences between the two kinds of theories, and a discussion of these can help to clarify still further the concept of an interpretive theory of religion.

Full-blown theories in physics can be said to consist of the following ingredients: (1) some sort of deductive calculus, i.e., a mathematical system, from which logical entailments in precise quantitative terms can be drawn; (2) a theoretical model, which postulates theoretical entities and processes and interprets them in terms of the deductive calculus; (3) correspondence rules, which link the calculus and model with certain known empirical laws and with predictive statements, so as to make these deducible from the calculus and model; (4) the empirical laws so deduced; and (5) the predictive statements so deduced. When the predictive statements are successfully tested in practice through application of the theory, then it is said to be validated or empirically confirmed. (For a fuller development of the characteristics of theories in the natural sciences see Hempel 1966, especially Chapter 6, 'Theories and Theoretical Explanation'.)

Such a theory is explanatory in at least the following senses. First, it coordinates, and therefore affords a central conceptual perspective on, a range of laws and phenomena previously uncoordinated. Second, these laws and phenomena are coordinated in a way that is highly impressive to the rational mind, viz., as entailment relations. Third, if the theory can be shown to be coherent with previously established theories, or if it can be shown that some of these are subsumable under it, then this coherence bestows explanatory significance on the theory. Fourth, the theoretical entities and processes posited by the theory can give a plausible account of the character and workings of events which before were opaque to understanding. And finally, the successful predictions of a theory, sometimes of events or regularities not even discovered before its formulation (for examples of this see Hempel 1966:77) greatly enhance confidence in its explanatory power.

An interpretive theory of religion will differ from this kind of theory in at least the following respects. It will (at least typically) contain no deductive calculus, mathematical or otherwise. Instead of positing unobservable entities and processes as its theoretical categories, it will posit what might be termed categories of 'analysis'. Entities and processes are posited by theories in physics in the attempt to shed light upon the inner workings of natural phenomena, and so constitute part of a causal explanation. The categories of analysis in an interpretive theory of religion, by contrast, are ways of inquiring into the distinctive character of the human interest to which religious systems, practices, and institutions give cultural expression.

Implicit in the fact that it does not seek to give a causal explanation of religion is the further difference that empirical laws and predictions do not come within the purview of an interpretive theory of religion. As has already been noted, such a theory will provide us with a way of rationally coordinating and understanding generalizations and descriptions. But the generalizations it concerns itself with will not be in the form of statements about lawlike behavior (except perhaps indirectly), and its descriptive aspect will not take the form of predictions. As for correspondence rules, these may or may not be stated by an interpretive theory of religion, but there will be the need for some sort of procedure, even if informal and only assumed, for moving back and forth from the descriptive data to the theoretical categories. A matter of some importance for an interpretive theory of religion, as we have already seen, is the extent to which it can incorporate or build upon important insights made available in previous theories. In this respect interpretive theories of religion and theories in physics are of course similar.

A final difference between interpretive theories of religion and theories in physics is also a difference from theories in religion. While intepretive theories of religion are theories about the nature of religious interest, theories in physics are not theories about the nature of scientist interest. They express scientific interest, just as theories in religion (theories about God and Brahman, for example) would express religious interest. This does not mean that interpretive theories of religion cannot also express religious interest, even as they seek to interpret the nature of religion. But they need not. They may express philosophical interest, as when they are developed from the standpoint of analytical philosophy of religion. Or they may express some combination of religious and philosophical interest. The case is similar with explanatory theories of religion, which typically would express a scientific interest but might also express a religious or philosophical interest, or perhaps even some combination of all three.

7. INTERPRETIVE THEORIES OF RELIGION AND THE EPISTEMOLOGY OF RELIGION

The search for an interpretive theory of religion can be viewed as part of the epistemology of religion, and when so viewed its task dovetails with the larger tasks of philosophy of religion and philosophy as such. Religious claims, and doctrinal schemes comprising such claims, pose certain epistemological problems which are of vital interest to the philosophy of religion. These claims and schemes can be approached as the outcome of a process of religious inquiry. And when they are, an understanding of the logic of religious inquiry becomes an important step in the direction of understanding the logic of religious discourse.[5]

Religious inquiry, like all fundamental lines of inquiry, presupposes a fundamental sort of interest, i.e., a religious interest. But what is a religious interest? Call it an interest in 'F', where 'F' is a predicate variable expressing the distinctive focus or object of religious interest. Religious inquiry, then, is the active pursuit of an answer to the question, 'What is it that is F'? The answer, once arrived at, will then be the basic claim of a given religion. For example, Judaism would have as its basic claim, 'Yahweh is F'. Theravada Buddhism would have as its basic claim, 'Nirvana is F'. And so forth. Each religion's doctrinal scheme can now be construed as an extensive elaboration of the meaning of this basic claim, spelling out its implications for thought and action.

It is obviously important for this kind of analysis that there be some content for the predicate variable 'F'. And this is where an interpretive theory of religion comes in. It supplies us with a predicate or set of predicates to go with the logical subjects proposed by the different religions. This predicate or set of predicates will be common to all religions, while the subject will vary, depending on the religion. Each religion has its own distinctive subject, such as 'Yahweh', 'Nirvana', 'Brahman', 'Ohrmazd', 'Allah', etc.

What holds true for the analysis of particular religious systems also holds for the analysis of the relation of various religious systems to one another. Without consensus on a common predicate or set of predicates for the basic claims of different religions (e.g., 'the Holy', as a predicate supplied by Otto's theory), we cannot even formulate those claims, much less proceed to analyze respects in which they differ or concur. But when we understand that Judaism is claiming that Yahweh is the Holy; Hinduism, that Brahman is the Holy; and so on (presuming for the moment that we had settled on Otto's theory of religion as being the most adequate one), then we have an important basis for comparison. So an interpretive theory of religion is one key to problems which arise when we try to make a comparative analysis of the meanings of different basic claims of religions, and of their doctrinal schemes to the extent that each rests upon or explicates a different basic claim.

But a good theory of religion ought to do more for the epistemology of religion than supply us with a common predicate or set of predicates for basic religious claims, as important as that is. It ought also to suggest some of the possible lines of development open to religious schemes, helping us to understand why, with the exercise of some options, others are closed, or why certain tensions and problems tend to be characteristic of religions as such, while other ones are more characteristic of some religious system or systems than of others. Provision of this kind of clarification and under-standing of religious schemes is a kind of explana-tion, but it is not the causal type of explanation, which has been reserved for what I call explanatory theories of religion. Of course, no theory of religion will be able to give this kind of understand-ing by itself, but it should function as a useful point of departure for obtaining it. Herein will lie a significant part of its heuristic contribution.

8. SOME CRITERIA FOR INTERPRETIVE THEORIES OF RELIGION

Implicit in the preceding discussion were some criteria for interpretive theories of religion which can now be given explicit formulation. These criteria can serve as a summary of what has been said in this chapter about the task of an interpre-tive theory of religion. In the next chapter these criteria will be supplemented with some additional ones which become relevant in the process of think-ing about various theoretical options for fulfilling the task of an interpretive theory of religion. This task will therefore not have been completely defined until we have had occasion to develop the need for and to present those additional criteria. But its basic outline can be drawn as follows:

(1) An interpretive theory of religion should not contain norms of religious judgment.
(2) It should supply us with a structure of categories whose conceptual interplay, tensions, and

connections can illuminate the nature of religious interest.
(3) It should encompass, build upon, or complement previous theories which have value and importance for clarifying the nature of religion or significant aspects of religion.
(4) It should not give a causal explanation of why man is religious.
(5) It should prove heuristically fruitful for investigating the logic of single religious systems.
(6) It should prove effective for helping to bring into perspective some of the grounds of difference and similarity among various religious systems.

Criteria (1) and (4) set off the task of an interpretive theory of religion from the tasks of normative and explanatory theories of religion, respectively. Criterion (2) states the character of a theory as such, as over against definitions, descriptions, and descriptive generalizations, as well as expressing the subject matter of an interpretive theory of religion, which is the nature of religious interest. Criterion (3) reminds us that a new theory of religion need not be constructed in a vacuum but that it can and should profit from dialogue with the work of previous theorists. Criteria (5) and (6) suggest two uses to which we should be able to put such a theory in the study of religions, particularly in the philosophical study of religions.
The phrase 'logic of single religious systems' in criterion (5) perhaps needs some explanation, for I do not mean for it to refer only to implicative relations which might hold among propositions. I mean for it to designate the patterns of reasoning, of whatever sort, which give unity and cohesiveness

to a particular system, so that it can properly be called a 'system', rather than being taken simply as an aggregate of disconnected sentences.[6] The following statement of Ninian Smart is instructive in this regard, although it may downplay too much the role of implicative relations in at least some religious systems (1958:13, Note 1; see also Smart's discussions of 'Organic Justification', 1958:40,127,199; 1970:122-124).

It should...be remarked that the notion of <u>premiss</u> is hardly applicable to doctrinal schemes, though there are some more or less central propositions from which others in a loose manner follow (perhaps it is best to say the former <u>suggest</u> rather than <u>imply</u> the latter); and indeed the discovery that an inference suggested by these more central propositions is allowable (and not, say, conducive to heresy) throws light on the sense of these propositions in a way in which the performance of an inference in a deductive system does not throw light on the sense of the premisses.

9.   SOME VALUES OF THIS KIND OF STUDY

One value of the kind of study offered in this book has already been discussed in section 7 of the present chapter, where we looked at the bearing of the search for an interpretive theory of religion upon problems in the epistemology of religion. Since such problems fall within the province of philosophy, this constitutes a philosophical value. Two other values of this kind of endeavor can also be briefly cited. One of these is again philosophical, while the other might be called educational or moral.

The second philosophical value of a study of this kind is the light it can shed on the place of religion within the whole context of human knowing, valuing, and acting. In other words, the construction of an interpretive theory of religion is relevant to the task of developing general theories of cultural interests and their interrelations. While not exclusively a philosophical problem, this is one to which philosophers through the years have devoted a good deal of attention.

A third value of this kind of study is educational or moral. It is educational because the task of trying to arrive at a theory which can bring into clearer focus that underlying interest to which all religions give expression is a difficult one, and its very difficulty underscores the rich variety of the religions of the world and the diversity of options they present to the religious seeker. We are thus delivered from too parochial and narrow a view of what religion is and of what it has meant and can mean in the life of man. Involvement in this task can contribute toward that generality of outlook and breadth of vision which is the final goal of all education.

And as Alfred North Whitehead reminds us, 'morality of outlook is inseparably conjoined with generality of outlook' (1957:23). So this task has its moral significance too, in that it can be one way of freeing us from instinctive intolerance, suspicion, and distrust of people of different religious backgrounds by showing that their religious problems and concerns are not utterly alien to our own, that religion is a human phenomenon first, and only secondarily a culturally indigenous one. By stimulating us to think about religion in general, the quest for an interpretive theory of religion can deepen our awareness of religions in particular and our sensitivity to the very human longings and strivings of their adherents. The importance of such awareness need not be labored in a world where religious differences continue to pit person against person and nation against nation.

2

Some Theoretical Options

Some different types of interpretive theories of religion will be sketched in this chapter. This list of types is not meant to be exhaustive, but only to point to some of the more obvious logical alternatives. There is also some overlap of the types, so we can speak of different theories as incorporating different combinations of types. While each combination may well have value for one purpose or another, one combination would seem to be the most appropriate kind of theory for the purposes of analytical philosophy of religion. Reasons for this conclusion will be brought out as the discussion proceeds. Largely on the basis of this discussion some additional criteria for appraising interpretive theories of religion (at least from the standpoint of analytical philosophy of religion) will be formulated.

The types of theories to be discussed are as follows: experiential, ontological, functional, reductive, and autonomic theories of religion. Each type can be briefly characterized, then we will go on to look at each one in greater detail. An 'experiential' theory is one which gives an account of the nature of religious experience, as compared and contrasted with other types of experience. In this way it tries to get at the nature of religion. An 'ontological' theory depicts religious interest as being an interest in a certain kind of ontological entity or entities with specific defining attributes. Or it may regard the focus of religious interest as being-itself or the infinite power of being which grounds and sustains all particular beings. A 'functional' theory provides an account of the work or performance that is peculiar to objects of religious interest. A 'reductive' theory tries to make a case for the reducibility of religion to some more fundamental kind of interest (e.g., moral, philosophical, aesthetic), while an 'autonomic' theory views religious interest as autonomous, i.e., as not as reducible because fundamental in its own right.

I will argue that the most promising kind of theory of religion for our purposes is one which will be functional and autonomic. But I will distinguish between two senses of 'functional', opting for what I term the 'role-functional' type of interpretive theory of religion.

1. EXPERIENTIAL THEORIES OF RELIGION

This first sort of theory seeks to isolate and specify a certain state (or combination of states) of consciousness which, when present in human subjects, marks them as being religious or as undergoing religious experience. Schleiermacher's theory of religion, at least in terms of its basic tendency and emphasis, can be cited as an example of this sort of theory. Schleiermacher points to 'the feeling of absolute dependence' as the uniquely religious mode of consciousness, and his theory examines this mode and its relationships to nonreligious modes like the feeling of freedom and the feeling of partial dependence. He goes on to make reference to God as the 'Whence' of the religious consciousness and to ascribe attributes and modes of operation to God. In addition, he makes claims of a theological nature concerning the constitution of the world. But neither of these topics have any specifically religious import, he insists, except to the extent that they can be shown to grow out of or to be rooted in the feeling of absolute dependence, as the uniquely religious type of experience. So the essence of religion lies in this type of experience, and nowhere else.

Experiential theories of this sort have the value of giving insight into the way religion looks from the 'inside', or from an immediate personal perspective. By conveying something of the tone and impact of first-hand religious experience, such theories serve to remind us that no account of religion can be adequate or complete which concentrates simply on the externals of various dogmas and practices. As Schleiermacher observes, these are not 'pious' (religious) merely in themselves, but need to formulated, entertained, or performed with a certain kind of motive. And a consideration of the character of that motive, and of the modes of consciousness which underlie or comprise it, is an important way of contributing to an understanding of the nature of religion (Schleiermacher 1928:8-10, 12-26, 125-128).

But there is one main disadvantage of this type of theory, so far as its usefulness for analytical philosophy of religion is concerned. And that is that it is too one-sided. Religious systems do stress the importance of having certain kinds of experiences, and they frequently insist on the experiential rootage of their central claims. But they are as intent, if not much more intent, on exploring the objective meaning of what is disclosed in the experiences, i.e., what it is that the experiences are experiences of. In other words, they expound on the cosmic nature or role of some object of religious interest, such as God, Nirvana, or Tao. Experiential theories fail to take this cosmic side of religion sufficiently into account in their preoccupation with the traits of experiencing subjects.

Suppose, for example, that the feeling of absolute dependence came to be focused by someone on his parents. Would the mere possession of the feeling be sufficient to mark that person as being religious, i.e., as having his parents as the object of his religious concern? I do not think that it would. We would be much more likely to speak of such utter dependency as pathological rather than religious (of course, one can be pathologically religious, but that is another matter). For however much the parents might satisfy the meaning of religion on its personal side in such a case, they would still lack the cosmic status accorded by religious systems to such objects of interest as God, Nirvana, or Tao. Schleiermacher does state (1928: 18) that to have the feeling of absolute dependence center on particular perceptible objects (such as one's parents) would be a 'corruption' of true religion. But the issue being raised here is whether the case cited would count as religion at all. And his theory seems to require that it would.

Since analytical philosophy of religion undertakes the task of trying to understand as fully as it can the meaning of religious claims, both singly and in the context of religious systems, it would be remiss if it gave the whole, or even the bulk, of its attention to only a part of those claims and systems, that part having to do with the traits of religious experience. Religion has an objective and a subjective side, or as I shall term them, a 'cosmic' and a 'personal' side. And an interpretive theory of religion should try to do justice to both. This can be considered a seventh criterion for interpretive theories of religion:

(7) An interpretive theory of religion should give equal stress to the personal and the cosmic sides of religion.

The experiential type of theory would be more appropriate if our philosophical concern were that of trying to achieve a precise phenomenological analysis of what religious experience is like. In other words, it seems more appropriate to phenomenological than to analytical philosophy of religion. Such a theory is also quite appropriate for the descriptive side of the psychology of religion.

2.   ONTOLOGICAL THEORIES

Examples of ontological theories of religion would be theories which center on such entities as 'God', 'gods', 'spirits', 'superhuman beings', 'supernatural beings', and the like. Thus the anthropologist Melford Spiro, after asserting that all institutions consist of belief systems, action systems, and value systems, contends that religion 'differs from other institutions in that its three component systems have reference to superhuman beings' (Spiro 1966:96).[1] A theory which accepted this contention and then went on to devise as its theoretical categories a variety of types of superhuman beings and to provide some kind of conceptual ordering or interpretation of the rational interplay of these types, would be an ontological theory of religion, as I am here using the term. It should be noted that in interpreting religion by reference to such beings, a theory should not imply any judgment about whether they do in fact exist (if it is to remain an interpretive theory). So while its categories would be types of superhuman beings, it would not settle any question about their actual ontological status. For if it did, it would be to that extent normative in implication, i.e., deciding some important question bearing on the truth or falsity of religious claims.

The ontological type of theory could be said to have at least two advantages. On the one hand, it combines a considerable breadth of application with a means of making a sharp differentiation between religion and nonreligion. And on the other hand, it does considerable justice to the way the term 'religion' tends ordinarily to be used, at least in Western culture. Certainly it is true that many, if not most, religions have 'gods' or 'superhuman beings' as the focus of their interest. And systems like humanism or Marxism could easily be demarcated from those systems which presuppose the existence of such beings, thus resolving the chronic problem of whether they are or are not 'religious'. It might turn out, in terms of such a theory, that there are cultures without religion, but perhaps there is no compelling reason for thinking every culture must have religion. So we would trade some breadth of application for an appealing precision (Spiro 1966: 88-96).

And a glance at the dictionary will confirm quickly that the ordinary use of the term 'religion' assumes that it has to do with a being or beings of the sort referred to in Spiro's definition. Webster's New World Dictionary of the American Language: College Edition (1964), for example, has as its first entry under 'religion': 'belief in a divine or superhuman power or powers to be obeyed and worshiped as the creator(s) and ruler(s) of the universe'.

But offsetting these two advantages are some distinct disadvantages, at least as far as the purposes of analytical philosophy of religion are concerned. The most obvious disadvantage is that, while the ontological approach provides breadth enough, perhaps, for the methodological purposes of anthropologists who want a convenient and pragmatic way of distinguishing religious from nonreligious aspects of cultures they have under study, it is still too restrictive to satisfy the demands of analytical philosophy of religion, where a truly generic sort of theory is required. Implicit here is another criterion of interpretive theories of religion, the eighth in our growing list:

(8) An interpretive theory of religion should be adequately general, not provincial, in its scope.

An ontological theory of the kind discussed so far would not encompass Theravada Buddhism, Zen Buddhism, or Taoism, to mention but three systems of thought and practice widely regarded as religious even though their objects of primary interest cannot be thought of as a being or beings. And such a theory would force us to brand as nonreligious, systems like those of Plotinus and Paul Tillich, which would normally be taken as paradigms of religious philosophy. Spiro makes a rather weak attempt to include Theravada Buddhism in the scope of his ontological definition of religion by saying that the Buddha is a 'superhuman' being in the sense that he points the way for others to

enlightenment and final release (Spiro 1966:92).
But this surely is to stretch the meaning of the
word 'superhuman' too far, particularly since it
implies a distinction between human and superhuman
power for salvation that is alien to Theravada
Buddhism's whole outlook. Zen is equally devoid of
a focus upon spirits, gods, superhuman beings, and
the like. And the Tao which is central in Taoism is
not a being, but the source and ground of all
existent beings, a concept akin to Plotinus' 'One'
and Tillich's 'being-itself'.

We might be tempted in light of examples like
these to want to take a different route still within
the general type of ontological theories of religion,
and to claim that the ontological category of being
qua being, rather than any distinct being or
beings, is the root preoccupation of religions.
Victor Turner takes this approach in his Chihamba:
The White Spirit (1962; for a criticism of his
approach see Horton 1964:88-95), arguing that
religions with distinct spiritual beings can be
understood, on a deeper level of analysis, to be
concerned with the power of being-itself. But this
tack runs us afoul of those theological systems,
undeniably religious, in Judaism, Christianity, and
Islam, which insist that the object of worship be
regarded as a distinct being. The fact of the
matter seems to be that there is no ontological
category common to all religions. This version of
the ontological approach to an interpretive theory of
religion, as well as the other version, founders on
this fact. (For a detailed treatment of basic
ontological differences in the Christian, Buddhist,
and Hindu religions see Puligandla 1971.)

A second major disadvantage of the ontological
approach is that it tends to gloss over the

possibility that concentration on gods, spirits, superhuman beings, etc., may not arise out of religious but out of some other kind of interest, for example, a scientific, historical, or literary concern. There is also the alternative possibility that they may be in some cases only the means to the realization of a religious interest and not the direct object of the interest. Spiro's concern was with a characterization of religion as an institution, so this problem is not as acute for him as it would be for the sort of theory which tries to understand the nature of the interest that underlies and gives rise to religious institutions.

Another way to get at this second disadvantage of the ontological type of theory is to note that it has the opposite deficiency from the experiential type. That is, it is also one-sided in that it stresses the cosmic side of religion to the virtual neglect of its personal side. It fails to specify precisely what it is about personal concern with God, gods, being-itself, etc. that qualifies as peculiarly religious concern.

3.　FUNCTIONAL THEORIES

Disadvantages like these count against theories of religion which take the ontological approach. Another alternative, however, is to take a functional approach. A functional theory of religion would interpret for us what ends religion is instrumental to, and in that way clarify its nature; or it would try to shed light on the kind of role the object of religious interest plays in the religious person's life and in the cosmos as he conceives it. The first of these I will call the 'goal-functional' approach, and the second, the 'role-functional' approach in the development of theories of religion. The former, as we shall see, does not usually qualify as an example of an interpretive theory of religion. But the latter does. In fact, I take it to be the best kind of theory for our purposes, for reasons I will give as the discussion proceeds.

The functional approach in general seeks to characterize what religion is by giving us an account of what it does. And the goal-functional approach, in particular, tries to give us understanding of what religion does by specifying certain goals or ends it is said to fulfill, for individuals and/or for societies. Thus, on this account, the objects of religious interest are but means to the real objectives of religion. The terms 'goals', 'ends', and 'objectives' can be misleading, however, for the usual goal-functional theory is not meant to imply consciously entertained purposes but to put its finger on effects of religious systems that are but dimly understood by their adherents, if at all. Still, it is in terms of these effects that the nature of religion is to be analyzed and its presence explained.

A good example of the goal-functional approach to a theory of religion is contained in an article by the sociologist Robert Bellah, entitled 'The place of religion in human action' (1958). According to Bellah, religion has two great functions for society and for the individual personality. The first of these he calls the 'superego function', and its goal is to provide 'a set of symbols which stand above and give meaning to the values institutionalized in society'. Religion thus holds the line 'against meaninglessness at the highest level', giving a context of ultimate purpose and value to the young

adult as he emerges from the shelter of his family
into the challenges of the larger world.   Should
religion fail in this goal of 'pattern maintenance',
social norms and institutions would be undermined,
and in time, society itself would be destroyed
(Bellah 1958:145-146).

The second function Bellah terms the 'id
function' of religion, and its goal is controlling and
channeling the frustrations and tensions that come
inevitably with the living of life, and that stem from
things like troubles in work or in marriage, the
failure to live up to the moral standards sanctioned
by religion in its first function and internalized by
the individual from childhood, and the ultimate
threat of death.   By comforting and guiding the
individual in times of crisis, shame, and disappoint-
ment, religion performs a function for the adult re-
markably similar to that performed by the parents
for the child.   This is well borne out in its central
symbols, especially those having to do with re-
concilation with an offended deity or reunion with
a whole of which one is viewed as a separated part,
for these are replete with family images and
allusions.   The viability of a society depends in
large measure, in Bellah's analysis (1958:146-151),
on the ability of its religious traditions to achieve
this second goal of 'tension management'.   The
consequences of failure to achieve it can be
'cataclysmic'. [2]

The categories of a goal-functional theory,
then, will be specified individual and/or social ends,
and aspects of religious systems which are said to
conduce to those ends; and the theory itself will
explore the interconnections of means and ends.
This sort of theory has important values.

First, it can serve as a powerful reminder that religious systems and institutions do not exist in isolation, nor can they be fully understood if studied in isolation. Their influence on personal psychic life is profound, and they enter into the very fabric of social existence. Theories which help us to appreciate this fact, and to understand it in more detail, have a valuable contribution to make.

A second value of the goal-functional approach is the light it can perhaps shed on the nature of society itself, which helps to explain its particular appeal to students of culture such as anthropologists and sociologists. To the extent that a functional analysis of religion stressing its bearing on the needs and requirements of society is accurate, to that extent we can gain comprehension of the inner workings of social institutions, norms, and customs. Goal-functional theories might have a similar kind of relevance to our attempts to understand psychic processes.

Nevertheless, there are two defects in this approach, when viewed from the perspective of the task of interpretive theories of religion, as laid out in the previous chapter, and as far as the purposes of analytical philosophy of religion are concerned. The first defect is that the goal-functional type of theory is much closer to being a member of the class of explanatory theories of religion than the class of interpretive theories. It is usually employed as an attempted explanation of the presence and persistence of religion in human life and societies, as is so clearly shown by the example of Bellah's theory. But the task of an interpretive theory of religion, as we have seen, is not to explain why human beings are religious, but only what it means to say that they are religious. Goal-functional theories are therefore better suited to the endeavors of social scientists or psychologists than to those of analytical philosophers of religion.[3]

A second defect is that the goal-functional approach, while it can bring out the extent to which religion is tied in with the various elemental problems and needs of life, does not go nearly as far in clarifying for us the nature of religious interest as something deliberate and conscious, and not merely blind and groping; something pursued for its own sake, and not just instrumentally. Since the focus of this approach is commonly on the 'latent' meanings of religious systems, and not on those which are central and apparent for their adherents, it does not give us much assistance in getting clear about the conscious intent of religious inquiry, and it tends to bypass or even prejudge questions about the cognitive significance of religious claims. It is in the very nature of this approach that it does not focus on the face-value significance of religious claims but takes their significance to lie elsewhere, in the social or psychic goals to which they are said to conduce. The usefulness of the goal-functional approach for analytical philosophy of religion would seem to be much more restricted, therefore, than that of the role-functional approach, to which we now turn.

In his book Explanation in the Social Sciences (1963:44), Robert Brown notes that there are two sorts of questions that can be answered in a functional manner. The first is a question such as 'To what goal is this a means?' And the second is a question like 'What is the function of throwing rice at weddings?' The second question need make no request for a specification of means and goals; it asks only for a clarification of how the custom of throwing rice fits into the whole set of practices which make up the marriage ceremony. This too is a question about function, because it asks about the role, function, or mode of operation of some one thing within the context of a total system.

It is this second sense of 'function' that William Christian presumably has in mind when he says that one type of theory of religion refers 'to some function the religious object has in the experience of the religious person, some place it has in his universe'. And Christian's own definition of religion is a functional one in this second sense, for he defines it as an interest in what 'matters most' or what is 'most important' for a person, out of the whole range of his concerns (Christian 1957:33, 1941:415, also 1964, Chapter IV). We can note that the emphasis of this definition is on the psychic or personal side of religion, not on its cosmic side. But the phrase 'some place it has in his universe' can allow for a cosmic role accorded by the person to the focus of his concern, i.e., for his conception of its place and importance within the objective universe.

A role-functional theory of religion, then, is one which seeks to specify the role played by objects of religious interest within some larger context, such as the entirety of a person's aims, interests, or experiences; or such as the cosmos as a whole, viewed or interpreted in such a way as to accord a certain definite place to an object of religious concern. If both of these aspects are kept in balance, we will have a role-functional theory which abides by the seventh criterion for interpretive theories of religion, and which is able to incorporate the personal emphasis of experiential theories and the cosmic emphasis of ontological theories of religion. I contend that both of these aspects must be given justice if we are to understand the nature of religion. An outlook which lacks either aspect will not be religious in the full sense of the term.

The categories of a role-functional theory and their structure of interrelations will be designed to interpret the role which an object of interest has when it is an object of religious interest, much as (to use rather prosaic examples) a job description or a playscript will delineate the roles of persons filling that particular job or acting in that particular play. One way to clarify this concept of role-functional theories of religion is to contrast the logic of the categories of such a theory with the logic of attributes ascribed to the logical subject of a religion's basic claim.[4] The categories of the theory can serve as a set of predicates for such a claim, but their logical use is to assign a function or role to the logical subject, not to ascribe attributes to it. To revert to Brown's example of throwing rice at weddings, suppose it were the case that corn, salt, or sand were proposed as substitutes. Of course such customs usually just grow up, so the example is somewhat artificial. But it can be used to make the point. We might be able to interpret the function of this practice quite independently of a discussion of the different characteristics of rice, corn, salt, or sand. This would give us an answer to the question:

(i) What is the function of throwing something over the heads of the bride and groom at a particular point in the wedding ceremony?

Having decided upon the function of the practice, i.e., its role in the context of the total ceremony, we might then move to consider three other questions:

(ii) Does rice have this function, i.e., is it in fact used in this way?
(iii) Is it claimed that, of all candidates for performing this function, rice is best suited to perform it?
(iv) Is the claim justified, assuming that it is made?

Let us suppose that question (i) is answered in the following way: 'symbolizes the wishes of those in attendance for the fertility of the bridal pair, at the point where they leave the scene of the marriage rite, bound, as it were, for their nuptial bed'. Noting that the throwing of rice does perform this function by tradition would give us an affirmative answer to question (ii). We might then try to ascertain if anyone wishes to defend the tradition, perhaps by claiming that, of all candidates for performing that function (rice, corn, salt, sand, etc.), rice is best suited to perform it (question (iii)). Our next question might be whether this claim can be justified (question (iv)).

One thing to note about this series of questions is that only the fourth one would involve us directly in a consideration of the attributes of the various substances which might be alleged best to perform the function at issue. For instance, we might decide that rice is better than salt or sand, because a seed is a better fertility symbol than either of the other two substances. But we would not have as easy a time deciding between rice and corn, and a more detailed comparison of their attributes would

be required. And even then we might not be able
to make a clearcut decision between the two.

If we apply this schema of questions to an
analysis of the task of a role-functional theory of
religion, its primary task would be that of providing
an answer to a question similar to (i) above,
namely:

(i') What is the function of objects of religious
interest, i.e., what distinctive role can they be
said to play?

Having answered that question by means of our
theory we would then be in a position to pose other
questions:

(ii') Does Allah have this function in some system
of thought or practice?
(iii') Is it claimed that, of all candidates for
performing this function, Allah is best suited to
perform it?
(iv') Is this claim justified, assuming that it is
made?

An affirmative answer to (ii') identifies Allah as an
object of religious interest. The claim alluded to in
(iii') would be the basic claim of a religion, in this
case, Islam. But an important thing to note, again,
is that only in the case of question (iv') would we
get involved in a direct consideration of the attributes of Allah, as compared with the attributes of
other candidates for filling the role at issue
(Nirvana, Nature, the gods, Tao, Brahman,
Ohrmazd, the Triune God, Yahweh, or whatever).
In the case of Allah, this would mean
considering such ascribed attributes as 'Infinite

Power', 'Infinite Love', 'Infinite Mercy', 'Infinite Justice', and so forth, as well as the claim that Allah is the Creator and Ruler of the heavens and the earth and that he is a personal being. But these attributes and claims have a different logical use than the categories of a role-functional theory, even though both could be predicated of Allah. The role-functional theory does not tell us anything directly about Allah's nature (though it might imply something about what his nature is assumed to be by adherents of Islam), but only informs us of Allah's role as an object of religious interest. The question of whether Allah is best suited to fill the role or perform the function made explicit by the theory is quite another question. And it is a question which lies beyond the bounds of analytical philosophy of religion. Only in considering this question does the ascription and discussion of specific attributes become relevant.

The theory of religion which I will propose in Chapter 7 is a role-functional theory of the nature of religion. I find this type of theory to be better suited to the particular purposes of analytical philosophy of religion than any of the other types of theories discussed thus far, chiefly because it does not suffer from the disadvantages of those theories which I have pointed out. But I should add that no one type of theory can be completely adequate for all purposes, simply because each must emphasize some aspects of religion at the expense of other aspects. So there is a built-in limitation on each type of theory, namely, its selectivity, its restriction to only one approach and method. Accordingly, absence of some of the advantages of the other kinds of theory which have been cited will be disadvantages of the role-functional kind.

4.   REDUCTIVE THEORIES

By a reductive theory of religion I mean one which would make religious interest a subset of some other interest or interests taken to be more fundamental than it is. For example, religion might be subsumed under art, morality, science, philosophy, or a combination of some or all of these. But this reduction, to remain within the scope of interpretive theories of religion, would not be done for normative reasons. For example, it would not represent an attempt to eliminate religion from consideration as a fundamental type of interest on the ground of the deleterious effects it is alleged to have for individuals or societies, or on account of its alleged uselessness when standing alone.

Not only is (a) this normative sense of 'reductive' excluded from my use of the term, but some other possible meanings of it are also excluded. A specification of these might help to make my use clearer, as well as to point up ambiguities in the term which need sorting out.

(b) I do not mean a reduction of data. There is a sense in which every theory of religion will be reductive, i.e., it will reduce a mass of descriptive data to the interpretive categories of the theory itself. These categories and their interconnections will provide a way to view this mass of data as an ordered whole, as a relatively simple structure of relationships. But this reduction of data is not what is meant by a reductive theory of religion, because all theories by their very nature will be reductive in this sense.

(c) I mean a reduction of theories, rather than of data (in making this distinction I am following a suggestion of Hans Penner 1971:92), but only of theories of a certain type, viz., theories of cultural interests, where a theory of religious interest takes the form of an attempt to demonstrate the subsumption of this interest under a more encompassing theory of another kind of interest. This subsumption would be demonstrated if all that is essential in religion, e.g., its most typical sorts of problems, concerns, or claims, could be shown to admit of derivation from or translation into broader characteristic problems, concerns, or claims of another cultural interest, the nature of the latter having itself been delineated by a theory. A theory which interprets or explains religion in terms of theories of psychological or social behavior would not, therefore, be a reductive theory in my usage. This excludes goal-functional theories as such from the term 'reductive'.

It might be thought that goal-functional theories would be reductive in that they reduce religion to certain ends or goals, elaborated in the matrix of psychological or social theories. But it is evident that any basic human interest might be so interpreted or explained, with no necessary bearing on the question of its autonomy or reducibility to some more basic cultural interest. Melford Spiro alludes to a widespread methodological conviction among social scientists when he says that explanation of phenomena in terms of their social and psychological bases 'is precisely the task of the student of culture'. And he is right in arguing that this kind of explanation need not destroy the 'essential quality' of religion any more than analysis of a Brandenburg concerto in terms of its physical properties or constituents need destroy its essential quality for a lover of Bach's music (Spiro 1966:123, Note 3).

(d) Implicit in Spiro's way of making his point is a fourth sense of 'reductive' I mean to exclude from my use of the term. This sense would imply comission of the reductive fallacy. Reductive theories, as I am regarding them, need not succumb to this fallacy, though of course certain ones might. The reductive fallacy is committed whenever one argues in this way:

A is dependent on B (or B,C,D, etc.) for its occurrence. Therefore, A is nothing but B (or B,C,D, etc.).

If one were to infer that the reductive fallacy is committed whenever one attempts to understand one kind of phenomena in terms of other kinds of phenomena, or in terms of theories about those other kinds of phenomena, this would be to make many causal explanations fallacious, and this would be an egregious error. Similarly, to say that an interpretation of religion in terms of its putative ends or goals is necessarily to make it identical with those ends or goals would be a mistake. And finally, the reductive fallacy would be committed by a theory of religion which reduces religion to some other cultural interest only if the fallacious mode of reasoning were employed. And it need not be employed in making such a reduction, since the reduction could be argued for on other, more plausible, grounds. By this last statement I do not mean to suggest that reductive theories of religion correctly interpret the nature of religion, but only that they are generally not so obviously fallacious as the fourth sense of 'reductive' would imply.
    Let us now take a look at an example of a reductive theory of religion, one which in effect

subsumes religious interest under a theory of moral
interest. The theory is that of R. B. Braithwaite
(1955), as set forth in his Eddington Lecture, 'An
empiricist's view of the nature of religious belief'.
A theory of the nature of moral interest is implicit
in Braithwaite's notion of what constitutes a moral
assertion. A moral assertion is one which declares
a speaker's intention to act in certain ways, and
'the policy of action intended by the asserter should
be a general policy (e.g., the policy of utilitarian-
ism)' or it 'should be subsumable under a general
policy which the asserter intends to follow and
which he would give as the reason for his more
specific intention' (Braithwaite 1955:13). It would
seem to follow from this that a moral interest would
be characterized by Braithwaite as an interest in
general policies which can express one's intention to
follow certain broad courses of action, and which
can serve as reasons for intending more specific
actions.

The relationship between religious assertions
and moral assertions is brought out by this passage
in Braithwaite's lecture (1955:32):

A religious assertion, for me, is the assertation of
an intention to carry out a certain behavior policy,
subsumable under a sufficiently general principle
to be a moral one, together with the implicit or
explicit statement, but not the assertion of,
certain stories.

The basic difference between the two types of
assertion, then, is that in religious assertions an
intention to act in certain ways is associated with
(though not logically derivable from) certain
'stories', such as the Christian story of justification

by means of the atoning work of Christ. Belief in the truth of these stories is not necessary for their religious functioning. What is necessary is that they be entertained in a way which helps to focus and strengthen the resolve to carry out a policy of action. Differences among religions are claimed by Braithwaite to come down to differences in the stories with which intentions to act are associated, as well as to different patterns of life which may be intended.

From this we can infer that a religious interest would be an interest in general policies which can express one's intention to follow certain broad courses of action, and which can serve as reasons for intending more specific actions, and in stories with which these policies and intentions can be associated.[5] On this account, religion is a species of morality or an adjunct to morality, rather than being founded on an autonomous interest. Braithwaite's theory of religion is therefore an example of a reductive theory of religion.

I do not wish to criticize at length Braithwaite's theory of religion, although it is vulnerable to a number of criticism, most notably in its failure to take seriously enough the element of belief (or claims to truth) in religious discourse, and in its lack of consideration of the very real possibility that there are 'distinctively religious valuations', and not merely moral valuations, implicit in religious statements of intention to follow certain policies of action and in religious recommendations of those policies.[6] Rather, I want to make some criticisms of reductive theories of religion in general, criticisms which suggest that they create more problems than they give promise of solving.

Such a reduction seems inevitably to yield a narrow and lopsided view of the nature of religion, leaving out of account or minimizing in the extreme aspects of it to which a nonreductive approach would be more likely to give due consideration. The omissions in Braithwaite's theory, already alluded to, are a case in point. With regard to all theories which would reduce religion to morality, Willard Arnett makes the observation (1966:129) that from 'the strictly moral point of view, nothing is more obviously superfluous than many religious practices and teachings'. And he notes (ibid.) that

descriptions of the world and of how man is in the world and what he is and can hope for are no less fundamental and functional elements in the religious perspective than are prescriptions concerning what ought and ought not to be done... .[7]

Reductive theories, like Procrustes' bed, have a tendency to truncate a body of facts so as to force them into the theories, instead of accommodating theories to the demands of the facts. We often learn as much, if not more, about the nature of religion from what such theories minimize and over-look as from what they highlight and include. Another weakness of reductive theories is their inability to do justice to the fact that the relation between religion and other aspects of thought and life is not merely one-directional, but reciprocal. Granted that philosophic, moral, scientific, and aesthetic considerations often figure prominently in religious systems and practices, there is also ample evidence that the reverse is true. The profound influence of religious outlook and belief in the history of philosophy, morality, art, and even science in the West hardly needs detailed documentation (for a recent attempt to exhibit the presence of elements of religious interest in contemporary scientific thought see Gilkey 1970, Chapter II). Reductive theories are right in the stress they lay on the intricate connections of religious interest with other interests, but wrong in not recognizing that it is a matter of interconnections and interdependence, rather than a one-way street.

Finally, reductive theories of religion have the effect of broadening beyond recognition the type of interest to which they do reduce religion, when the attempt is made to include all the dimensions of religion. (I discuss this point in more detail in the context of Immanuel Kant's theory of religion, in Chapter 4).

5.   AUTONOMIC THEORIES

The alternative to a reductive theory is an 'autonomic' theory of religion. By this term I mean a theory which can do justice both to the autonomy of religious interest and to the many complex ways in which it can influence and be influenced by other kinds of human interest. Not only will such a theory avoid what seems to me to be the mistake of making religion a mere epiphenomenon of some other interest or interests. It will also steer clear of the even less defensible position which would portray religion as something so radically set apart from the rest of life that its connections with other interests are tangential rather than intimate. This suggests a ninth criterion of interpretive theories of religion:

(9) An interpretive theory of religion should enable us to distinguish religious interest from other basic types of human interest, and yet to do justice to the interdependence of religious and other interests.

6. A FINAL CRITERION

I also want to stress the importance of a tenth and final criterion for interpretive theories of religion, which runs as follows:

(10) An interpretive theory of religion should tell us what it means <u>not</u> to be religious, all or a part of the time, and aid us in deciding problematic cases.

A theory which made it impossible in principle for a person to be nonreligious would suffer from an implausible breadth, since by all indications there are nonreligious people, i.e., people who give little or no attention to religious problems or concerns, either at certain times in their lives or throughout their lives. This is a fact to which a theory of religion ought to be able to do justice. The kinds of 'problematic cases' I have in mind are those systems of thought or programs of life (e.g., Marxism, humanism, Confucianism) which we might have difficulty in classifying as either religious or nonreligious. An adequate interpretive theory of religion should be of some assistance in helping us to make up our minds about such problematic cases. And it should not preempt in advance the possibility of there being nonreligious alternatives to religious systems or programs (for a discussion of such alternatives from a sociological perspective see Campbell 1972, esp. Chapter IV).

With these remarks we can bring to a close our discussion of some of the possible types of interpretive theories of religion. Our conclusion, as supported by the reasons presented in this chapter, is that the type of theory which most closely accords with the purposes of analytical philosophy of religion will be one which is role-functional and autonomic. The material of this chapter and the preceding one, and especially the ten criteria for interpretive theories of religion, will provide the critical perspective we need in Part Two, where we will be examining and assessing four past theories of religion. And it will also provide a background and context for the constructive work of Part Three. For ease of reference, the ten criteria are listed in an appendix.

Part Two

Historical

Spinoza: Religion as Obedience to God

In Part One I have sought to provide a methodological perspective on the problem of constructing interpretive theories of religion by talking about the task of such a theory, some possible types of such a theory, and some criteria which might be used in criticizing or constructing such a theory. In this second part I wish to supplement the methdological perspective with a historical one. My way of doing this is to offer a detailed analysis and criticism, in a chapter each, of four major theories of religion which have been presented over the past few centuries: the theories of Benedict Spinoza (1632-1677), Immanuel Kant (1724-1804), Rudolf Otto (1869-1937), and Paul Tillich (1886-1965).

My selection of these particular theories for critical examination has been somewhat arbitrary, but not entirely so. Each theory is the work of a first-rate philosophical mind, so it is not surprising that each is provocative and illuminating in its own right. None of the theories is without its defects, but these are themselves instructive and can provide us with some concrete examples of the kinds of pitfalls which lie in the way of attempts to arrive at adequate interpretive theories of religion. Moreover, our investigation of these four theories and their interconnections should give us some sense of the historical development of thinking on the subject of our study, at least in the modern period. As we

move from the earliest theory, that of Spinoza in
the seventeenth century, to the latest one, that of
Tillich in the middle of the twentieth century, we
can witness definite progress in the direction of
much greater subtlety and breadth in the understanding of religion and of its complex interrelations
with such other basic types of human interest as
philosophy, morality, science, and art. There are
no doubt many reasons for this progress, which
would have to include new developments in
philosophy itself, as well as a growing awareness
and knowledge of the teachings of the many world
religions as we come down to the present time. But
this progress was also made possible by the fact
that our later theorists were able to profit from the
insights and mistakes of their predecessors, including those in our list.

Finally, these four theories of religion have
made significant contributions to my own reflections
on the nature of religion, contributions which will
be evident in the theory of religion I will offer in
Chapter 7, and to which I will make explicit reference in Chapter 8. Let this much suffice, then, by
way of rationale for this historical part and for the
selection of these four theorists. We now turn to
our first theorist, Spinoza.

Spinoza had a compelling reason for trying to
distinguish religion from other fundamental types of
interest and endeavor, especially philosophy. The
reason was that he was ardently committed to the
vocation of philosopher and determined to follow the
pronouncements of reason wherever they might lead.
And he was anxious to show, as against the de-
tractors of philosophy, that freedom to philosophize
was not detrimental to piety or the public weal but,
in fact, was essential to their maintenance[1] (Spinoza

1951 (hereafter referred to as "E"), Vol. I, 6). In
order to substantiate this claim, he sought to define
the boundaries of religion and philosophy in such a
way as to make it plain that the aims of the one
were radically distinct from the aims of the other.
This meant that when the nature of each was
properly understood, there could be no conflict
between them, and each could be allowed to flourish
unthreatened by the other.

   Spinoza develops his theory of religion in a
work called Tractatus Theologico-Politicus (1673),
and it can best be approached in terms of a contrast he draws there between 'faith' and philosophy.
This contrast will be explicated under four main
headings: the different aims of faith and philosophy; their different foundations; the difference in
meaning of their respective forms of discourse; and
their different kinds of clientele.

1.   THE DIFFERENT AIMS OF FAITH AND
     PHILOSOPHY

The aim of faith is what Spinoza calls 'obedience',
which in general 'consists in acting at the bidding
of external authority' (E,I,74).   In the specific case
of faith the obedience is to God.   To obey God is to
believe in him and to honor him, and to honor him
means nothing else than to love one's neighbor and
to practice justice and charity (E,I,183,185).   This
is the 'main precept' of the Bible, according to
Spinoza, a thesis he finds to be confirmed by the
fact that, while the biblical writers differed widely
in 'matters speculative', they concurred to a man in
teaching a common basic morality (E,I,184,33).   And
not only is this the main precept of the Bible, it is

'the only standard of the whole Catholic faith', by which expression Spinoza evidently intends to include all historical religions, for he insists in one of his letters that Turks and other non-Christian peoples have salvation 'if they worship God by the practice of justice and charity' (E,I,184;E,II,368). So where justice and charity are practiced in obedience to God, there is faith to be found, and where they are lacking, there will faith be absent, no matter what speculative doctrines may or may not be taught. The aim of faith has nothing to do with promulgating or assessing the truth of speculative-doctrines but is entirely a matter of teaching and fostering such obedience (E,I,184-185,189-190).[2]

By contrast with the aim of faith, 'philosophy has no end in view save truth...' (E,I,189). So speculative doctrines come entirely under the jurisdiction of philosophy, and he who concerns himself with defending or attacking the truth of any one or more of them is doing the work of a philosopher. Since he views these two aims as being 'as wide apart as the poles', Spinoza concludes that there is no basis for conflict between philosophy and faith (E,I,189,194; italics my own).

2. THE DIFFERENT FOUNDATIONS OF FAITH AND PHILOSOPHY

Not only do faith and philosophy have different aims, they also have different foundations. The foundation of faith Spinoza usually calls 'revelation' or 'prophecy', and while he almost always employs these words in connection with the Bible and the Jewish and Christian religions, they can also be taken as designations of the basis of statements of faith in general, as witness his references to prophecy in the religions of the Magi, Nebuchadnezzar, and Mohammed, and his efforts to show that the gift of prophecy was not peculiar to the Hebrews (E,I,30,43-56;E,II,368). Revelation is conveyed by prophets, and a prophet is recognizable by three traits, traits which constitute his religious authority. First, he is possessed of an unusually vivid and active imagination. Second, his utterances are confirmed by 'signs'. And third, his mind is given wholly to what is right and good (E,I,29,196).

In saying that prophets must have lively imaginations Spinoza means to assert that their special gift is not speculative reason but a capacity to conceive and clothe their thoughts in dramatic sensuous images which have marked power to move the heart to obedience.[3] What he means by 'signs' is mainly the fulfillment of predictions made by the prophet. Successful predictions give evidence of divine origination of the prophetic message to the philosophically unsophisticated, which includes the prophet himself as well as the vast majority of his hearers and readers. And since his message gains its significance for faith wholly from its effectiveness in teaching and fostering obedience, the prophet's moral discernment, commitment, and example will obviously figure importantly in an assessment of his religious authority.

Spinoza puts the foundation of faith somewhat differently when he says that it is 'history and language' (E,I,189). By this phrase he means to call attention to the need for what we should now call historical criticism of prophetic documents. They were written with particular purposes in mind, to particular audiences, and under the pressure of particular historical circumstances. They have undergone changes in their transmission from one

generation to the next. They are couched in a
style that is often fanciful and obscure, because of
its rootage in idiosyncrasies of the prophet's nature
and temperament and in the archaic patterns of
thought characterizing his times. Even the ancient
languages in which they are written pose their own
difficult problems of interpretation. All of these
factors must be taken carefully into account if we
are to interpret the sacred writings of a religion
in their own terms and on their own ground
(E,I,27-42,98-119).

The central message of these writings is
really quite simple and can be apprehended by all,
for it is the message of obedience. But it needs to
be demonstrated by intensive study that this is
indeed the end to which all else is the means.
Without such study we are likely to mistake for
revelation that which is only its ephemeral trap-
pings, its historically conditioned methods of communication and motivation. Spinoza's historical
criticism of the Jewish and Christian Scriptures in
the Tractatus purports to provide this demonstration, so far as those sacred writings are concerned.

Philosophy's foundation, on the other hand, is
nature or reason (E,I,189-199). Philosophy seeks
truth, as we have seen. And it appeals for the
adjudication of its truth claims, not to that which is
relative to particular times and places, but to that
which is universal and timeless. Its method, as
Spinoza conceives it, is rational demonstration,
perspicuous deductions of conclusions from self-
evident axioms. For those with intelligence enough
to construct or follow its trains of reasoning it
yields a surety and lucidity of thought and expression that contrasts sharply with the vargaries and
obscurities of the prophetic idiom. Resting on the

foundation of precise ratiocination, philosophy is suited to the task of determining truth in a way that faith, with its appeals to revelatory experience, could never be (see E,I,77-78,175).

3. THE DIFFERENCE IN MEANING OF THE FORMS OF DISCOURSE OF FAITH AND PHILOSOPHY

Turning now to the difference in meaning between the respective forms of discourse of faith and philosophy, it is evident that while philosophical discourse is cognitive for Spinoza, the discourse of faith is not. It is not cognitive because it does not make claims to truth but offers only 'modes of expression calculated to instil with efficacy, and present vividly to the imagination the commands of God' (E,I,159). In other words, the discourse of faith is directive and evocative. It is directive in that it issues commands, and it is evocative in that the dogmas it teaches are not to be construed as assertions of fact but as imaginative devices for evoking the resolve to obey these commands as divinely decreed.

In Chapter fourteen of the Tractatus Spinoza poses the intriguing problem of trying to decide just what dogmas are necessary and sufficient for motivating people to a life of obedience, and can therefore be regarded as the 'dogmas of universal faith'. The dogmas he decides upon are seven in number and can be listed as follows (E,I,186-187):

I.   That God, meaning a supreme being sovereignly just and merciful, or an exemplar of true life, exists.
II.   That he is one.

III. That he is omnipresent, or that all things are open to him.
IV. That he has supreme right and dominion over all things, and that he does nothing under compulsion, but by his absolute good pleasure and grace.
V. That worship of God and obedience to him consists entirely in justice and charity, or love towards one's neighbor.
VI. That all those, and those only, who obey God by their manner of life are saved; the rest of mankind, who live under the sway of their pleasures, are lost.
VII. That God forgives the sins of those who repent.[4]

To most of these dogmas Spinoza appends a reason designed to show why it is indispensable to faith or the life of obedience. His reason for the first dogma is that if one did not know (nescit) or did not believe in (credit) God, one could not obey him or know him as judge. But what is the force of nescit and credit in this passage? Clearly, if these terms mean that there is at least one claim to truth essential to faith, namely, that there is a God who is merciful, just, and a judge, then Spinoza's whole distinction between faith and philosophy breaks down.

But his use of the phrase 'exemplar of true life' implies that it is not the claim to truth of the existence of God that is indispensable to faith but the effective functioning of this conception of God as an imaginative device. What Spinoza is saying is that a life of obedience requires the stimulus of a model of human life at its best and fullest, a model which can inspire people as a powerful example and serve as their highest standard for distinguishing good from evil. It might seem incongrous at first to think of God as being an exemplar of <u>human</u> life, but Spinoza's point is that the idea of God as being just and merciful, and a judge, is an anthropomorphic symbolization, a symbolization of humanity writ large. In one of his letters he remarks that 'theory frequently, and not unwisely, represents God as a perfect man...' (E,II,347; see also E,II,306;E,I,64). And in his <u>Ethics</u> (published posthumously in 1677) he speaks of the need for a 'type of human nature' by reference to which persons can form notions of good and bad, even though from an ultimate philosphical perspective, reality and perfection mean the same thing (E,II,189). God, so to speak, lives the moral life that humanity called upon to emulate; he embodies the justice and charity which is faith's aim.

Philosophical interpretations and appraisals of this symbol of God as the exemplar of true life have no bearing whatever upon its indispensability for faith, because what matters for faith is not how God comes to be the exemplar of true life or what God is in his nature ('fire, or spirit, or light, or thought, or what not...' (E,I,187), or even, we might add, whether on philosophical grounds we can know that there is such a thing as God. What matters for faith is that this symbol has the power to elicit and sustain the resolve to live a life of obedience. Whether it is fiction or fact is irrelevent, for it is not a claim to truth in the first place (for further elucidation of this point see Christian 1965).

Spinoza's defense of the indispensability of the other dogmas to faith turns likewise on their power to move people to obedience. God must be regarded as one if he is to be wholeheartedly obeyed, for entire devotion, admiration, and love spring from

the superiority of one over all else. He must be
thought of as omnipresent, for if things could
happen unnoticed by him, people might doubt of
the equity of his judgment as directing all things,
and fail to obey him on that account. He must be
viewed as having supreme right and dominion over
all things, else all things would not be bound to
obey him. Humans must think of their salvation as
consisting exclusively in obedience to God, for
otherwise they would have no reason for obeying
him rather than succumbing to lives of pleasure.
Lastly, God must be thought of as forgiving, for
unless he were, all people having sinned, would
despair of being saved. And in their despair they
would have no impetus to obey him.

Faith is unaffected, on the other hand, by
speculative questions which might arise in connection
with these dogmas, such as (E,I,188):

whether we hold that God is omnipresent essentially
or potentially; that he directs all things by
absolute fiat, or by the necessity of his nature;
that he dictates laws like a prince, or that he sets
them forth as eternal truths; that man obeys him by
virtue of free will, or by virtue of the necessity
of the Divine decree; lastly, that the reward of the
good and the punishment of the wicked is natural or
supernatural... .

These are questions of truth and lie wholly within
the sphere of philosophy, marking its form of
discourse, in contrast to that of faith, as having
cognitive significance.

4. THE DIFFERENT KINDS OF CLIENTELE OF FAITH AND PHILOSOPHY

Such questions as those above can be resolved by reason, Spinoza thinks, but only the gifted few will have the patience and ability to follow the requisite arguments and proofs to the end. These few constitute the clientele of philosophy. The clientele of faith is the masses of ordinary people, who have no talent for philosophizing and no interest in pursuing philosophy's problems. Such people are incapable of comprehending philosophical truths (which Spinoza seeks to prove in the Ethics) such as that God and nature are one; that the laws of God are not arbitrary acts of his will but eternal truths, since his will and understanding are the same; that there is nothing that is contingent, since all things are conditioned by the necessity of the divine nature; that the salvation to which reason leads, the intellectual love of God, is eternal yet does not involve duration, imagination, or recollection (E,I, 62-65;II,68-69,264). Spinoza speaks in one place of the 'feeble intelligence' of the masses and holds that they 'are only bound to know those histories which can most powerfully dispose their mind to obedience and devotion' (E,I,79).[5] Frederick Pollock puts the difference in clientele between faith and philosophy quite succinctly when he says, 'Obedience is within every man's power but not wisdom. This is the burden of the Tractatus Theologico-Politicus...' (Pollock 1899:318). For those who have the power to reach wisdom by the path of philosophy, faith, as characterized by Spinoza in the Tractatus, is entirely superfluous. But for the rest it is a necessity, at least if they would attain fullness of life and peace of soul.

5.   'FAITH' AND 'RELIGION'

To what extent does Spinoza's conception of the
nature of faith constitute his view of the nature of
religion? In general, the two coincide, particularly
if we mean by 'religion' what is exemplified by the
existing religions of the world. But the matter is
complicated somewhat by certain passages in his
writings where he seems to have in mind a religion
of reason, i.e., a philosophical religion. Let us
consider the character of this philosophical religion,
so as to see how it relates to positive religion, as
described in Spinoza's analysis of faith.

Towards the end of the Tractatus he tells us
that 'religion is one and the same, and is equally
revealed by God', whether it 'be apprehended by
our natural faculties or by revelation' (E,I,247).
This implies the possibility of a religious outlook
being founded on reason, rather than on revelation.
In the Ethics we come across passages to the same
effect, such as this one (E,II,212):

But he, who endeavours to lead men by reason, does
not act by impulse but courteously and kindly, and
his intention is always consistent. Again, whatsoever we desire and do, whereof we are the cause in
so far as we possess the idea of God, or know God,
I set down to Religion. The desire of well-doing,
which is engendered by a life according to reason,
I call piety.

And in a letter written in 1671, Spinoza responds
in the following manner to the charge that in the
Tractatus he had 'thrown off all religion' (E,II,365):

I would ask whether a man throws off all religion, who maintains that God must be acknowledged as the highest good, and must, as such, be loved with a free mind? or, again, that the reward of virtue is virtue itself, while the punishment of folly and weakness is folly itself? or, lastly, that every man ought to love his neighbor, and to obey the commands of the supreme power?

Both of these passages, like the one in the Tractatus, suggest that doctrines of religious import can be founded on reason. But then in what does their religious import consist?

Evidently, it consists in the fact that the true conception of God, as discovered by philosophy, can be said to conduce, like the imaginative dogmas of faith, to a life of obedience. At least there is a certain sense in which this is so, provided that we give to the term 'obedience' an extended, nontechnical meaning.[6] Technically speaking, 'reason... leads us to love God, but cannot lead us to obey him', since in the light of reason his laws are not decrees but necessary truths (E,I,277,Note 26). But these truths can still loosely be spoken of as commands of God, 'because they proceed, as it were, from God himself, inasmuch as he exists in our minds...'. And the plan of life centered on the philosophical or rational aim of the knowledge and love of God may with some fitness be called the 'law' of God (E,I,60). To follow these so-called 'commands' and this so-called 'law' is, in the same loose manner of speaking, to 'obey' them.

In strict correctness, then, religion and philosophy are to be distinguished along the lines of Spinoza's distinction between faith and philosophy, and his view of the nature of faith amounts to his view of the nature of religion. This is borne out by the parallelisms 'religion and faith' (Religio & fides) and 'religion and piety' (Religio & pietas) in Chapter fifteen of the Tractatus, as well as by the strong contrast Spinoza draws there between religion (Religio) and reason (E,I,192). But since both faith and philosophy center on God and both ensue in patterns of life whose outward manifestations are the same, even though their foundations are vastly different, the term 'religion' can, on occasion, be used to cover them both. This extended sense of the term served Spinoza particularly well in fending off the emotive charge that he had discarded all religion.

6. CLASSIFICATION AND CRITICISM OF SPINOZA'S THEORY

We can now raise three questions about Spinoza's theory of religion, by way of tying it into our discussion in Part One of the task and types of interpretive theories of religion. (A) Can it be properly construed as an interpretive theory of religion? (B) If it can, what type of interpretive theory can it be said to be? (C) What critical assessment of it can we make, in light of the ten criteria previously set forth?

(A) That Spinoza's views on religion constitute a theory, and not merely a definition or a catalogue of independent traits, is shown by the seven dogmas of universal faith in Chapter fourteen of the Tractatus. For there he posits a scheme of inter-locked categories ('exemplar of true life', 'one', 'omnipresent', 'supreme', 'worshipful', 'saving', 'forgiving': would be one way to list them) designed to characterize the object of religious interest and to show how preoccupation with it, and it alone, conduces to the aim of religion (that is, to obedience, in the narrow, technical sense of the term indicated in the previous section).

And that his theory is interpretive, rather than explanatory or normative, in its main thrust and intent is indicated by the following considerations. He makes little attempt to explain why human beings are religious, giving most of his attention to the question of what being religious means. And his theory does not concern itself primarily with the question of whether religion is good or bad, or of which religion is the best one for people to follow. It is true that he assumes that religion is good for human beings, at least for those not able to handle philosophical arguments. And it is also true, as we shall see, that there is some normative bias built into his theory. But he does not set it forth as an evaluation of religion or religions, but as an interpretation of the nature of religion as contrasted with the nature of philosophy. So it would seem that we are justified in discussing Spinoza's theory as an example of an interpretive theory of religion.

(B) As for fitting his theory into our schema of theoretical options, it might be alleged that Spinoza has offered an ontological theory of religion, where the object of interest peculiar to religion is said to be a being with certain attributes. But a little reflection will convince us that what he has set out to do is not to decide what attributes are common to God or to religious objects in various religions, even though the categories of his theory do look very much like attributes. Rather, he has sought to interpret the common function of objects of religious interest, and the categories have a functional significance.

It will be recalled that a distinction was drawn earlier between two types of functional theories of religion. The goal-functional type views objects of interest as being religious when they function as means to a specified end or goal, while the role-functional type views objects of interest as being religious when they have some stated mode of functioning in some larger context, when they play some specified intrinsic role. It is apparent that Spinoza's theory is an instance of the goal-functional type. It differs from the goal-functional theories which are usually constructed in anthropology, sociology, or psychology, however, in that its intent is not to explain why humans are religious, but rather to interpret what it means to say that they are religious. The goal in question in Spinoza's theory is a certain pattern of life, i.e., one in which deeds of justice and charity are performed in the spirit of obedience. And he has sought to determine just what combination of imaginative ideas, coalescing in the symbol of an exemplar of true life, can function as the necessary and sufficient conditions for inducing people to adopt this pattern of life, with its underlying spirit of obedience.

If it will be allowed that Spinoza's theory of religion is goal-functional, rather than experiential or ontological, we are left with the last of the theoretical options laid out in Chapter 2 above to be decided upon. Is his theory an instance of the reductive type of theory or of the autonomic type?

Could a case for his theory's being reductive be built around the claim that it reduces religion to morality? It might seem so, since his theory puts such stress on justice and charity in its specification of religion's aim, and since these are commonly regarded as moral ends. But the matter is not quite that simple. For one thing, as was pointed out in Chapter 2, to give an interpretation of religion in terms of its putative end or goal is not necessarily to make it identical with that end or goal. And for another, the aim of religion as Spinoza conceives it is not justice and charity <u>per simple</u> but a life embodying these virtues which <u>is</u> inspired and sustained by the imaginative idea of God as the exemplar of true life.

We would be justified in saying of Spinoza's theory that it is one-sided, in that it downplays far too much the role and importance of speculative and ceremonial aspects of religion in favor of what might be called religious ethics. To this extent his theory has some tendency towards reduction in the direction of morality. And that tendency is not mitigated by his speaking at times as though, wherever justice and charity <u>per se</u> are found, there will be faith or religion (see, for example, E,I,185). Still, religious ethics is not the same thing as morality as such. And unlike Kant, Spinoza does not have a well-worked-out theory of what constitutes the specific domain of morality or of moral judgment, in contradistinction to other fundamental types of judgment. So we are not really in a position to say that his theory of religion is subsumable under his theory of morality.

A clearer case can be made for the claim that Spinoza's theory of religion is reductive in that it makes religion subsumable under philosophy. That is, the proper pursuit of philosophical interest can accomplish both the aim of philosophy and the aim of religion, at least when the latter is construed in the wider, nontechnical sense explained in section 5 above. When philosophical understanding is attained, as was noted in section 4, religion becomes entirely superfluous. Thus philosophy can encompass and include religion in a way that religion cannot encompass and include philosophy, for religion can lay no claim to truth. And there is no question that Spinoza regards it as better to live the life of justice and charity as based on firm <u>knowledge</u> than it is to live it as based on mere appeals to the imagination which cannot qualify as being literally true or even as having any cognitive significance. Another way of putting this case is to note that the essential problems and claims of religion, as Spinoza conceives them, are translatable without any important residue into the problems and claims of philosophy, at least for those who have the intellectual capacity for comprehending the reduction. Considerations like these support the conclusion that Spinoza's theory is an example of the reductive type of theory of religion, and that he makes religious interest subsumable under his theory of the nature of philosophical interest.

(C) Some weaknesses of Spinoza's theory, seen in the light of our set of criteria of interpretive theories of religion, can now be indicated. Then we can go on to say something about its positive contributions.

There is a normative bias built into the theory, which runs counter to the first of our criteria. For the theory would seem to contain the evaluation either (a) that all religions are good, since all foster the desirable ends of justice and charity, or (b) that a given religion can be judged to be good or bad depending on the extent to which it contributes to these ends. There is also the bias built into the theory that if one has a choice, it is better to be philosophical than religious.

Criterion (4) and the first part of criterion (2) have already been taken into account in our classification of Spinoza's theory. As for the latter part of criterion (2), the extent to which the theory illuminates the nature of religious interest, I think that Spinoza's theory suffers from the second defect of goal-functional theories to which I called attention in Chapter 2. Criterion (3) is satisfied to at least some degree by the affinities and connections between Spinoza's theory and the thoughts of some of his Jewish and Muslim predecessors on the nature of religion, as rooted in prophecy or revelation, and on the relations between religion and philosophy. I have called attention to some of these affinities and connections in the notes to this chapter.

It would be my judgment that Spinoza's theory falls seriously short of criterion (5). Its denial of cognitive significance to the notion of God as the exemplar of true life is unconvincing, partly because it is doubtful that this conception would function on the scale and with the effectiveness the theory attributes to it unless it were believed in as true. Spinoza is right in holding that there is considerable latitude for different interpretations of what is implied by this notion, but wrong in denying to it altogether the status of a belief.

His theory is also unpersuasive when it tells us that as soon as one undertakes the kind of interpretation mentioned above and tries to defend it on the basis of reason, he is suddenly doing philosophy and has stepped wholly outside the boundaries of religion. For this is to introduce an arbitrary cleavage into the continuum from faith to faith-seeking-understanding, as though this search did not comprise a large and essential part of the literature of religion, and as though the worship of God did not include the passionate desire, at least on the part of some religionists, to separate the chaff of error from the pure kennel of truth. Theologians may be mistaken in their truth-claims and theoretical interpretations of fundamental religious commitments, but they make them nonetheless. And they make them in the interest of religious, and not merely philosophical, nurture and comprehension. A theory which does not give due weight to considerations such as these cannot do justice to the logic of religious systems.

Why, then, was Spinoza so adamant in denying cognitive status to the notion of God outlined in Chapter fourteen of the Tractatus? I think that one has to turn to the Ethics for the line of argument he perhaps had in mind. It would run as follows:

A typical interpretation of the conception of God as outlined is that God 'directs all things by absolute fiat', 'that he dictates laws like a prince', and so forth, which means that God is thought to possess free will. But to attribute free will to God is self-contradictory and absurd. So either this interpretation of God's nature is empty and has no good use, or it has some noncognitive use. For many people it has a good use, i.e., this view of God's nature plays an important and positive part in their lives. Therefore, the function or use of this view must be a noncognitive one.[7]

But there are some obvious difficulties with this line of argument.

For one thing, the truth of the second premise is debatable, particularly to the extent that it rests on the starting assumptions and basic definitions of Spinoza's system. For these are not as <u>self-evidently</u> true or correct as he seems to have <u>thought</u> them to be. But perhaps more fundamentally, the argument shows at best only that one interpretation of the divine nature is noncognitive and yet has a religious use, not that all interpretations which have a religious use must be non-cognitive. Spinoza would not want to deny cognitive status to the view that God directs all things 'by the necessity of his nature', or that he sets forth his laws 'as eternal truths', for he considers these claims to be perfectly consistent. But these claims can also have a religious use for someone. In fact, I think that they played a profoundly religious role in Spinoza's own outlook and life. So some views of God's nature are both cognitive and of religious significance. And I see no need sharply to separate their religious significance from their cognitive character.

Another weakness of Spinoza's theory is exposed by the sixth criterion. For while he tries to marshal massive support for his thesis about the respect in which all religions agree, namely, their stress on obedience to God, his theory sheds little or no light on the grounds of disagreement among religions. This defect grows partly out of his apparent assumption that only where religious spokesmen concur is the core of religion to be found. But it is also an important question as to what alternative possibilities for interpretation and development lie latent in their common object of concern. In other words, respects in which spokesmen for the same or different traditions disagree are also of crucial significance for clarifying the nature of religion. Spinoza's failure to bring this side of the problem into clear focus is of a piece with his rejection of cognitive significance in religious discourse. For much that would be grist for religious disagreement is shunted by his theory into the province of philosophy.

What about the seventh criterion? Does Spinoza's theory give equal stress to the personal and the cosmic sides of religion? In a way it does, and in a way it does not. In one sense, the imagery of God as exemplar of true life, as presented in the form of the universal dogmas of religion, gives expression to the notion of a divine being with certain definite characteristics. And these characteristics, in their turn, are connected with certain responses on the part of the individual person. In this way the focus of the theory is on both the cosmic and the personal sides. But in a more fundamental and accurate sense, Spinoza's theory cannot give equal stress to the two sides, because its entire focus is on the personal side, i.e., on the end or goal served for a person by his object of religious interest. That end or goal is its power to motivate that person to a life of obedience. To speak of the object of religious interest as being accorded a cosmic status is already to grant to it the significance of a belief, i.e., it is believed to be of a certain ontological nature or to have a certain real function in the universe as a whole. By denying any cognitive significance to the notion of God in the context of religion, Spinoza has in effect preempted the possibility of any genuine stress on religion's cosmic side.

Contrary to the eighth criterion, Spinoza's theory of religion suffers from provincialism or the lack of adequate generality, because: (a) it is defended on the basis of a thoroughgoing analysis only of the Jewish and Christian scriptures (though it also reflects some influence of Muslim religious philosophers); (b) it incorrectly assumes the centrality of God to all religions; and (c) it has the ironical implication of branding Spinoza's own constructive views as nonreligious, except in a nontechnical, extended use of the term 'religion'. But it was apparent to Spinoza himself that his is a religious philosophy. So a more adequate theory of religion is needed to show why this is so.

His theory can be faulted by the ninth criterion in that it either creates an impassable gulf between philosophy and religion (all the facts of their histories to the contrary), in the interest of shielding philosophical arguments from religious attack, or it simply reduces all that is important and valuable in religion to philosophy, as has already been argued. Spinoza would in all probability want to take issue with the ninth criterion itself. This would shift the debate back to arguments for this criterion, such as those in Chapter 2. But here we are simply trying to apply the ten criteria, not justify them.

Finally, as for the tenth criterion, being nonreligious would presumably mean for Spinoza failing to live a life of obedience as inspired by the symbolism of God as the exemplar of true life. There is no reason to assume that this would be impossible, or even that it would be uncommon. And systems of thought like Marxism or humanism, lacking this kind of symbolism, would be clearly nonreligious by the test of Spinoza's theory. So these and other problematic cases could probably be rather easily decided. Unfortunately, cases that

are not all that problematic but are commonly
accepted as religions, such as Taoism and Theravada
Buddhism, would also have to be branded as
nonreligious by Spinoza's theory, which shows that
its precision in terms of the tenth criterion is
bought at the price of its lack of adequate generality (the eighth criterion).

The weaknesses in Spinoza's theory that we
have called attention to are important ones, but we
ought not to allow them to blind us to the really
great achievement which his theory represents in
the history of thought. Although he does not
adequately solve all the problems he raises, he
deserves much credit for having so forcibly raised
them, and for having bequeathed to his successors
a legacy of provocative questions and stimulating
suggestions. He has emphatically posed the problem
of interpreting the nature of religion in generic,
cross-cultural terms, and of puzzling out its relations to other basic types of human interest. With
his stress on religion as having its focus in a
pattern of life he has offered a needed corrective to
the common tendency, particularly pronounced in
his own century, to think of religion simply as a
repository of doctrines demanding intellectual
assent. Even the one-sidedness of that stress is
a contribution, for it throws into sharp relief the
task of explicating both the practical and the
theoretical sides of religion in their distinctively
religious character, so that religion is not simply
reduced to morality, on the one hand, or to
speculative philosophy, on the other, or to a mere
combination of moral and philosophical pursuits.

Spinoza's functional approach to the nature of
religion lays out a promising route for future
theorizing, and there is much that is suggestive in

his seven dogmas of universal faith, despite the
fact that they fall short of being truly generic.
Finally, he has made important forays into the
difficult area of analyzing the meaning of religious
discourse, and his emphasis on the role of imagination and symbol in that discourse is important, even
if carried too far. These are some of the positive
contributions of Spinoza's theory of religion, some
important respects in which future generations of
philosophers of religion stand in his debt.

4

Kant: The Route From Morality to Religion

Immanuel Kant's most mature and sustained reflections on what he calls 'the theory of religion as a whole' or 'the definite concept of religion' are presented in a book he wrote late in his life (1793) entitled Religion innerhalb der Grenzen der blossen Vernunft (hereafter referred to in citations as 'G-H', above quotes from pp. 10,7).[1] As he himself notes in the Preface to its second edition, this book is largely self-contained (G-H, 12-13), and the theory of religion it sets forth is fully developed. Accordingly, we shall use this book as the principal source for our discussion of Kant's theory of religion, alluding to his other works only when they can serve to provide needed clarification of points under discussion.

For our purposes, the most significant statement that Kant makes in the Religion is that 'morality leads ineluctably to religion' (G-H,5,7, note). Once we have understood precisely what he means by this statement, we will have grasped his theory of religion. Let us consider, then, the several ways in which, for him, this statement holds true.

1. MORALITY AND GOD AS HOLY LAWGIVER

The first of these is that there is inherent in the idea of duty a sense of holiness which points to the religious doctrine of God as holy lawgiver and to the religious disposition to regard all duties as his commands. Kant never ceased to wonder that man, a being dependent upon nature in so many ways, should yet be raised far above it by his possession of a reason which through the categorical imperative binds him unconditionally to the call of duty, as if in complete obliviousness to the lure of his sensual desires and his tendency toward narrow self-love. What reason thus sets before man is the ideal of holiness, the holiness of complete and utter conformity to the moral law, not from fear of punishment or expectation of reward, but simply from love of the moral law for its own sake. This predisposition to holiness man finds in himself is at once awesome and inexplicable, making him 'the holiest of beings in this world' (G-H,147,note; see also 44-45, 142).

But man's holiness is a holiness of obligation and potential, not a holiness of fact. He is capable of responding to and making continual progress toward the moral law, but not of achieving absolute conformity to it. Kant is not very explicit about the reasons for this, but he does mention in one place that a certain kind of moral inadequacy is 'inseparable from the existence of a temporal being as such', and in another place he speaks of 'such moral perfection as is possible to an earthly being who is subject to wants and inclinations' (G-H,61, note,55). Such factors as the following, we can therefore suppose, would account for man's never quite reaching the goal of complete holiness. In the first place, because of his life in time, it must always be said of man that he is in the process of becoming moral, never that he simply is moral, because his actions tomorrow, the next day, and so forth, must be taken into account in assessing the moral quality of his outward life. Secondly, not only must the necessary incompleteness and uncertainty of the futurity of human actions be recognized, but there is also the contingent fact that all men start from evil, on account of what Kant calls 'radical evil in human nature' (more will be said on this below). And even when this evil is overcome by the adoption of a good disposition, it still leaves a taint of guilt from the past to mar man's future progress. Thirdly, as one subject to wants and inclinations, each man's capacity for rationalization and self-deception is great, and there is always the possibility of his performing an act or acts for disguised sensual, rather than purely moral, reasons. Fourthly, given his finite perspective and necessarily limited experience, a man might not always have the wisdom to apply the moral law rightly to the available concrete courses of action. This is especially true since, in a sensate existence, conflicts of good often arise to perplex even the most well-disposed persons. So even at its very best, man's life is 'virtue striving toward holiness', rather than holiness itself (G-H,123; see also 60-66, cxx).

The consciousness in man of the unconditioned binding force of the law of morality, and of its contrast with the conditioned character of even the most resolute human responses to it leads quite naturally, in Kant's view, to belief in one whose conformity to the moral law is absolute, i.e., God as holy lawgiver. 'Yea, it leads thither so naturally that, if we care to try the experiment we shall find that it can be elicited in its completeness from anyone without his ever having been instructed in it' (G-H,170). He does not so much argue for this connection between morality and religion as point to it as an obvious fact.

Kant speaks often in the Religion (as elsewhere) of the profound respect (Achtung) which every man must feel for the moral law, and he links this respect with the feeling of fear of God as moral lawgiver (G-H,170; see also 136 note). Fear is the appropriate feeling toward this aspect of the divine nature because God's perfect conformity to the moral law stands in scathing indictment of the extent to which each man falls short of it, and because this divine conformity sets before man an ideal which he must struggle throughout his life to attain, at no matter what cost to his comforts, ambitions, or desires.

It is not God's power which the morally sensitive man fears, for the authority of the moral law stems from no arbitrary imposition of the divine might but is autonomous, being rooted in dictates of pure practical reason which are as binding upon God as they are upon man. What man fears is rather the majesty and awesome authority conferred upon God by the moral law, when he is seen as its complete embodiment and exemplification. Far from being arbitrary and wholly unrelated to man's own concepts of morality, the laws of God are 'laws addressed to man's holiness' (G-H,132), and as such, their claim upon man is total and inescapable. They search his heart, not merely his overt acts, calling for a purity of disposition which alone can render him well-pleasing to God. One facet of man's fear of God as holy lawgiver, we can therefore conclude, is the fear of failure, failure to measure up to what reason itself tells man is his true destiny and end. Since without conformity to the moral law one cannot be free (autonomous) or

function as a person (G-H,22-23,xc-xci,cv), part
of the meaning of the fear of God as moral lawgiver
is the fear of the self-destructive consequences of
slavery to the evil principle and of the shame of a
truncated and ineffectual life. Seen from this
perspective, the fear of God is a corollary to what
Kant calls 'moral self-love' (GH,41,note).

Thus the moral law as the doctrine of morality
leads inevitably to the concept of the holy lawgiver
as a doctrine of religion. And similarly, the moral
disposition strictly to fulfill one's duty (G-H,19
note) culminates in the religious disposition to fulfill
all duties as divine commands (G-H,79,96,100).
This is the first way in which, for Kant, morality
leads to religion.

So far we have spoken only of the ideal which
morality sets before man and which God exemplifies.
But how is it possible for man to attain this ideal?
This question brings us to the second connection
and one aspect of the third connection between
morality and religion Kant adduces, namely, the way
in which moral experience points to the need for
God as 'Preserver of the human race, its benevolent
Ruler and moral Guardian', and the way in which it
implies the need for him as 'Administrator of his
own holy laws, i.e., as righteous Judge' (G-H,130).

In asking how man can live up to the searching
requirements of the moral law and of God as holy
lawgiver, we are really asking two questions. The
first one (I will call it Q.I) is: how can man find
the strength of will to pursue and attain that degree
of holiness of which he is capable qua man? The
second one (which I will call Q.II) is: since it is
inevitable (as we have seen) that even the most
well-disposed and morally advanced persons will fall
short of complete conformity to the moral law, how

are we to understand the injunction in the gospels
(which accords with our consciousness of moral
obligation) to 'be...holy even as your Father in
Heaven is holy'? (Matt. 5:48; quoted G-H,60).
Each of these questions relates to one side of a
polarity which Kant (G-H,60) expresses as follows:

the distance separating the good which we ought to
effect in ourselves from the evil whence we advance
is infinite, and the act itself, of conforming our
course of life to the holiness of the law, is
impossible of execution in any given time. Nevertheless, man's moral constitution ought to accord
with this holiness.

The 'evil whence we advance' is for Kant 'a <u>radical</u>
innate <u>evil</u> in human nature' (G-H,28), and it therefore becomes problematic in the extreme to understand how man can hope to extricate himself from
it, so as to set out upon a path of steady progress
toward holiness. And 'the good which we ought
to effect in ourselves' is none other than a state of
holiness like unto God's, and as such, would appear
to be unattainable even if we made steady progress
toward it throughout our lives. So how can man be
obligated to attain it? Let us consider each one of
these questions in turn, as Kant addresses them,
for in so doing we can reveal the second way and
part of the third way in which he links morality and
religion.

2. MORALITY AND GOD AS BENEVOLENT RULER

How, then, can men find the strength of will to
pursue and attain that degree of holiness of which

they are capable as men, especially in view of the state of radical evil in which all men find themselves to be mired?   (Q.I) Kant describes this state of radical evil as a propensity to make 'the incentive of self-love and its inclinations the condition of obedience to the moral law', rather than allowing simple respect for its authority to be the sole incentive for obedience to it (G-H,32).   This state is 'radical' because it implies a perversity at the very root of all actions, i.e., a corrupt disposition. It is 'innate', not in the sense that it is unavoidable or necessary (it must have originated in each man's freedom, since each man is held accountable for it), but in the sense that it is to be found in all men 'as early as the first manifestations of the exercise of freedom' (G-H,33).   And it is 'evil', because it treats the moral law as though it were binding upon man only conditionally, thus violating the sanctity of its categorical character.

The disposition to obey the moral law only when it is convenient or profitable to do so, and to override it when it is not, is made all the more menacing and insidious by the fact it is so often advantageous to conform one's actions to it (Kant cites the example of truthfulness: truthfulness has the advantage of enabling us to avoid the anxiety of making our lies agree with each other).   The result is that a man may well appear to others, and even to himself, as reasonably virtuous, despite the perversity of his heart.   So the radical character of his plight will be hidden from him, and he will be deluded into thinking that his problem is merely one of fighting against overt acts of vice one by one, 'leaving undisturbed their common root' (G-H,43-44).

But why, if it originates in each man's personal freedom, is radical evil so universal? Why is it to be found in all men without exception? From one aspect, this question is unanswerable, for freedom is 'incomprehensible' (G-H,179,133) and does not admit of explanation in terms of causes. But we can talk of factors in human experience which provide opportunities for the misuse of freedom. And the most fundamental of these, so far as each man's lapse into radical evil is concerned, is his life in society. Kant comes to this conclusion after considering and rejecting two other hypotheses.

The rejected hypotheses are either (a) that radical evil is grounded in man's senuous inclinations themselves, or (b) that somehow a corruption of the morally legislative reason in men has occurred. Kant rejects the first hypothesis because sensuous inclinations, considered in themselves, are good and necessary. And if each man lived in isolation from his fellows, these inclinations would pose no real threat to the rule of reason, for they are few and rather easily satisfied (G-H,30,51,85). He rejects the second hypothesis because it would take away the very possibility of human freedom, and also because he is firmly convinced that no matter how corrupt men may become, they never lose the incentive of respect for the moral law. In fact, 'were such a thing possible, we could never get it again'. The presence of this incentive in all men Kant calls 'the original predisposition to good in us', and it provides the basis for moral renovation of man's character and acts (G-H,30,42).

The hypothesis Kant does adopt and defend is that man's social existence has the unfortunate effect of distorting and magnifying out of all proportion the senuous side of his nature, for in

society each man's susceptibility to self-
aggrandizement is reinforced manyfold by that of
the others, and passions are aroused for which
there would be no occasion in the lives of men
living alone.

Envy, the lust for power, greed, and the malignant
inclinations bound up with these, besiege his
nature, content within itself, <u>as soon as he is
among men</u>. And it is not even necessary to assume
that these are men sunk in evil and examples to lead
him astray; it suffices that they are at hand, that
they surround him, and that they are men, for them
mutually to corrupt each other's predispositions and
make one another evil. (G-H,85)

Each individual is not thereby <u>forced</u> into evil, but
his freedom is powerfully enticed to succumb to it.
And succumb to it all men do, without exception.
    Since each man is enmeshed in the state of
radical evil by his life in society, it follows that the
remedy for his plight must also be societal. That
is, the 'rabble of the evil principle', which rein-
forces his tendencies to dishonor the moral law,
must be replaced by 'a society, enduring, ever
extending itself, aiming solely at the maintenance
of morality, and counteracting evil with united
forces...' (G-H,91,86). Kant terms such a society
an 'ethical commonwealth'.
    An ethical commonwealth has the following
traits. (a) The laws on which it is predicated are
not statutory laws, but are the laws of virtue growing out of the moral law as an <u>a priori</u> principle.
(b) Observance of these laws in an ethical commonwealth goes beyond a legality of overt acts to a
radical purity of the inner disposition, for only in

this way can an ethical commonwealth be the antidote for radical evil. (c) An ethical commonwealth is not be conceived of as restricting individual freedom for the sake of the common good, but as maximally enhancing the true human freedom grounded in respect for the sovereignty of the moral law as a law of reason. (d) An ethical commonwealth encompasses all mankind, and is thus one and universal, for it aims ultimately to exclude all social influences making for evil, and to impress the laws of virtue in all their scope upon the human race as a whole. (e) Its only proper ruler is God, therefore it can be alternatively termed 'a people of God under ethical laws' (G-H,90). In each of these respects the concept of an ethical commonwealth differs from the concept of a juridical or political commonwealth.

We are now in a position to answer the question (Q.I) with which we began our discussion of this second way in which, for Kant, morality leads to religion. That question, it will be remembered, was: How can man find the strength of will to pursue and attain that degree of holiness of which he is capable, qua man? As we have seen, this question also involves the problem of how man can extricate himself from the snare of radical evil. Kant's answer to this question is twofold. First, since radical evil is a corruption of the inner disposition, and since each man fell into his evil disposition through an act of freedom, so must he freely choose a new disposition of making the moral law the absolute standard of all his actions. This new choice is as inscrutable as the first one, and all that can be said about it in the final anaysis is that man is obligated to make it, therefore he is capable of making it (G-H,43). But second, an ethical commonwealth can surround a man with a new social environment wherein he can find incentive to choose a new disposition, and encouragement and support to persevere in an outward course of life which makes steady progress toward holiness.

What is of most interest to us in all of this is Kant's claim that God is the only proper ruler of an ethical commonwealth, for this points to God in his character of benevolent ruler and preserver of the human race; God as not merely calling men to the ideal of holiness, but as providing them with the necessary means to this end. As such, God is not only an object of <u>fear</u> for the morally sensitive person. He is also an object of <u>love</u>.

There are at least three reasons why God is the only proper ruler of an ethical commonwealth. First, every commonwealth needs a ruler or head, and the very nature of an ethical commonwealth requires that its head be one who is entitled to rule, not by virtue of his might, nor by virtue of an authority conferred upon him by consent of the governed, but solely by virtue of his perfect conformity to the moral law. As we have already seen, this can only be God. Second, since an ethical commonwealth is based on something inner, namely, the <u>morality</u> of actions, and not just their legality, it requires a ruler who can see into the innermost parts of the disposition of each individual. As Kant is reported to have said in one of his courses of lectures at Königsberg,[2] the consciousness of God as such an all-knowing One is an indispensable motivation to the moral life.

...the preeminent consideration in morality is purity of disposition, and this consideration would lose its force it there existed no being to take notice of it. Without belief in the existence of such a being man could not possibly attain to and be conscious of the highest moral worth. Only God can see that our dispositions are moral and pure, and if there were no God, why ought we to cherish these dispositions? Our conduct might be the same, we might still go on doing good, but not from any pure motive... . It is, therefore, impossible to cherish morally pure dispositions without at the same time conceiving that these dispositions are related to the Supreme Being to whom alone they can be an open book. (Kant 1930:80-81)

Third, since an ethical commonwealth is designed to include all men everywhere, and the duty of establishing it is different from ordinary moral duties in that it is a duty, not of men toward men, but of the human race toward itself, it is unlikely that human effort alone will suffice to bring it fully into being. 'We can already foresee', says Kant, 'that this duty will require the presupposition of another idea, namely, that of a higher moral Being through whose universal dispensation the forces of separate individuals, insufficient in themselves, are united for a common end' (G-H,89). But he hastens to add that men should in no wise slacken their own efforts to carry into effect the rational idea of such a commonwealth, even while recognizing that theirs is 'a task whose consummation can be looked for not from men but only from God himself' (G-H,92).

Fortunately, men do not have to begin from scratch in their endeavors to bring an ethical commonwealth into being. Vehicles or frameworks for its furtherance and spread already exist, to some extent in each of the religions of the world, but especially in Christianity, at least to the extent that it bases itself upon the teachings of Jesus (see G-H,144,147-151,121-122). Kant prefers not to use the term 'religion', however, in speaking of historical religious communities, because he wants to reserve this term for 'pure religious faith', i.e., the religion of reason to which moral experience ineluctably leads. Instead, he speaks of particular religions as 'statutory faiths', or 'ecclesiastical faiths'. The difference between the singular and plural forms of these terms is significant. For while there can be only one pure religious faith, and only one universal church (the ethical common-wealth) founded on it, there are various statutory faiths, each with its specific churchly structure and tradition. The relationship between pure religious faith and these statutory faiths is one of the more intriguing features of Kant's theory of religion.

He suggests that we can construe the nature of this relationship along the lines of a concept he introduced in the Critique of Pure Reason, viz., the concept of 'schematism'. A 'transcendental schema' in the first Critique provides a bridge between the pure categories of the understanding and appearances, making application of the categories to the appearances possible. Such a schema, in order to perform this mediating function, must be in one respect intellectual and in another, sensible (Kant 1929, 'Transcendental Analytic', Book II, Chap. I). In a somewhat similar vein, Kant tells us in the Religion that to 'schematize' is to 'render a concept intelligible by the help of an analogy to something sensible' (G-H,59). The concept in question here is the concept of pure religious faith, and the schemata which are required to make this intelligible to men and to further its realization in human society are the scriptures, symbols, rites, doctrines, institutional forms, and experiences through time of particular religious communities. Kant holds that whatever in these schemata does not admit of a moral interpretation is either religiously useless or a snare and a delusion, for the schemata can have no religious justification other than as means to the end of establishing the ethical commonwealth. As he expresses it in one place, 'every partial [ecclesiastical] society is only a representation or schema' of the ethical common-wealth as 'an absolute ethical whole' (G-H,88).

Such schemata are required, at least for the present, because of 'a peculiar weakness' of human nature, stemming largely from its sensuous side (G-H,94,92). The concept of pure religious faith is too abstract, austere, and cerebral to commend itself immediately and directly to the general run of men. So statutory faiths and their accoutrements are needed to prepare the way for the comprehen-sion and acceptance of pure religious faith by setting it forth in a manner that is concrete, vivid, and experiential, thus adapting it to the conditions of man's sensuous nature.

Kant leaves open the possibility that actual divine revelations lie at the basis of the religions of the world, but his reasoning on this second way in which morality leads to religion does not require the belief that such revelations have in fact taken place (see G-H,122-123,96-97). The essential idea is rather that man is led, on the basis of his moral experience, to an acute sense of his need for an ethical commonwealth to be the societal remedy for radical evil as a societally induced and sustained malady. And the concept of an ethical common-wealth, in turn, implies belief in God as its head, God in his capacity of benevolent ruler and

preserver of the human race. So far as statutory
faiths are concerned, they link up with our moral
experience and become vehicles of the ethical
commonwealth when we learn to interpret their
scriptures, teachings, traditions, etc. along moral
lines. Such interpretations might at times seem to
be forced, and indeed will be forced (G-H,101), but
the religious value of statutory faiths depends
entirely on the extent to which they can be made
conducive to the goal of bringing about morally
upright conduct on earth. Kant cites examples of
such moral interpretations of the lore of Judaism,
Islam, and Hinduism, as well as Christianity, to
back up his point (G-H,102).
      Although he is not oblivious to the extent to
which religions like Christianity have failed to exert
a beneficent moral influence upon their adherents in
the past, Kant feels that his own time is religiously
the best of times, because he sees increasing
numbers of thoughtful people becoming critical of
ecclesiastical dogmatism and exclusivism and beginning to recognize the distinction between religion's
moral core and its statutory wrappings (G-H,121-
123). And he envisions a day when all men will
have reached such an advanced stage of religious
development that they will no longer have to rely
upon statutory faiths but will have attained the
stability and freedom of pure religious faith. As
vehicles, statutory faiths might then still be made
use of, but they would no longer be indispensable
(G-H,126 and notes). In this expectation he
exhibits a confidence in the whole of mankind's
potential for religious progress which Spinoza
lacked. For the latter, as we have seen, reserved
the possibility of such growth to maturity for only
the highly intelligent.

3. MORALITY AND GOD AS RIGHTEOUS JUDGE

A. Belief in God as Righteous Judge and Q.II

The third and final way in which morality leads to
religion for Kant turns in part upon the question
which was raised earlier and called Q.II. How can
sense be made out of the injunction, implicit in the
moral law, to be perfect even as God is perfect, in
view of the fact that no amount of moral progress
could ever bring man wholly up to the level of the
moral perfection of God? Or put another way, the
question is, how can man avoid falling prey to
frustration and despair in the face of this rigorous,
and seemingly impossible, demand of the moral law?
Careful reflection on this question and its implications leads us, Kant thinks, to trust in God as
'Administrator of his own holy laws, i.e., as
righteous Judge' (G-H,131). And because it is this
trust which points the way out of moral despair,
God in this aspect can be viewed as an object of
hope.
      Kant divides into three parts this question of
how man can hope to become morally pleasing to an
awesomely holy God, so as to show how belief in
him as righteous judge is implied in the answer to
each part. The first part deals with the problem
arising from the fact that a certain kind of moral
deficiency is inseparable from the existence of a
temporal being as such. The second part has to do
with the problem of how the well-disposed man can
know that he is well-disposed, and thereby gain
confidence that he will continue to make moral progress as long as he lives, and not lapse fatally in
the face of some future temptation or temptations.
And the third part relates to the problem of how

satisfaction can be made for those sins previously committed in the state of radical evil and for those new sins which will crop up even in the midst of a life of steady progress toward moral goodness. This last part of the question is especially poignant in view of the dictum, which Kant takes to be axiomatic, that this debt of sin 'can never be discharged by another person' (G-H,66).

It was noted early in this discussion of Kant's theory of religion that, on account of man's life in time, it must always be said of him that he is in the process of becoming moral, never that he simply is moral, because his future actions, which are as yet unknown, must be taken into account in assessing the moral quality of his outward life as a whole. This element of incompleteness, of 'not yet', can only be reconciled with the strict demand of the moral law, Kant reasons, if there is belief in a God who can judge man's inner disposition, regarding the future good actions implicit in a good disposition as if they were already performed. By judging a person's disposition, God can see that person's moral life as a unity, as a completed whole, rather than as an as yet unfinished sequence of acts.

So when the moral law demands that man be holy as God is Holy, one way of understanding this is to see that its emphasis is upon man's disposition, and therefore that an incompleteness or uncertainty of future actions is not a fundamental barrier to the present holiness of which man is capable, namely a holiness of disposition. But a just appraisal of a person's disposition can only be made by God, not even by the person himself. For only God can know full well what is in that person's heart; God alone is qualified to judge the quality and tendencies of the core of man's moral being.

Trusting in God, therefore, the well-disposed person need not despair on account of the finitude and incompleteness that is his lot as a man.

The need for this trust is also implied by the second part of the question with which we began this section. For even though the emphasis of the moral law is upon the disposition, it also demands as much conformity to divine holiness in the outward pattern of man's life as is humanly possible. And given the fact that a person can never know with complete certitude what the tendencies of his heart are, how can he achieve what Kant terms 'moral happiness', i.e., the confidence that, as his life goes on, he will be able to go from strength to strength in bringing his actions into ever closer approximation to the rigor of the moral law? (G-H,61,69,note). This confidence can be derived partly from the accumulating evidence of one's deeds, but Kant warns that it is dangerous to put too much stock in this, given the human tendency to complacency when some moral progress has been made or to undue self-condemnation when moral setbacks occur. A more dependable source of confidence is belief in God, whose judgments do not involve precarious estimates of future deeds on the basis of past deeds but rest on a direct knowledge of the human disposition. Thus belief in God as righteous judge is required to give man the kind of perspective he needs to forego 'anxious fantasies' about the remote future and to focus his energies on the opportunities for moral progress each day affords (G-H,62).

Kant also suggests, though he does not develop the idea, that the moral law's demand for conformity of man's outward actions to divine holiness contains the implication of an afterlife for

man. For man could more nearly approach the
infinite holiness of God if he continued to improve
morally throughout infinite time. Seen from this
angle, the afterlife is a means in Kant's thinking,
not only to a conjoining of virtue and physical
happiness (a notion that we will look at later), but
also to man's everlasting moral happiness. And
belief in God as righteous judge is connected with
belief in an afterlife.[3]

The third part of the question presently under
discussion raises the problem of how satisfaction can
be made for those sins which the well-disposed man
has committed in his former state of radical evil,
and for the new sins which will sometimes crop up
in the course of his outward progress toward
goodness. Belief in God as righteous judge is
implicit in the resolution of this problem, because
in the eyes of God the man with a new disposition
is 'morally another person' (G-H,67). And the
struggles of this new person, as he strives to bring
his deeds into accord with his good disposition, can
be thought of as punishment for the sins of the old
person (and presumably, for relapses into sin of
the new person, since these sinful acts are not
really characteristic of him). And yet, since the
'two' persons are, from another aspect, one and the
same, the principle is not violated that the debt of
sin cannot be discharged by another person. Kant
admits that this line of reasoning is rather speculative, but he thinks (G-H,71) that it has the practical value of making it utterly plain that

only the supposition of a complete change of heart
allows us to think of the absolution, at the bar of
heavenly justice, of the man burdened with guilt;
that therefore no expiations, be they penances or

ceremonies, no invocations or expressions of praise (not even those appealing to the ideal of the vicarious Son of God), can supply the lack of this change of heart... .

Kant is completely unyielding in his insistence that expiation for past sins can be made only by the man who has comitted those sins, and by no other. And he believes that to think otherwise is to destroy the moral import, and thereby the only proper meaning, of religious teachings. He has no sympathy for the notion that there are special duties men owe to God over and above their duty to be moral, and that performance of these duties is necessary or can be effective to persuade God to forgive men for their past sins. There is no value to the external forms and ceremonies of religion so far as an effect upon God is concerned. Their sole value is the vivification of the demands of the moral life which, when taken as schemata, they provide for men. Kant allows that men are perhaps entitled to hope that God, in his grace, will supplement their deficiencies at the end of life, provided that they have done all that is humanly within their power to improve themselves morally, but he argues that it would be the crassest kind of 'fetishism' and 'idolatry' to think that there are nonmoral shortcuts to satisfying the claims of divine holiness, or that outward forms are anything other than mere schemata of the moral life. God is not an earthly lord or king to be swayed by courtly performances, special petitions, or excuses. The moral law which he embodies and expresses lays a radical claim upon the human heart which permits of no evasion or escape.

An example of the application Kant makes of this uncompromising outlook is his interpretation of the Christian notion of the atoning work of Christ. Men are not saved by their faith in what Christ has done for them. Rather, Christ is an archetype of the life of unending moral struggle and sacrifice which all men must undergo if expiation is to be made for their sins. This is the moral lesson in the symbolism of Christ's life and death, viewed as a schema. As Kant states it, 'the suffering which the new man, in becoming dead to the old must accept throughout life is pictured as a death endured once for all by the representative of mankind' (G-H,69).

B.   God as Righteous Judge and the Need for Worthiness to be Happy to be Conjoined with Actual Happiness

Up to now we have been discussing ways in which the answer to the question of how finite and imperfect man can hope to measure up to the standard of divine holiness implies the need for belief in God as righteous judge. But there is another way as well in which moral experience leads to this particular belief, a way which Kant develops in his second Critique and which he comments further upon in the Preface to the first edition of the Religion. This way has to do with the demand of human rationality that worthiness to be happy (virtue) be conjoined with actual physical happiness.

This demand can be understood only when we take into account both the rational and the sensuous sides of man's nature and recognize the need for harmonizing these into an all-encompassing final end for man's moral life. The rational side sets forth a

moral law which is purely a priori, and applies as
much to God as it does to man. In other words, it
gives no notice to man's natural desires and
inclinations. It is entirely deontological, command-
ing obedience quite apart from any consideration of
the physical consequences which might follow from
that obedience.

But the sensuous side of man's nature sets
forth the end of physical happiness for man. This
is not a moral end, for it contains no note of
obligation. It simply reflects the fact that man has
a nature dependent on sensuous objects. All propositions based on this end are empirical, growing
out of and applying to contingent facts of human
experience.

The rational side of human nature can be
indifferent to whether or not a life of virtue will
result in eventual happiness, but the sensuous side
cannot. If man's nature in its twofold aspect is to
be fulfilled, therefore, there must be a reconciling
of these two tendencies. This reconcilement is
brought about, Kant thinks, when we construe
virtue as worthiness to be happy and say that all
men should seek as the final end of their moral
striving to bring about the kind of world in which
worthiness to be happy will be conjoined with
physical happiness. Because it merges the rational
and senuous aspects of man, the proposition which
states his obligation to pursue this goal as his final
end is a synthetic a priori proposition.

But unfortunately, man is not the author of
the cosmos and does not have the capability of
bringing about a union of the purposiveness of
freedom (whose end is the moral law) and the
purposiveness of nature (whose end is physical
happiness, as the end of natural desires). If man

has only his own resources to call upon, and has no assurance that he lives in a universe where moral values will be ultimately vindicated, he must be reduced to despair. For he can have no firm hope of realizing that final end which alone can fulfill his nature as a man.

It is just at this point that Kant marks another transition from morality to religion, as these words from the Critique of Practical Reason (1956:134) will indicate:

Therefore, morals is not really the doctrine of how to make ourselves happy but of how we are to be worthy of happiness. Only if religion is added to it can the hope arise of someday participating in happiness in proportion as we endeavored not to be unworthy of it.

Where religion comes in is in the implication of the need for God as righteous judge. For God has both the power and the wisdom to insure that worthiness to be happy will be conjoined with actual physical happiness. We know that this harmonization of man's rational and natural ends does not take place in this earthly life for many persons. So we are led by moral experience to hope for an afterlife in which it will become a reality. God must preside over such an afterlife to determine who is worthy of happiness and who is not, and to see to it that each receives his just deserts. Here again God's ability to discern the character and tendencies of each person's inner disposition means that he alone is qualified to make a fair and just appraisal.

Kant is very specific, of course, in insisting that men should not seek virtue for the sake of happiness, for that would be morally contemptible.

But he is equally persuaded that men's moral confidence does depend crucially upon the hope for ultimate cosmic justice. Belief in God as righteous judge he holds to be the only sure ground for this hope.

This discussion of Kant's theory of religion has disclosed three main ways in which morality leads ineluctably to religion, and in so doing it has characterized the object of religious interest in a threefold way: as holy lawgiver, benevolent ruler, and righteous judge. 'These three attributes', Kant tells us in the second Critique (1956:136,note) 'contain everything wherein God is the object of religion'. The universality of the conception is confirmed, he thinks, by its presence in such diverse religions as Zoroastrianism, Hinduism, the religion of Egypt, Gothic religion, and late Judaism, to say nothing of Christianity, where the doctrine of the Trinity can be viewed as its schematization (G-H,131-132 and note,136-138 and note).

Kant informs us that these three attributes of God which loom so centrally in his theory of religion are not to be construed as theoretical notions of what God is in himself. They tell us what he is for men as moral beings. There are 'natural' attributes which can be inferred from these moral ones (e.g., omniscience, omnipotence, omnipresence, unity), but the only status these can have for practical reason is their seeming necessity for God's carrying out his divine will with regard to the moral life (Kant 1930:79-80).

Corresponding to each of the moral attributes of God, as we have seen, is a distinctive attitudinal response, showing that Kant gives some attention to the personal side of religion, as well as to its cosmic side. Thus, connected with God as holy lawgiver is the response of fear; to him as benevolent ruler, the response of love; and to him as righteous judge, the response of hope.

4. CLASSIFICATION AND CRITICISM OF KANT'S THEORY

The same questions which were raised about Spinoza's theory of religion can now be raised about Kant's. (A) Can it be properly construed as an interpretive theory of religion? (B) If it can, what type of interpretive theory can it be said to be? (C) What critical assessment of it can we make, in light of the criteria presented in Part One?

(A) The theoretical character of Kant's views on religion can be seen in the fact that he offers a set of conceptually interrelated categories designed to characterize the object of religious interest on both its personal and its cosmic sides. It might be thought that his theory is explanatory, in that it explains why human beings are religious; namely, because they are moral beings and morality leads necessarily to religion. But the explanation is not so much causual as it is conceptual. That is, Kant has tried to show the necessary conceptual relations between the two human interests, morality and religion. He does not adduce physiological, psychological, or sociological causes in an attempt to show that religion can be viewed as the effect of such causes, nor does he base any predictive claims upon an analysis of religion's causes. So far, then, he offers us an interpretive theory of religion.

But is the theory entirely interpretive, or is it at least partly normative in its intent? In the Religion Kant notes that the threefold characterization of God, which assigns to him legislative, executive, and judicial functions, is the 'universal true religious belief', conformable to the requirements of practical reason (G-H,131, italics my own). And in the Lectures on Ethics he is reported to have viewed this conception of God as 'the theology which is to form the basis of natural religion...' (1930:79).[4] So it is evident that he conceives of himself, not only as giving a neutral interpretation of what is in fact common to all religions, but also as giving strong evidence, based on the practical demands of the moral life, for the truth of this common core. To this extent his theory combines normative and interpretive intentions. But though these two aspects are commingled in his presentation, they are not so entwined as to be inseparable. His theory can be assessed in part as an interpretive theory of religion, though certainly he should have kept the two facets of his enterprise more clearly distinct than he did.

(B) Which of the various types of interpretive theories of religion is Kant's theory most like? It is not an experiential theory, for its basic thrust is not that of giving us a detailed analysis of the distinctive qualities of religious experience, as compared and contrasted with other sorts of experience. But could it be viewed as a theory of the ontological type, given the fact that Kant regards the object of religious interest as a certain kind of being, with specific defining attributes? There is certainly something to be said for this interpretation. The being which is the object of religious interest for Kant is 'schematized' in different ways in different religions, but its essential nature he takes to be the same in all traditions. Since he does not deny cognitive status to the concept of such a being, he does not have Spinoza's motivation to perceive the religious object in a purely goal-functional manner. It can be taken seriously as an ontological conception, believed in as true by adherents of the various religions.

But Kant's theory also contains strong overtones of the goal-functional approach. The manner in which he bases the natural attributes of God on his moral attributes and ties the latter to the needs of the moral life sounds a lot like Spinoza's treatment of the traits of God viewed as the 'exemplar of true life':

His natural attributes are necessary only in so far as they increase the effectiveness of the moral attributes. The omniscience, omnipotence, omnipresence, and unity of the Supreme Being are the conditions requisite to his moral attributes, and relate only to them. The being who is the most holy and the most benevolent must be omniscient if he is to give heed to that inner morality which depends upon our dispositions. For that reason, too, he must be omnipresent. But the principle of morality is inconceivable except on the assumption of a supremely wise will which must be one and so must be the will of a single being. (Kant 1930:80)

Moreover, Kant, like Spinoza, thinks that the objects of religious interest in all religions do have a common function. In Kant's case it is that of conducing to the needs or ends of the moral life. And he spends a lot of time developing a case for this contention. So I think that we will have to conclude that Kant's theory combines the ontological and the goal-functional approaches to a theory of religion, and that it does not come down decisively on the side of either. His theory seeks to elucidate both the common attributes and the common goal-function characteristics of objects of religious interest.

Is Kant's a reductive or an autonomic type of theory? It has been commonly assumed that the theory is reductive, because it subsumes religion under morality. Some of the evidence which might be marshaled in support of this assumption is implicit in the preceding pages of this chapter. Let us cite it again, in order to assess its bearing on our question. We have seen that Kant holds that whatever in the schemata of statutory faiths does not admit of a moral interpretation is either reli-giously useless or a snare and a delusion. It was also noted that, for him, the religious value of these statutory faiths depends entirely on the extent to which they can be made conducive to the goal of bringing about morally upright conduct on earth. And a distinction was drawn between what Kant takes to be religion's moral core and its statutory wrappings. Finally, we saw that the moral import of religious teachings if claimed by Kant to be their only proper meaning, and that he asserts that men have no special duties to God over and above their duty to be moral. Such statements as these give formidable support to the conclusion that, for Kant, the problems and claims of religion are translatable without any significant remainder into the problems and claims of morality, and there-fore that for him religion is reducible to morality.

A counter to this thesis would run somewhat along the following lines. It was seen above that Kant at one place speaks of the need for religion to be added to morality, implying that religion itself is something more than morality. And rather than

holding that the problems and claims of religion
reduce to those of morality, he seems to insist that
the problems and claims of morality point beyond
themselves to those of religion. In other words, we
are led by the requirements of the moral life beyond
morality proper into the domain of religion. Kant
has elucidated an intricacy of connection between
morality and religion without reducing one of these
basic interests to the other. Even this defense of
the autonomy of religion in Kant's theory would
have to admit, however, that the theory as laid
down in the Religion is very one-sided in that he
comments at length only on the extent to which
moral interest points to religious interest, and not
on the extent to which other basic interests
(philosophical, scientific, aesthetic, etc.) might also
point in that direction.

Such a defense of the autonomy of religion in
Kant's theory is attractive, and perhaps it could be
given fuller development. But on balance I think
it will have to be admitted that Kant's theory, like
Spinoza's, is an instance of the reductive type of
theory of religion. If Kant did intend to uphold
the autonomy of religion he did not succeed. And
he certainly does not address the question of its
autonomy with the same persistence and incisiveness
that he gave to defending the autonomy of morality.
Kant's theory of religion can be classified, then, as
a theory which combines the ontological and the
goal-functional approaches and which is reductive in
character.

(C)   What critical assessment can we make of
Kant's theory in light of our set of criteria for
interpretive theories of religion? It is apparent
that his theory does not quite measure up to
criterion (1), given the the normative element in it

which has already been spoken of. It would not be fair, of course, to hold Kant strictly to this criterion, since his principal interest in the Religion (as is indicated by the work's full title) was to determine what religious truth can be arrived at on the basis of reason alone. But he often speaks in this book as though he were offering a theory which can interpret the nature of religion or clarify the common concern of the various religious systems in a more neutral way. So he can be faulted for not keeping the two tasks sufficiently distinct. Implicit in any judgment as to which form of religion is the most true or most rational is some notion of what religion itself is. And the more explicit this notion is made, the better. But the interpretive and the normative are two distinct stages of inquiry, and the effect of running them together can only be confusion. There is a logical priority of interpretive to normative theories, just as there is of interpretive to explanatory theories of religion.

With respect to the second criterion, Kant has shed important light on the nature of religious interest by indicating how it is tied up with moral interest, or at least by showing some of the ways in which it might be linked to moral interest. As we shall see later, Tillich was very much influenced by Kant's insistence on the inviolable sanctity of the moral imperative in arriving at his own conception of religion as 'the dimension of depth' which underlies both morality and culture. So Tillich, for one, finds Kant's account of religious interest to be an illuminating one.

While Kant's theory shares with Spinoza's a legitimate (though one-sided) stress upon the relations between religion and the practical demands of the moral life, he does not go so far as Spinoza does in denying all cognitive significance to religious doctrines. To this extent his theory exhibits a continuity with Spinoza's theory while still making an advance over it, thus satisfying criterion (3). But as was the case with Spinoza, Kant's theory does not satisfy criterion (6), since it does not enlighten us about the grounds of difference among religious systems. Also like Spinoza's theory, Kant's falls short of criterion (8), because it incorrectly assumes the centrality of the concept of God in all religions, and also because it leaves no room for the traditional Christian doctrine of the Atonement. As for criterion (5), the theory would be of help in investigating the logic of particular religious systems to the extent that ethical principles in those systems are connected with the character of the religious object. We have already indicated Kant's fulfillment of criteria (4) and (7).

So far as criterion (9) is concerned, Kant's allowance of cognitive import to religious systems makes possible interactions of religion with other cognitive interests like science and philosophy which are not possible from the standpoint of Spinoza's theory. Kant's theory also falls short of this criterion, however, in its failure to uphold the autonomy of religion, with the consequence that a clear distinction of religious interest from other basic types of interest (especially moral interest) cannot be drawn. Kant's reply to this criticism might be simply to state that religion is not as 'basic' an interest as this ninth criterion assumes, so the focus of debate would be shifted once again, as with Spinoza, to the appropriateness of the criterion.

A corollary of Kant's tendency to reduce religion to morality and hence (I would claim) to conceive of it in too narrow and confined a manner, is that his view of morality is too sweeping and broad. When he speaks of the problem of radical evil in man's nature and of man's need for a fundamental transformation and reorientation of life, for example, he seems to have made a transition, though not recognized as such, to problems which are more characteristic of religion than of morality per se. This would also seem to be the case when he lays such heavy stress on the need for purity in the inner disposition of man, a theme which is more typically religious than moral. In my own theory of religion I have tried to highlight such matters as being of crucial religious importance, implying that they do not loom as centrally in morally, at least as the latter is most commonly understood. These are of course debatable points. I raise them here only by way of suggesting that Kant tends to accord too much to morality and too little to religion, and that this fact helps to explain the domineering role played by morality (as he understands the term) in his conception of the nature of religion. Kant is certainly well within his rights, however, as Spinoza was, in emphasizing the practical side of religious commitment—its character as a way of being and living—and in not allowing it to be regarded merely as a matter of giving intellectual assent to a certain set of doctrines.

What would it mean for a person to be nonreligious (the tenth criterion) in Kant's theory? It would have to mean not taking the moral imperative seriously. The nonmoral man is at the same time the nonreligious man, for lacking interest in morality, he would have no appreciation of his need for religion. And the nonmoral man can be defined as one who gives no consideration to the claims of the moral law upon his actions or his disposition, and who has no sense of that law's awesome sanctity. Kant does not state for us what it would mean to be moral but nonreligious, although perhaps it would simply mean being blind to the religious implications of one's moral endeavors. Presumably it would be impossible, in his view, to be religious but nonmoral.

With these critical remarks we can take leave of Kant, turning our attention next to Rudolf Otto, who was indebted to Kant in countless ways and yet tried assiduously to avoid some of the deficiencies in Kant's theory of religion which we have been discussing.

5

Otto: Religion as Experience of the Holy

Rudolf Otto develops his theory of religion in his well known work Das Heilige, which appeared in 1917 (translated as The Idea of the Holy, 1923, 2nd ed. 1958, hereafter referred to as 'H'). Here he expounds the thesis that 'the innermost essence of religion' is 'the idea of holiness as such' (H,173). This idea Otto sees as very complex, and he believes that far too much attention has been given to what he terms its 'rational' aspect, with the consequence that its important 'nonrational' side has been slighted or has even tended to go unrecognized. The rational aspect of the holy (or of the 'divine' as he sometimes calls it) is that which is 'clearly to be grasped by our power of conceiving, and enters the domain of familiar and definable conceptions', most notably those of morality, art, and philosophy. But 'beneath this sphere of clarity and lucidity lies a hidden depth, inaccessible to our conceptual thought', which deserves much more attention than it has received, because it is 'the basis upon which and the setting within which' the rational meanings of holiness are unfolded (H,59,75). This 'hidden depth' is the main focus of Otto's book, as its subtitle indicates: 'An Inquiry into the nonrational factor in the idea of the divine and its relation to the rational'. We will give our attention first to the nonrational aspect of the holy, as that is conceived by Otto, looking next at its rational aspect, and then at the interrelations of the two aspects. A

fourth section will be devoted to Otto's defense of
the autonomy of religion.

1.   THE   IDEA   OF   THE   HOLY   IN   ITS NONRATIONAL (NUMINOUS) ASPECT

The original and basic meaning of the holy is just
its nonrational aspect, according to Otto.   And he
devises a special name to designate it: the 'numinous' (from the Latin numen, meaning 'spirit').   His
fuller characterization of it is mysterium tremendum
et fascinans ('aweful and fascinating mystery').
But the terms of this characterization, and others
related to them which will be discussed shortly, are
not intended by Otto to be taken as descriptions of
the numinous which make it comprehensible to the
speculative mind.   For that would be impossible,
given its nonrational or suprarational character.
The numinous cannot be taught or abstractly conceived.   It must be felt or experienced at first
hand if it is to be known at all.   Thus the most
that terms such as these can do is to function in an
'indirect' manner, serving as symbols, analogies, or
'ideograms' for the felt sense of the numinous,
helping to evoke it into clearer consciousness, but
not actually describing it or transmitting a conception of it (H,61f,59).
    We have no terms in our language which
belong originally to the numinous sphere itself, so
we must rely when speaking of it on terms derived
from the 'natural' sphere which are most nearly
analogous to it.   'Natural' is apparently the complement of 'numinous', for Otto, meaning simply
those feelings, experiences, or dimensions of life
which are nonnuminous, i.e., which do not pertain

exclusively to the idea of the holy in its nonrational aspect. He is careful to note that the passage from natural to numinous feelings[1] which can occur when natural terms are given a numinous significance does not involve merely a change in the intensity of the natural feelings. He takes Schleiermacher to task, for example, for speaking of 'the feeling of absolute dependence' as though it differed only in degree from feelings of relative dependence (H,9). Numinous feelings are entirely sui generis, differing in quality or kind from natural feelings. Hence there can be no derivation of numinous from natural feelings and no direct passage from one to the other in discourse.

How is it possible, then, for terms designating natural feelings to arouse consciousness of the numinous? The possibility rests, Otto thinks, on a law of analogy or principle of the association of feelings rooted in the very nature of the human mind. Given sufficient 'resemblance' between a feeling of one sort and a feeling of another sort, the mind has the capacity, when presented with the one feeling, to become aware of the other. For example, the feeling of constraint by custom and the feeling of moral obligation resemble one another closely enough (partly in that both are restraints upon conduct) for the former to arouse the latter in the mind. The feeling of moral obligation itself cannot be taught or empirically derived, as Kant rightly saw, but it can be awakened into clearer consciousness through the stimulation of feelings with close affinity to it. Otto goes on to apply the lesson of this example to the feeling of the numinous:

It too is not to be derived from any other feeling, and is in this sense 'unevolvable'. It is a content of feeling that is qualitatively sui generis, yet at the same time one that has numerous analogies with others, and therefore it and they may reciprocally excite or stimulate one another and cause one another to appear in the mind. (H,44)

The mind's capacity for this reciprocal stimulation or excitation is the basis of any and all discourse about the complex category of the holy in Otto's theory. It makes possible the kind of talk about its nonrational side which we are now ready to inquire into, and it also explains the possibility of bringing out its rational side, viz., its amenability to moral, aesthetic, and philosophic interpretation and evaluation. In both cases the language is indirect; it is the language of metaphor, analogy, and allusion, not to be confused with literal description.

Even though experience of the numinous must always elude complete analysis by concepts, and even though the language used to designate it must of necessity be metaphorical and allusive, Otto does not see this as in any way excusing a loose or careless terminology. 'We are bound to try', he says, 'by means of the most precise and unambiguous symbolic and figurative terms that we can find, to discriminate the different elements of the experience so far as we can in a way that can claim general validity' (H,59). Let us look, then, at some of the terminology he devises for speaking of the holy in its nonrational aspect. This can be discussed under the general headings of Tremendum, Mysterium, and Fascinans.

Tremendum

'The nature of the numinous', Otto asserts, 'can only be suggested by means of the special way in which it is reflected in the mind in terms of feeling' (H,12). His task is therefore that of giving as precise and clear an indication as he can of each of the determinate affective states whereby the numinous reality grips and stirs the human mind. Or put another way, he seeks to capture as best he can 'the essence of each several state of mind' (H,17) through which the numinous is encountered and made known. This can only be done, as we have already noted, by adducing those natural feelings which are most closely akin to the numinous ones in question, in order to use terms designating the former as metaphors and symbols of the numinous states, with the intent that these latter will 'ring out, as it were, of themselves' (H,12).

Otto begins his discussion of the numinous states with an investigation of the adjective tremendum, contending that this is more easily analyzed and understood than the substantive idea mysterium. Tremendum itself he breaks down into three component elements: (1) 'awefulness', (2) 'overpoweringness' (or majestas), and (3) 'energy' (or 'urgency').

(1) Numinous awefulness can be suggested by its analogue, the natural emotion of fear, but differs from it in that it has 'something spectral in it'. It is 'a terror frought with an inward shuddering such as not even the most menacing and overpowering created thing can instil' (H,14). In the mood of awefulness one has the distinct sense of being in the presence of something 'absolutely unapproachable', something so 'eerie', 'uncanny', or

'weird' as to make one 'stand aghast' before it (H,19,14). Otto tries to capture the difference between this feeling and the feeling of ordinary fear in one place by contrasting the two expressions, 'My blood ran icy cold', and 'My flesh crept'.

The 'cold blood' feeling may be a symptom of ordinary, natural fear, but there is something non-natural or supernatural about the symptom of 'creeping flesh'. And any one who is capable of more precise introspection must recognize that the distinction between such a 'dread' and natural fear is not simply one of degree and intensity. (H,16)

One of the most important and persistent indicators of the feeling of awefulness in the literature of religions, Otto thinks, is the stress placed upon the 'wrath', 'ferocity', or 'jealousy' of God or the gods. From one perspective these are but naive analogies from the domain of ordinary experience, i.e., from the ordinary passional life of man; but viewed as ideograms of awefulness they become 'most disconcertingly apt and striking' (H,18). In their most original religious meaning such terms are fundamentally independent of any moral significance, such as swift requital or punishment for moral transgressions (H,107,19). They refer instead to the dreadful and daunting character of the divine, the awesome power and might with which, as St. John of the Cross expresses it, the holy God 'destroys, crushes, and overwhelms' the soul (from The Ascent of Mount Carmel, quoted in H,106). Other areas in which Otto finds intimations of numinous awe are reactions to the dead (especially the dead of one's own species); the religious sense of impurity or pollution; and the fear of daemons. There are two main <u>natural</u> reactions to the dead, according to Otto. First, there is disgust at the corpse's putrefication and stench, and second, there is the feeling of its threat to one's own will to life. Even animals are capable of experiencing these natural reactions. Of an entirely different order, however, is the reaction to the dead as something 'horrible', or 'grisly', for this approaches the numinous response of deep dread or awe (H,119-120). A similar distinction can be drawn between the oridinary sense of disgust at being confronted with something seen as repulsive or loathesome (e.g., flowing blood) and the numinous sense of horror or dread in the presence of that which is believed to be polluted or profane. There is enough affinity between the two sorts of feeling for the one to arouse the other, but they remain feelings of an entirely different quality (H,122-123).

The fear of daemons is an especially effective means for 'the spontaneous stirring of numinous emotion' (H,125). One example of this cited by Otto is the horror of Pan (H,14), and the experiences of Jacob at Bethel and Moses at the burning bush are others. Quite vivid is Jacob's exclamation, to which Otto refers several times, 'How dreadful is this place!' (Gen.28:17). This expresses in a very direct manner the awesome and unnerving recognition of a place as 'haunted', as daemon- or numen-possessed. In such experiences of the lurking presence of daemons we have a 'really separate beginning' of religion, Otto believes, because in contrast to such things as magic, fairy tales, <u>mana</u>, and belief in souls or spirits, these divine-daemonic powers are 'pure products of the religious consciousness itself' (H,125-129,122-124).

(2)   Closely related to and yet distinct from awefulness is another element of the feeling of tremendum: 'overpoweringness' (or majestas). One way in which Otto tries to bring this element into focus is by discussing what he terms 'creature-feeling'. Otto thinks that Schleiermacher came close to a proper appreciation of this element with his emphasis on the 'feeling of dependence', but that he treated the phrase too rationally, converting it into a speculative concept instead of seeing it as an ideogram. The correlate of 'dependence' for Schleiermacher was 'causality', i.e., God as all-causing and all-conditioning. But Otto insists that in the first-hand experience of creature-feeling the notion of divine causality does not enter in at all. This is a later rational interpretation of it. The immediate feeling is not one of createdness or of the fact of having been created, as Schleiermacher thought. Instead, it is the feeling of creaturehood, of the lowly status of a creature (H,20-21). Otto sums up his own understanding of creature-feeling in this way:

It is easily seen that...this phrase, whatever it is, is not a conceptual explanation of the matter. All that this new term 'creature-feeling', can express, is the note of submergence into nothingness before an overpowering, absolute might of some kind; whereas everything turns upon the character of this overpowering might, a character which cannot be expressed verbally, and can only be suggested indirectly through the tone and content of man's feeling response to it. And this response must be directly experienced in oneself to be understood. (H,10)

'Overpoweringness' or 'absolute might' are therefore the correlates of creature feeling, taken as 'the consciousness of the littleness of every creature in face of that which is above all creatures' (H,22). The element of overpoweringness can also be spoken of under the rubric of majestas or 'majesty'. This term captures very well, Otto thinks, the sense of 'might', 'power', or 'absolute overpower- ingness' in this second element of the feeling of tremendum. In fact, it contains in its own right 'a last faint trace of the numinous', perceptible to anyone with a feeling for language (H,19). In an autobiographical aside Otto recounts that he borrowed from Luther's expressions divina maestas and metuenda voluntas ('divine majesty' and 'fearful will'), in De Servo Arbitrio, in choosing his own key terms majestas and tremendum. These expres- sions rang in his ears from the time of his earliest studies of Luther, causing him to understand the numinous and its difference from the rational long before he came to identify it with the Hebrew qadosh ('holy') or to recognize its centrality in the history of religions in general (H,99-100). It is obvious from even the most cursory reading of Das Heilige, especially the chapter on 'The Numinous in Luther', that Otto's indebtedness to the founder of the Protestant Reformation is very great indeed. Otto also detects a strong note of overpoweringness, and its correlate, creature-feel- ing, in the doctrine of predestination and in the feeling of uncleanness or profaneness, which we have already had occasion to speak of. He argues that predestination really has nothing to do with

the issue of freewill vs. determinism. Its true
import or experiential basis is creature-feeling,
'that self-abasement and the annulment of personal
strength and claims and achievements in the presence of the transcendent as such'. So great is
the sense of distance between the creature and the
overpowering divine might that he feels that all his
activities, be they ever so vigorous and free, are
overborne and made to seem as nothing when compared to the stupendous operations of the divine
purpose (H,88-89). And the sense of uncleanness
and sin, such as expressed by Isaiah in the temple
('Woe is me! For I am lost; for I am a man of
unclean lips...', Isaiah 6:5), is not in the first
instance anything like a moral depreciation. It
belongs to a quite special and unique category of
valuation, the religious. Therefore, the sense of
profaneness is not so much a judgment one passes
on his moral character, on account of individual
immoral acts, but is a judgment 'upon his own very
existence as creature before that which is supreme
above all creatures'. The feeling of creaturely disvalue or unworth, in other words, stems from the
sense of surpassing worth and majesty, or supreme
religious worth, in the numinous object (H,51).

(3) The third element in the feeling of
tremendum Otto calls 'energy' (or 'urgency'). With
these terms .and others similar to them (e.g.,
'vitality', 'passion', 'will', 'force', 'movement',
'excitement', 'activity', 'impetus'), most of them
drawn from man's conative and emotional life, Otto
tries to kindle an appreciation for the experience
of the numinous as 'a force that knows not stint nor
stay, which is urgent, active, compelling, and alive'
(H,24). He sees recognition of this element of
numinous experience as an important dividing line

between the God of the philosophers and the God of
the religionists, i.e., between those who construe
the idea of the divine as something which admits of
consistent intellectual formulation and which can
therefore be quite rationally conceived; and those
who insist that this idea is of a vital force or
energy which continually overreaches the bounds of
speculative understanding and can only be referred
to with the approximate and rather perplexing
language of symbol, analogy, and paradox. He
uses the example of Luther's controversy with
Erasmus to illustrate the point (H,23).

The 'wrath' of God or the gods is an ideogram,
not only of the awefulness of the numinous but also
of its overbrimming energy and vitality, experienced
as a capricious and baffling 'ferocity' that knows no
bounds. Otto suggests that this aspect of numinous
experience is the origin of the idea of Lucifer, and
of the devilish in all religions. Viewed in that guise
it can even be spoken of as mysterium horrendum,
or as that which is 'negatively numinous'. It is in
one way opposed to the divine and yet has something very much in common with it (note 2,106;23).

And an especially important way in which the
idea of urgency or energy enters into discourse
about the divine is in the weight given to the will
of God by voluntaristic mystics and theologians like
Jacob Boehme, Meister Eckhart, Duns Scotus, and
Luther himself. For example, the supracomprehen-
sible or inexpressible in Boehme, as Otto interprets
him (H,106),

stands...not for Being and Above-being, but for
Stress and Will; it is not good and above-good, but
a supra-rational identification of good and evil in
an Indifferent, in which is to be found the

potentiality for evil as well as for good, and therewith the possibility of the dual nature of deity itself as at once goodness and love on the one hand and fury and wrath on the other.

The last line of this quotation suggests the continuity between 'will' and 'wrath' seen as ideograms of the divine.

Mysterium

In its natural or conceptual sense, the substantive term *mysterium* has a purely negative significance. It 'denotes merely that which is hidden and esoteric, that which is beyond conception or understanding, extraordinary and unfamiliar' (H,13). A problem which admits of no conceivable solution would be 'mysterious' in this sense, as would any happening which persistently defies rational explanation. But in its religious or ideogramatic sense, *mysterium* has an entirely positive meaning. Here it does not refer to the negative feelings left in the wake of unresolved problems or unexplained events but to the intensely positive experience of the numinous as something 'wholly other', something which belongs to an order of being that contrasts radically with our own.

The possibility of this ideogramatic use of the term *mysterium*, which involves such an abrupt shift from a negative to a positive significance, illustrates again the law of the association of feelings, which figures so prominently in Otto's conception of religious language. He explains (H,27) that this feeling or consciousness of the 'wholly other' will attach itself to, or sometimes be indirectly aroused by means of objects which are already puzzling on the 'natural plane' or which are of a surprising or astounding character; such as extra-ordinary phenomena or astonishing occurrences or things in inanimate nature, or in the animal world, or among men. But here once more we are dealing with a case of association between things specifi-cally different—the 'numinous' and the 'natural' moments of consciousness... .

The important role played by miracles, or tales of the miraculous, in the history of religions can be largely explained, Otto thinks, on the basis of this transference of feelings, i.e., the tendency of occurrences which are terrifying or baffling to the intellect to arouse in man a sense of the numinous in its character of <u>mysterium</u> (H,64).

The feeling of response to numinous mystery is not one of mere perplexity, bafflement, or amaze-ment, though these terms suggest something of its tonality. It is more like 'blank wonder and astonishment' or 'a wonder that leaves us still and dumb' (H,26,28). By far the most fitting ideogram to express it, Otto believes, is the term 'stupor'. He insists that this feeling differs in kind from that of <u>tremor</u>, and that it is quite possible to exper-ience the one feeling without the other, or to downplay sharply the one in favor of the other (H,26-27). Western mysticism, for example, exhibits little sense of the <u>tremendum</u> aspect of the numinous but a great deal of its <u>mysterium</u> aspect. By contrast, certain forms of <u>Eastern</u> mysticism (e.g., some forms of Shiva and Durga worship and of Tantrism) give a lot of emphasis to the <u>tremendum</u> aspect, so much so that they can be called examples of 'a mysticism of horror' (H,105).

Otto cites the 'void' of Eastern mysticism and the 'nothingness' of Western mysticism as ideograms of the <u>mysterium</u> aspect of the numinous (H,29-30). And he shows that the climax of the Book of Job in the Hebrew Scriptures is not a theodicy, as we might have been given to expect, but is rather a citation of numerous examples from nature which heighten further the sense of the strangeness and marvel of the Creator which has already been brought into perspective by Job's inexplicable suffering. So the 'wholly other' character of God is powerfully portrayed (H,77-80). Even the experience of utter meaninglessness and blind destiny, as depicted in a novel by Max Eyth, Otto interprets as a kind of confrontation with the divine <u>mysterium</u> (H,81).

Fascinans

This last element in the experience of the numinous Otto calls the 'Dionysiac' element. Whereas <u>tremendum</u> suggests the daunting and fearful side of the divine, <u>fascinans</u> calls attention to a side of it which is alluring and joyful. Here it is 'something that captivates and transports' the creature 'with a strange ravishment, rising often enough to the pitch of dizzy intoxication...' (H,31). Although this element admits of 'schematization' in moral and aesthetic categories—a matter to be discussed in the next section—it is in itself a unique and distinctive species of value, entirely numinous or religious in character, and therefore not to be subsumed under moral or aesthetic valuations. It appears in the

history of religions 'as a strange and mighty
propulsion towards an ideal good known only to
religion and in its nature fundamentally nonrational,
which the mind knows in yearning and presentiment,
recognizing it for what it is beyond the obscure and
inadequate symbols which are its only expression'
(H,36). Man's proclivity toward this uniquely religious ideal testifies to a part of his nature 'which
can find no satisfaction in the mere allaying of the
needs of...sensuous, psychical, or intellectual
impulses and cravings. The mystics called it the
basis or ground of the soul' (H,36). Otto refers
often to this 'basis or ground of the soul' under its
Latin name fundus animae, and it is for him the
deepest part of man's makeup, that which explains
his religious sensibilities and his capacity for
numinous experience.

As was the case with mysterium, the element
of fascinans often finds expression in terminology
which is negative in its conceptual significance and
which yet refers to experiences of an intensely
positive sort. These experiences are so 'rapturous',
'exuberant', or 'overbounding' as to defy positive
verbal description. One can only speak weakly of
them as experiences of that which cannot be seen or
heard, that before which 'all images fall away', and
so forth. Otto cites the words of St. Bernard of
Cluny in praise of the City of Zion as an example
of the negative language used by those who have
known the bliss and transport of numinous experience: 'None can disclose or utter in speech what
plenary radiance fills thy walls and thy citadels. I
can as little tell of it as I can touch the skies with
my finger, or run upon the sea or make a dart
stand still in the air' (H,35,note). The fact that
the element of fascinans cannot be proclaimed in

words or conceived in thought, and that it can be
known only by direct experience, is for Otto clear
indication that it belongs to the nonrational or
numinous side of the idea of the holy (H,33-34).
     Otto perceives two values within the element of
fascinans which he is careful to distinguish. The
first is the subjective value of the numinous, i.e.,
the beatitude it promises or brings to man. The
second is its objective value, i.e., recognition of
it as possessing in itself surpassing worth which
claims man's highest homage. This distinction is
comparable to ones noted earlier in discussing other
elements of numinous experience, namely, 'creature-
feeling' as the correlate of 'overpoweringness', and
'stupor' as the correlate of mysterium. The objective value implicit in fascinans Otto thinks can best
be designated by the term 'august' (H,52,14). And
the subjective value finds its most notable expression in the idea of 'salvation', which he believes to
lie 'at the base of all higher religion everywhere'.
This idea is operative in Zoroastrian eschatology,
for example, and in the Islamic ideal of surrender
to Allah, with its hope, not only of attaining a
future paradise, but also of entering upon the
'Allah' state of mind here and now (H,166). And
what (H,38)

Christians know as the experiences of grace and the
second birth have their parallels also in the
religions of high spiritual rank beyond the borders
of Christianity. Such are the breaking out of the
saving 'Bodhi', the opening of the 'heavenly eye',
the Jñána, by Iśvaras presada, which is victorious
over the darkness of nescience and shines out in an
experience with which no other can be measured. And
in all these the entirely nonrational and specific

element in the beatific experience is immediately noticeable.

Otto's insistence on the 'nonrational and specific' character of the idea of salvation in the higher religions is an implied counter to those who, like Kant, would interpret this idea along merely rational or moral lines. The nonrational side of the idea of the holy in general looms so large in the history of religions for Otto, and in the very nature of religion, as he conceives it, that Kant's quest for a 'religion within the limits of reason alone' is rendered entirely implausible (H,37,note). Spinoza's religion of reason would fall under this same criticism.

The elements of fascinans and tremendum, though they are in one sense opposed, are nevertheless brought together in the actual experience of the numinous, so as to exhibit what Otto calls 'a harmony of contrasts' (H,41). For example, experience of the 'wrath' of God makes all the more desperate the creature's craving for salvation as its summum bonum, because of its felt need for a shield or covering against the awefulness and overpoweringness of the numinous, and for a transcending of its separating unworthiness (H,54-55,85-86). And in a strange and wonderous way, as Luther saw, the numinous satisfies this need by altering its face from something unapproachable to something approachable, from consuming majesty to healing intimacy and familiarity (H,160). This harmony of contrasts is also implicit in the phrase Tu solus sanctus, as Otto interprets it. For 'Thou alone art holy' does more than give quaking expression to a sense of the overwhelming divine might and supremacy. It also (H,51-52) recognizes and extols a value, precious beyond all conceiving. The object of such praise is not simply absolute might, making its claims and compelling their fulfillment, but a might that has the supremest <u>right</u> to make the highest claim to service, and receives praise because it is in an absolute sense worthy to be praised.

Holiness, as the unique quality and possession of the numinous, therefore encompasses both its character as 'dreadful' and its character as 'august', or as spontaneously eliciting the deepest admiration, respect, and yearning. Both of these facets can and frequently do enter into religious experience at the same time.

This completes our discussion of the idea of the holy in its nonrational aspect. We are now ready to consider Otto's views on its rational aspect.

2. THE IDEA OF THE HOLY IN ITS RATIONAL ASPECT

Thus far we have looked in some detail at Otto's attempts to characterize the nonrational aspect of the idea of the holy, i.e., the holy as an object of immediate awareness or experience, prior to any appreciable conceptual interpretation or evaluation. In order to accomplish this characterization Otto argues that he must have recourse to symbols, metaphors, or ideograms which, by bringing to mind certain natural or nonnuminous feelings, can also stimulate into consciousness those uniquely religious feelings which they most nearly resemble or with which they are most closely associated.

An important implication of this conviction that the holy in its nonrational aspect can be an object of immediate awareness and that it can be characterized in nonconceptual ideograms is that knowledge and conceptual understanding do not come down to the same thing, and that it is quite possible to have the first without the second.

Something may be profoundly and intimately known in feeling for the bliss it brings or the agitation it produces, and yet the understanding may find no concept for it. To know and to understand conceptually are two different things, are often even mutually exclusive and contrasted. The mysterious obscurity of the numen is by no means tantamount to unknowableness. (H,135)

And far from downplaying the importance of this nonconceptual knowledge in religion, Otto insists that it provides the essential substrate on whose basis the rational meanings of the idea of the holy are consummated (H,75).

But how can such a consummation take place? Given the fact that one aspect of the holy 'can be firmly grasped, thoroughly understood, and profoundly appreciated, purely in, with, and from the feeling itself' (H,34), the problem is posed of how the transition can be made from this kind of knowledge to knowledge of the conceptual sort. What kind of bridge is there, in other words, between the nonrational and the rational aspects of the holy? Otto answers this question by drawing upon a concept already encountered in our discussion of Kant's theory of religion: the concept of 'schematization'.

We saw that for Kant, in the first Critique, schemata are in one respect intellectual and in another, sensible; and that they have the role in thought of mediating between the pure categories of the understanding and appearances (or sensate experiences), making application of the categories to the appearances possible. And we noted how, in the Religion, Kant views the scriptures, dogmas, rites, institutional forms, etc., of the various religions as schemata of the concept of pure religious faith, setting that concept forth in a manner that makes it more vivid and concrete, thus adapting it to the conditions of man's sensuous nature. Otto's conception of schematization is similar to that of Kant in the first Critique, with the difference that in his case the schemata operate as bridges between the numinous and the rational spheres of the mind, instead of between sensate experiences and categories of the understanding. And his view has an affinity with that of Kant's Religion in that he seems to regard the different doctrinal schemes of the various religions as containing complex sets of schemata which serve to evoke a sense of the holy in its relations to such nonnuminous spheres of life as the moral, the aesthetic, and the philosophical.

Two distinctions will help to clarify further Otto's concept of schematization. The first one is a distinction between 'numinous ideograms' (H,30) and schemata.[2] And the second is a distinction between 'genuine' or 'authentic' schemata and those which are 'wrong', 'illegitimate', or inadequate. We can call these latter 'inauthentic' schemata, for short (see H,45-46,134,48-49). Both numinous ideograms and schemata are made possible by the law of analogy or principle of the association of feelings which was referred to earlier. But the difference between the two is that, while numinous ideograms have the purpose of drawing atttention to the holy in its nonrational aspect, the purpose of schemata is to bring out its rational meanings.

Genuine or authentic schemata, for Otto, are those which exhibit 'an inner a priori principle', whereby the connection between schemata and the idea of the holy is 'felt as something axiomatic, something whose inner necessity we feel to be self-evident' (H,45,136). Inauthentic schemata, on the other hand, can be of two sorts. The first sort is when some form of rationalization is assumed to be schematic when in fact it lacks the necessary character of genuine schemata. That is, the connection between the mode of rationalization and the idea of the holy itself is only a chance or external connection and not a permanent and necessary one (H,134).

The second sort of inauthentic schematization of the idea of the holy occurs when that idea is allowed to 'evaporate' into the concept of the schema itself, so that the nonrational 'core' or numinous 'overplus' of the former is lost sight of (H,49,77,5). In other words, instead of being properly understood as a relation of analogy, the connection between the schema and that which it schematizes is mistaken as a relation of identity. This is the mistake of literalism or excessive rationalization in religion (H,76-77). What is at stake in such inauthentic schematizations is nothing less than the autonomy of religion, i.e., the fact of its rootage in a distinctive domain of experience whose special significance can never be completely explicated or unfolded by categories of interpretation taken from other domains.

The elucidation of authentic schematizations of the holy is of great interest and importance to Otto, not only because he considers them to be basic

motifs in the doctrinal schemes of all higher
religions, but also because he regards their necessary or a priori character as providing a basis for
the transition from the numinous to the rational
meanings of the holy which can be readily understood and confidently affirmed. Whereas questions
may be raised about the appropriateness or
adequacy of contingent modes of rationalization
(e.g., some forms of imaginative myth having to do
with the concept of 'soul' or 'spirit', and the
'supernaturalism' of miracle; H,26-27,64), the
suitability and value of genuine schematizations is
beyond any doubt. The former may have some
adequacy, this would seem to suggest, but not the
complete and undeniable adequacy of the latter.
What kinds of genuine schematizations are there,
then, for Otto? They can be discussed under three
headings already alluded to: the moral, the
aesthetic, and the philosophical.

Moral Schematization

Moral schematization of the experience of the holy
proceeds along two main lines, the one relating to
the element of tremendum and the other, to that of
fascinans.

The tremendum, the daunting and repelling moment
of the numinous, is schematized by means of the
rational ideas of justice, moral will, and the
exclusion of what is opposed to morality; and
schematized thus, it becomes the holy 'wrath of
God', which Scripture and Christian preaching alike
proclaim. The fascinans, the attracting and
alluring moment of the numinous, is schematized by

means of the ideas of goodness, mercy, love, and, so
schematized, becomes all that we mean by Grace... .
(H,140)

The wrath of God as a schematization must be
distinguished, of course, from its use as a numinous
ideogram. We have spoken already of the meanings
it has for Otto in the latter sense. As a schematization it involves the notion of righteous requital
for moral transgressions which is explicitly
suppressed in its ideogramatic usage. Otto interprets the biblical term 'wrath of God', especially
from the time of Moses onward, as representing a
synthesis between the term's older numinous meanings and its subsequent moral meanings (H,19,75).
And he takes to task theologians like those of the
'Lutheran school' who, in his view, construed this
term along exclusively moral lines, and were therefore guilty of a distorted and one-sided explication
which leaves out of account its numinous significance. As important and inevitable as moral
schematization is in the development of religions, it
must not be forgotten that no purely ethical interpretation of the wrath of God can do justice to 'the
profound element of awefulness which is locked up
in the mystery of deity' and which is an indispensable feature of direct religious experience (H,100,
103,32).
  Similarly, it is quite legitimate and is in fact an
elucidation of a necessary connection of feelings or
ideas to regard the element of fascinans from the
standpoint of the 'love', 'pity', 'mercy', or 'comfort'
which a gracious God extends to man. This is a
genuine schematization of the meaning of fascinans,
as is the notion of God as one who possesses attributes of 'trustworthiness' and 'perfect goodness'

(H,31,103,110). But once again, such moral
schematizations fail to tell the whole story.   They
do not capture 'the profound element of wonderful-
ness and rapture which lies in the mysterious
beautific experience of deity' (H,32).   This is the
numinous side of fascinans, which forever resists
conceptual elaboration.   Otto criticizes Kant for
having been so preoccupied with moral explication of
fascinans, i.e., with the idea of God as exemplifying
a perfectly moral will, as to lose sight entirely of
its overplus of numinous meaning (H,5-6).

Aesthetic Schematization

A concept derived from aesthetic experience which
Otto considers most apt for schematizing numinous
experience is the concept of the 'sublime', to which
Kant devoted considerable attention in his third
Critique, the Critique of Judgment (1790).   Just as
moral and religious ideas resemble one another—for
example, in that both rest on feelings which are
qualitatively sui generis and underivable from other
feelings—so there are points of resemblance between
the idea of the holy and the concept of the sublime
which help to explain the latter's capacity to
schematize the former.
       One point of resemblance is that the feeling of
the sublime, like that of the numinous, cannot be
entirely explicated by any kind of rational analysis.
It is true that the feeling of the sublime is a con-
comitant of the experience of things which exhibit
mathematical or quantitative 'greatness', e.g.,
things which are spatially vast or display extra-
ordinary force or power.   But a thing does not
become sublime just by being great, any more than

a thing becomes numinous just by being fearful.
There is an overplus of meaning in each which
cannot be conceptually unfolded. A second point of
resemblance is that both the numinous and the sublime have a dual character, 'at once daunting, and
yet again singularly attracting'. They both humble
and yet at the same time they exalt (H,41-42).

Because of these and other resemblances, the
feeling of the sublime and the feeling of the
numinous are reciprocally related to one another.
That is, either can excite or be excited by the
other. Otto speculates in one place that the feeling
of the sublime was probably first aroused in man by
religious feelings (H,44). This reciprocal relation,
grounded in resemblance, explains why the concept
of the sublime can function as an authentic
schematization of the holy.

Two of the examples adduced by Otto to show
how experience of the sublime can excite a sense of
the numinous, in both its daunting (tremendum) and
its attractive (fascinans) aspects, are particularly
striking. The first one is the experience of Isaiah
in the temple, to which reference has already been
made in another connection. Speaking of this
experience, Otto notes that 'there is sublimity alike
in the lofty throne and the sovereign figure of God,
the skirts of his raiment "filling the temple", and
the solemn majesty of the attendant angels about
Him' (H,63). The second example is a type of
architecture. Imposing and magnificent artistic
creations like the Egyptian pyramids and the Gothic
cathedrals gain their singular capacity to inspire
deep feelings of the numinous, Otto thinks, from
their sheer 'pomp of sublime pose and gesture' (H,
66-68). He also contends that as religions have
developed from primitive to more advanced forms,

the category of the sublime has loomed ever more large in their portrayals of the divine, showing the intimate and lasting connection between the two conceptions (H,45,63).

Otto speaks often about the power of art (painting, architecture, literature, music) to arouse or give expression to numinous feelings (e.g., H,66-71,81,150-151). But he restricts his discussion of aesthetic schematization to the category of the sublime. He does assert that there is a 'magical' quality in some pictorial art, whereby it stirs the numinous feeling of mysterium, but the magical is not an aesthetic category. It is more akin to religion, being 'nothing but a suppressed and dimmed form of the numinous, a crude form of it which great art purifies and ennobles' (H,67).

Philosophical Schematization

The last of the three types of schematization of the holy is the schematization of its mysterium aspect by means of what I shall call 'philosophical' concepts, since Otto does not give them a distinctive name. The key philosophical concept involved in this type of schematization is that of 'absoluteness'.[3] As Otto states, 'The "moment" mysteriosum is schematized by the absoluteness of all rational attributes applied to the deity' (H,140). The concept of absoluteness closely resembles the awareness of the divine as mysterium, as it must if it is to serve as its schematization. For example, since our understanding can be adequate only to that which is relative, the absolute, like the mysterious, eludes our conceptual grasp. But still, the concept of absoluteness and the awareness of mysterium are not

entirely the same. They are related to one another
only in an analogical way.

The principal difference between the two is
that whereas divine attributes differ only 'formally'
from attributes applied to creatures, the qualitative
content remaining the same, the 'mysterious' 'is that
which lies altogether outside what can be thought,
and is, alike in form, quality, and essence, the
utterly and "wholly other"' (H,141). Human love,
knowledge, and goodness, for instance, are relative, admitting of degrees. But when these concepts are applied to the divine, they become
absolute or nonrelative, yielding such attributes as
omnibenevolence and omniscience. Such concepts
are familiar to us in their actual qualitative
character, but not in their formal character. We
know from ordinary experience what love, knowledge, and goodness mean, but we do not fully
understand what is meant by them as absolute.

It might seem that by the 'formal' difference
between relative and absolute attributes Otto means
only a difference of degree, the divine attributes
being human properties raised to the nth degree, as
it were. But he means more than this. The function of the absolute attributes is to draw a radical
contrast between the divine and the creaturely
which is far more than a difference of degree.
Their function is to call attention to the uniqueness
of the divine when compared with all that is merely
creaturely and mundane. Such attributes (H,60)

never give a positive suggestion of the object to
which the religious consciousness refers; they are
only of assistance in so far as they profess to
indicate an object, which they at the same time contrast with another, at once distinct from and

inferior to it, e.g., 'the invisible', 'the eternal'
(non-temporal), 'the supernatural', 'the transcendent'.

As schemata these absolute attributes express in
their own fashion and from a more conceptual direction what is ideogramatically characterized as the
'wholly other' nature of the divine. The formal
difference between relative and absolute attributes
comes down, therefore, to a distinction between two
entirely different orders of reality or levels of
value. Categories of interpretation taken from
creaturely experience can afford some inkling of
the nature of the divine, but it is only the vaguest
hint and suggestion, more to be prized for the
contrast it implies between the divine and the
creaturely spheres than for its elucidation of anything in common between them. Or put another
way, such categories are more valuable for what
they do not and cannot express than for what they
succeed in making clear.
    What this obviously means is that it is a
mistake to interpret the absolute attributes of the
divine in too literal or positive a way. For this
means failing to perceive that they 'imply a nonrational or supra-rational Subject of which they are
predicates', a subject 'which they qualify, but which
in its deeper essence is not, nor indeed can be
comprehended in them; which rather requires comprehension of a quite different kind' (H,2). Otto
deplores the kind of 'intellectualist Scholasticism' by
whose methods of interpretation 'the fundamental
fact of religious experience is, as it were, simply
rolled out so thin and flat as to be finally eliminated
altogether' (H,27).

An example of the too literal, overintellectualized interpretation of the absoluteness of divine attributes is the doctrine of predestination, as that is commonly conceived (see also the earlier discussion of this doctrine in connection with 'overpoweringness'). The absolute attribute involved here is that of divine omnipotence. Taken as an authentic schema, what this attribute does is to give conceptual expression to one sort of contrast between the human and the divine. It depicts the 'felt submergence and annihilation' of the creature 'as over against the numen...here impotence and there omnipotence; here the futility of one's own choice, there the will that ordains all and determines all' (H,89). But when used in an illegitimate and inauthentic way, omnipotence as a philosophical schema becomes converted into a literal doctrine of the fortuitous nature of the divine will, as that is emphasized in Islamic orthodoxy, for example, or in the voluntaristic theology which crops up in the Christian West. This line of interpretation makes nonsense of certain moral schematizations of the divine in ascribing the validity of the moral law only to chance and arbitrary divine decrees. It is a view productive of much fanaticism, Otto believes, and one which destroys altogether the delicate tension between the tremendum and the fascinans elements of numinous experience (H,90-92). Moreover, instead of maintaining a proper sense of the divine mysterium, it presents God in the entirely intelligible, if morally repulsive, guise of a capricious despot. The radical contrast between the divine and the human is then simply lost sight of.

The rule to follow in all such matters, according to Otto, is not that of simple logical deduction. Omnipotence, for example, is not to be taken as a premise to be approached in an ordinary intellectual manner. The right course is to focus upon those aspects of experience of the holy for which omnipotence is an authentic schematization, e.g., the felt contrast between awareness of oneself as a weak and insignificant creature, and the sense of the overwhelming strangeness and absorbing splendor of the divine. What Otto pleads for with respect to the concept of divine omnipotence is what he pleads for throughout his book: a theology firmly rooted in what he takes to be given in direct religious experience, instead of a theology based on mere abstract deduction and speculative surmise. Otto sees philosophical schematizations as being of great value for maintaining a strong sense of the mystery and uniqueness of the holy. But he also warns that when their analogical and schematic role is not kept clearly in mind the results can be disastrous for religious understanding.

3.   INTERRELATIONS OF THE NONRATIONAL AND THE RATIONAL ASPECTS OF THE HOLY

The previous two section have mainly emphasized the differences between the nonrational and the rational aspects of the holy. But how does Otto conceive the interrelations of these two aspects? Some start toward answering this question was made in our earlier discussion but now that answer needs to be made more explicit and drawn out in more detail.

We have already seen that the numinous or nonrational side of the holy must have a certain priority over the rational, because it provides the substrate or basis on which the rational meanings can be revealed. Or to put it another way, numinous experience and awareness, ideogramatically expressed, is the precondition for rational schematizations in religion. But we have also seen how awareness of the holy in its numinous aspects of tremendum, fascinans, and mysterium is deepened and enhanced by moral, aesthetic, and philosophic schematizations. So there is an important sense in which the two aspects of the holy interpenetrate one another and assist one another's fullest development. Therefore, Otto is not willing to give preference to one aspect over the other. Both are quite essential to the idea of the holy; so essential, in fact, that he frequently speaks of the nonrational as constituting the woof and the rational, the warp, of a tightly woven fabric (H,98-99, 135-136,46,142,153, etc.).

In Otto's eyes, history gives strong evidence of the intricacy of connection between the numinous and the rational parts of the holy. For it is not the case that the nonrational came full-blown onto the stage of history in primitive times, thence to undergo a gradual process of rationalization until the rational eventually overmastered and supplanted its numinous substrate. This is the reading of religious history given by its rationalistic interpreters, whom Otto castigates for failing to comprehend the enduring importance of the nonrational in the combined, complex category of the holy. The historical process as he sees it is rather that of two streams, the numinous and the rational, which sometimes run parallel and sometimes intersect. Each of these streams undergoes a continuing process of historical development which is enriched and furthered by their frequent interminglings.

Numinous development takes its rise, as has been noted, primarily from what Otto calls 'daemonic dread', where the numen is experienced simply as an object of horror and terror. Thence it proceeds to a stage of magical and shamanistic attempts to exploit the holy for the natural ends of man, until finally the distinctive value of the holy as a supreme good in its own right (fascinans) is perceived, and it is fervently sought for its own sake (H,32-33). Rational development parallels this numinous development, with the moral schematization of the punishing wrath of God or the gods as an earlier stage, to be supplemented by later stages in which the grace, sublimity, and absoluteness of the divine are also given their due. The directionality of this process of rationalization 'is in no wise suppression of the numinous or its supersession by something else...but rather the completion and charging of it with a new content' (H,109-111,140).

The fullest development of both the nonrational and the rational sides of the experience of the holy is so important to Otto that he finds in it what is perhaps the most basic criterion to be used in evaluating religious systems. 'The degree in which both rational and nonrational elements are jointly present, united in healthy and lovely harmony, affords a criterion to measure the relative rank of religion—and one, too, that is specifically religious' (H,141-142). By this measure Islam, Taoism, and both Eastern and Western forms of mysticism fall short, because they represent a preponderance of the nonrational over the rational (H,102,201,note 196,85,note). And as examples of the opposite deficiency Otto cites the theology of the 'Lutheran school', the thought of Albrecht Ritschl, and the views of the American transcendentalist, Theodore

Parker. All are found wanting, because they give such stress to the rational that the nonrational side of the holy is brought into virtual eclipse (H, 108,54,53,note). Applying his yardstick to the Christianity of the Bible, however, Otto comes to the happy conclusion that it 'stands out in complete superiority over all its sister religions'. It merits this status both by 'the continual living activity of its nonrational elements', which guard it from 'passing into "rationalism"', and by 'being steeped in and saturated with rational elements' which keep it 'from sinking into fanaticism or mere mysticality' (H,141-142).

One example of the precise blend of rational and numinous elements Otto detects in Christianity is its doctrine of God as transcendent Father and immanent Spirit. The first achieves a 'definiteness and fixity of representation' quite congenial to the rational mind. But the second is a continual reminder that no personalistic conception can 'quite comprise the full import' of the divine as 'the inapprehensible and unnameable', or as a mysterious power which indwells the creature and becomes a very part of him, rather than merely standing over against him as a transcendent being. Similarly, the Christian doctrine of God as Love, and not merely as One who loves, suggests the suprapersonal, nonrational side of the divine while yet retaining overtones of the personalistic, more rational view (H, 198-201). Further elaboration of Otto's reasons for judging Christianity to be the superior religion lies beyond the scope of our concern here, since we are interested primarily in the interpretive significance of his theory of religion, not its normative aspect.[4]

4.   THE AUTONOMY OF RELIGION

One of Otto's principal concerns in Das Heilige—
certainly as important as his delineation of the nonrational side of the holy in its relations to the
rational, or his defense of the superiority of the
Christian religion—is making as strong a case as
he can for the autonomy of religion. Thus would
he counter thinkers like Spinoza and Kant, who
subsume religion under some more basic mode of
judgment or dimension of experience, such as the
philosophical or the moral. Otto's strong resistance
to such reductionism has already been brought out
in our discussion of his claim that moral, aesthetic,
and philosophical interpretations of numinous experience can in no way substitute for or exhaust the
meaning of that experience. They serve only to
schematize it, that is, to suggest by means of
appropriate but approximate rational analogues what
it is in its own right and what relations it has to
other areas of life.

His defense of the autonomy of religion is also
intimately tied to his allegation that the idea of the
holy is a priori, and hence, underivable from ideas
in natural or nonnuminous spheres of thought and
awareness. In speaking of the holy as an a priori
category, Otto means to point to the presence in
man of an 'inborn capacity to receive and understand' matters religious, or an innate 'faculty of
receptivity and a principle of judgment and
acknowledgement' which is peculiarly religious.
This capacity or faculty he identifies with the
fundus animae spoken of by the mystics: the
innermost depth of the human soul and the 'hidden
substantive source, from which the religious ideas
and feelings are formed, which lies in the mind

independently of sense experience' (H,61,177,112, 114).

Man's possession of this propensity means for Otto that he has the ability to respond to religious reality and to make religious judgments on the basis of ideas or feelings which are absolutely 'pure', in Kant's sense of the term, and yet which must be distinguished from ideas belonging to the pure theoretical or the pure practical reason (H,112-114). Since the existence of a priori ideas or principles of a certain kind was the basis on which Kant erected each of his three Critiques, Otto is convinced that he has laid the groundwork for a fourth type of critique, namely, a critique of religious judgment. Religion, no less than perceptual knowledge and science, morality, and aesthetic and teleological judgment, has its own a priori foundations which set it off as a fundamental domain of experience and truth.

The whole import of Otto's attempt to trace out the elements essential to the numinous side of the idea of the holy (i.e., tremendum, mysterium, fascinans) was just to specify the essence of those feelings which belong exclusively to religious awareness and which are therefore entirely sui generis. He also takes the connection between these numinous elements and their moral, aesthetic, and philosophical schematizations to be a priori and necessary, as we have seen, so the rational aspect of the idea of the holy is also grounded in principles of judgment which are a priori in character. Hence the experiences and judgments of religion, for Otto, are mediated by a complex idea which is safeguarded on both its nonrational and its rational sides from any sort of derivation from ideas belonging to other spheres, or from reduction to such ideas.

But Otto can safeguard the autonomy of religion in this manner only if he can convince us that the complex idea of the holy does indeed have the a priori character he attributes to it. And he tries to do this by several lines of argument, some bearing on the numinous side of the idea and others, on its rational side. We will look first at two arguments relating to the numinous side.

The first argument is one from introspection. Otto confidently asserts that there 'is none of us who has any living capacity for emotion but must have known at some time or at some place what it is to feel really "uncanny", to have a feeling of "eeriness"'. So each of us has had intimations at first hand of the feelings of daemonic dread from which religion arose historically. And a bit of reflection will convince us that such feelings are not like any others, that they are quite separate, underivable, and unique. An example of this already noted is Otto's contention that a sharp separation can easily be made between our natural reactions to a dead body and the numinous feelings with which we respond to it (H,125,119).

The second argument takes as its premise Otto's observation that the external features stimulating numinous states of mind 'are often quite slight, indeed so scanty that hardly any account can be given of them, so disproportionate are they to the strength of the emotional impression itself'. This is proof, for Otto, that the feelings in question are not acquired from such external features or caused by them, but that they are simply occasioned by them. These feelings lie in wait, as it were, in the depths of the soul, waiting to be lifted spontaneously into awareness by the impetus of appropriate circumstances. 'For, if such meanings are not there at the start in some form or other, the mental and emotional disturbance could never take place' (H,125-126).

Other arguments of Otto are intended to show the necessary connection between numinous experience and its schematizations. The first argument to this effect turns upon the vague notions of 'high gods' (or a high god) in many primitive religions. Even though primitive tribesmen have hardly any day-to-day, practical relations with such high gods, they nevertheless sense that beyond their crude mythological images of deity there is a religious value which far surpasses them, 'a value which may well accord with the divine in the highest sense'. The connection between the tribesmen's numinous experiences and the exaltedness and absoluteness of the divine is thus already seen by them, albeit haltingly and unclearly (H,129).

A second argument is taken from the experiences of Christian missionaries. 'Once enunciated and understood, the ideas of the unity and goodness of the divine nature often take a surprisingly short time to become firmly fixed in the bearer's mind, if he show any susceptibility for religious feeling'. This readiness, and even eagerness, to accept higher concepts of the divine, once these are clearly presented, is strong proof, Otto thinks, that schematizations of the numinous carry their own internal warrant (H,139).

A third argument is that the development of all religious traditions tends to proceed along the lines of moral, aesthetic, and philosophical schematizations: 'wherever religion, escaping from its first crudity of manifestation, has risen to a higher type, this process of synthesis has in all cases set in and continued more and more positively'. That such

schematizations are genuine and inevitable 'may be
distinctly seen from the fact' that they 'do not fall
to pieces, and cannot be cut out as the development
of the consciousness of religious truth proceeds
onwards and upwards', but are 'only recognized
with greater definiteness and certainty' (H,139-140,
45).[5]

Supplementing these arguments from the
history of religions is a fourth and final argument
taken by Otto from one of the dialogues of Plato.
Socrates, in the Republic (II,382E) says to
Adeimantos: 'Then God is altogether simple and
true in deed and word, and neither changes himself
nor deceives others...'. And the latter replies, 'I
myself think so, ...when I hear you say it'. The
unhesitating and confident manner of Adeimantos's
response gives indisputable evidence, Otto believes,
of the unbroken line of continuity between numinous
experience and its schematizations, a continuity that
cannot be transmitted or taught, but that is simply
recognized for what it is on the testimony of each
person's inherent sense of rationality (H,137).

But if the fundamental feelings and concepts of
religion are a priori and hence, presumably directly
available to every reflective person, what role do
the founders of religion and the great religious
teachers have in Otto's scheme? He carefully distinguishes between the a priori capacities of men
unactualized and those capacities as actualized:
'...what is a universal potentiality of man as such
is by no means to be found in actuality the universal possession of every single man...' (H,149).
And he believes that only certain persons, highly
gifted in religious sensibility, or what he calls the
'faculty of divination', have the ability to make
those profound inroads into the a priori roots of

religious consciousness which give rise to new
religious systems or to radical new departures in
existing systems.   The great majority of mankind
are dependent on these few great teachers for
having their own innate religious predispositions
brought into full play.   So not only must the a
priori capacities of men be stimulated by appropriate
outward circumstances, such as the rustling of the
wind in the trees in a deserted place on a dark
night, or encounter with something uncommonly
strange and bewildering.   These capacities must
also await arousal by the presence and teachings of
the religious geniuses of history, if they are to be
developed to their fullest (H,143-154).

5.   CLASSIFICATION AND CRITICISM OF OTTO'S THEORY

For purposes of classification and criticism of Otto's
theory of religion, let us return to the three
questions asked about the theories of Spinoza and
Kant.   (A) Can this theory properly be regarded as
an interpretive theory of religion?   (B) If it can,
what type of interpretive theory can it be said to
be?   (C) What critical assessment of it can we make,
through use of the criteria set out in Part One?
     (A) Otto's views on religion have all the
earmarks of a full-blown theory, as against a mere
definition or a descriptive generalization.   He
presents us with several interrelated categories,
three of them delineating the numinous aspect of
the holy (tremendum, mysterium, fascinans), and at
least three demarcating its rational aspect (goodness, sublimity, absoluteness).   By means of these
categories he would have us to understand the

nature of religion, which comes down finally in his
judgment, to experience of the holy.

Otto's theory does have some explanatory
force. His contention that religion grows up out of
a priori elements in the human psyche would explain
its pervasive presence and influence in human
cultures and in human history. And he intends
this thesis to counter, as he makes explicit several
times, alternative attempts to explain man's
religiosity in some naturalistic or evolutionary
manner, as though religious feelings, for example,
could be said to develop gradually out of natural
emotions like puzzlement or fear, rather than being
of a unique and underivable quality. Just as
nature 'can only be explained by an investigation
into the ultimate fundamental forces of nature and
their laws', so, for Otto, the explanation of religion
must be rooted in certain fundamental predispositions, capacities, and inherent laws of the human
spirit which are simply given and do not require
further explanation (H,114,42-44,124).

Otto does adduce psychological causes of man's
being religious, therefore, and to that extent his
theory is explanatory in character. This is true
even though the explanation he offers does not move
along conventional scientific lines, since it offers no
predictive apparatus or means for its 'public' veri-
fication through evidence of the five senses. Its
final appeal is rather to what Otto terms the 'finer
and more pentrating psychological analysis that can
apprehend differences in quality', that is, to introspection (H,43).

There is also a normative thrust in Otto's
theory. On its basis he deduces the norm of religious judgment that the relative rank of religions
can be adjudged according to the degree in which

they bring to the fore both the nonrational and the
rational aspects of the holy and achieve a precise
balance between them. And using this norm, he
concludes that Christianity ranks highest among the
religions of the world. This conclusion is wholly in
keeping with Otto's profession as a Christian
theologian,[6] but the fact that he arrives at it on
the basis of his theory of religion shows that his
theory as he presents it is not entirely of the interpretive sort.

Still, the interpretive aspect of Otto's theory
is quite prominent, and can even be said to be
clearly predominant. Far from merely assuming out
of hand the nature of that which is to be explained
on the basis of its psychological causes, or that of
which he takes Christianity to be the outstanding
example, Otto makes an assiduous attempt to interpret the nature of religion by focusing on the
common threads of experience and conceptuality
which run through the religions of the world. In
fact, his is widely recognized as one of the truly
classical attempts in this direction. So it is entirely
proper to weigh the merits of his theory as an
interpretive theory of religion, while keeping in
mind that it cannot be called a pure example of the
genre, either in terms of the intent with which it
was fashioned or of its finished form.

(B) Otto's theory is first and foremost a
theory of religious experience, its main preoccupation being with the components and the structure of
such experience. It is a theory which tries to
grasp the essence of those several states of feeling
which can be said to be uniquely religious, to trace
out their interrelations, and to comment on the
extent to which they admit of rational elaboration
by means of schemata appropriated from other

domains. The focus of the theory is always upon what it feels like to be religious or what it is like actually to undergo religious experience. In this light, Otto's theory is mainly an example of an experiential theory of religion. But it also has overtones of the ontological type of theory, as we shall note presently.

What has already been said about Otto's vigorous efforts to defend the autonomy of religion will suffice to show that his theory of religion is a theory of the autonomic type. In him we meet strong resistance to the reductive results of the theories of Spinoza and Kant, along with illuminating discussions of some ways in which religion relates to morality, art, and philosophy. His theory can be classified, therefore, as basically experiential, though with some overlap into the ontological type of theory, and as autonomic.

(C) The normative thrust of Otto's theory has already been talked about, showing that it falls short of criterion (1), and its explanatory force indicates that it does not fully abide by criterion (4). But in fairness to Otto, we need to bear in mind that his theory was not intended merely as an interpretive theory of religion. The theory accords quite well with criterion (2), and since it is brought into explicit dialogue with previous theories like those of Kant and Schleiermacher, the intent being to take into account what is valid in those theories but to avoid their defects, Otto's theory also satisfies criterion (3).

With regard to criteria (5) and (6), Otto makes extensive applications of his theory to various religious systems, seeking thereby to illuminate the logic of single systems and also the ground of similarity and difference among systems. The applications to Christianity, as an example of a single religion, are particularly detailed, and many fresh and valuable insights into its structure are afforded. We saw earlier that neither Spinoza nor Kant gives us any insight, through their respective theories of religion, into the grounds of difference among religions. Otto, on the contrary, comments on this topic at many places in his book. One ground of difference he cites is the relative preponderance given in religious systems to the non-rational or to the rational sides of the holy. Examples have already been given of systems which differ from one another on this basis. Another ground of difference is the extent to which either the tremendum or the fascinans aspect of numinous experience is brought into prominence. A difference between Eastern and Western forms of mysticism which Otto notes is, as we saw, that the latter, in contrast to the former, gives little attention to the dreadful or daunting aspect of the divine, in its prcoccupation with the element of fascinans. And voluntaristic theologies differ from intellectualistic ones in the heavy emphasis placed by the former on the element of 'energy' or 'urgency' within the tremendum.

Otto insists that the significance of such differences cannot really be understood unless they are seen to originate in a single, common type of experience and concern 'which must itself have been grasped in its entirety before its parts [can] be properly apprehended' (H,133). No better statement could be given of the need for, and the contribution of, interpretive theories of religion! He also notes the arbitrariness of attempts to classify religions by genus and species before a viable theory of the nature of religion has been developed

(H,133). This suggests a view of the difference between interpretive theories of religion and descriptive generalizations similar to that sketched above in Chapter 1, section 4.

With regard to criterion (7), we have already seen that it is in the very nature of experiential theories of religion, which Otto's mainly is, that they give attention to the personal side of religion. But he also brings into consideration in his theory what it is that the religious experience is an experience of. He warns that the character of the holy or divine, objectively conceived, 'cannot be expressed verbally, and can only be suggested indirectly through the tone and content of a man's feeling response to it'. In other words, our talk about the holy is experiential through and through: we can only speak of it as it is mediated or communicated through our experience. And yet, Otto insists that in talking about the elements of our experience of the holy, we are not merely describing ourselves as experiencing subjects. The numinous is 'felt as objective and outside the self', and this feeling is immediate and indubitable, he holds, requiring no supplemental inference or interpretation. He criticizes Schleiermacher for thinking that such inference or interpretation is needed, i.e., from the states of feeling as effects to the character of the divine as their cause (H,10-11). Some states of feeling do have more of a reference to the nature of the objective presence made known in the experience, and others, more of a reference to the qualities of the subject undergoing the experience, even though the difference is only one of degree. Otto contrasts 'creature-feeling' with 'overpoweringness' (or 'absolute might'), 'stupor' with mysterium, and 'saving' with 'august' (both versions of fascinans), for example, suggesting that the former terms can be viewed as values (or traits?) of the experiencing subject, and the latter ones, as values (or traits?) of the object. And presumably, were the object disclosed in one's experience to lack such traits, it would not be an object of religious interest in the full sense of the term. So Otto's theory combines an ontological thrust (i.e., it ascribes certain attributes to the religious object, conceived from the cosmic side) with its basically experiential character, which helps to bring into line with the seventh criterion.

Some question can be raised about how adequately general Otto's treatment of religious experience or of the cosmic side of religion is (the eighth criterion). Ninian Smart discusses this question in a systematic and sustained way in Reasons and Faiths (1958), marshaling arguments to the effect that the numinous represents only one possible 'strand' in the discourse of world religions, and that it is not an all-encompassing category for interpreting religious experience or religious systems. Some systems, like Theravada Buddhism, have very little of the numinous strand in them (Smart 1958,passim). In truth, a Western, theistic bias does run throughout Otto's presentation of his theory. His utilization of it for the apologetic purpose of stressing the superiority of a Western religion, Christianity, only makes this bias all the more evident.

His theory comes off very well, however, as measured by criterion nine. Not only does he make a strong case for religion's having a distinctive domain and for its involving experiences, interpretations, and evaluations of a singular sort. He also offers a clarifying interpretation of ways in which

religion can interact with other domains of
experience and judgment, such as morality, art,
and philosophy.

Finally, what would it mean to be nonreligious
in Otto's theory (criterion ten)? This can rather
easily be surmised. It would mean having one's
innate religious propensities remain in an unculti-
vated and unattended state, just as if one were to
fail to develop an inherited talent. And this lack
of cultivation and attention would be reflected in
lack of interest in the concerns and claims of religious systems. Or put another way, one would be
uninterested in religious intepretations and valuations for the simple reason that he has little first-
hand acquaintance with the unique kind of experience to which they relate. Only when such experience is undergone and brought to the forefront of
consciousness can real religious inquiry begin and
genuine religious commitment be sustained.

The principal virtues of Otto's theory of
religion, as compared with the theories of Spinoza
and Kant, would seem to be three: the case he
makes for the autonomy of religion; the emphasis he
gives to the rootage of religious claims in religious
experience, and the success he achieves in giving
an interpretation of the nature of that experience;
and the resources in his theory for showing
grounds of difference, as well as similarity, among
religious systems. But beyond this, his theory as
a whole is one of the great milestones in the history
of attempts to understand the religious side of
human nature, as expressed in a variety of cultures
and traditions.

6

Tillich: Religion as Self-transcendence in the Direction of the Ultimate

The endeavor to understand the distinctive character of religion, as well as its modes of inter-relation with other fundamental types of human concern, was a life-long preoccupation of Paul Tillich and a theme which figures prominently in most of his writings. We can begin our analysis of the theory of religion which resulted from this persistent inquiry by looking at the account he gives of the relations between religion, on the one hand, and morality and culture, on the other, in the third volume of his major work, Systematic Theology (1951-1963, hereafter ST).

Tillich distinguishes morality, culture, and religion by claiming that the moral act is one of self-integration, the cultural act, one of self-creativity, and the religious act, one of self-trans-cendence. And each of these acts takes place within 'the dimension of the spirit', a term he uses to set off the personal and communal life character-istic of human beings from such other dimensions of being as inorganic existence, nonconscious life, and conscious life, all of which the dimension of the spirit presupposes, and whose combined poten-tialities it brings into full expression.

1.   MORALITY AND CULTURE

The basic thrust of moral action, as Tillich conceives it, is toward the constitution of the personal self, or the sense of one's individuality as a person, contrasting with a world outside oneself. Since the sense of personhood is of the very essence of the dimension of the spirit, morality is the function of life by which this dimension comes into being. The constitution of a human person requires in part the emergence of a center or focus from whose perspective all else in the universe can be viewed and to which all else can be related. To this extent the dimension of the spirit coincides with the dimension of conscious life, or what Tillich calls 'the psychological dimension'. That is, what has so far been said could also be said of conscious but nonpersonal animals.

The peculiarly human experience of personhood turns upon a distinction Tillich makes between 'environment' and 'world'. Conscious animals other than human beings experience their environment from the perspective of self-awareness, but only human beings experience a world, i.e., 'the structured unity of all possible content' (ST,III,36). Tillich clarifies this notion of a 'world' in The Courage to Be (1952,hereafter CTB) by stating that it is man's possession of language which gives him 'the power to abstract from the concretely given, and having abstracted from it, to return to it, to interpret and transform it'. By the unique powers of abstract conceptuality language confers, man gains his character of intentionality, or of 'being directed toward meaningful contents' (CTB,81-82; see also ST,I,170-171). The 'concretely given' of which he speaks here Tillich calls the 'merely given'

in Systematic Theology, and he identifies it there
with the environment (ST,III,39).   And the
'meaningful contents' toward which man is directed
comprise his 'world', as Tillich is using the term.
Total centeredness of self is dependent upon this
sense of being oriented toward a structured world
of meanings, for it means an ability to oppose
oneself to every part of the world, including even
oneself as part of the world (ST,III,39).

   This transcendence of self over its world
produces an awareness of freedom.   This awareness
is exhibited from one aspect as a profound drive
(which Tillich associates with Freud's 'libido') to
assimilate everything outside oneself into oneself,
so as to make use of everything else for one's
own purposes.   But from another aspect, this
awareness involves an openness to norms which can
regulate the exercise of one's freedom.   The two
aspects relate to one another in the following way.
The drive to incorporate everything into oneself
soon runs into limits.   One sort of limit is the
finitude of the self, which contrasts with the vast-
ness of the world—its resistance to being taken up
completely into any single perspective.   But a more
significant limit is the encounter with other selves.
These other selves are centered perspectives and
loci of freedom in their own right, and as such they
resist being assimilated into the content of one's
own selfhood.   In other words, each personal center
is unique and a counterforce to the will to domina-
tion.   So each self must come to terms with the fact
of other selves, and it can do so only when those
other selves are accorded the respect their uniqueness and dignity require.

   The experience of this second limit to one's
own self-centeredness and exploitative drives 'is the

experience of the ought-to-be, the moral imperative'. Only when this normative factor is taken fully into account can a social context be established in which it is possible for each self to achieve its maximum personhood or self-integration. 'Personal life emerges in the encounter of person with person and in no other way' (ST,III,40). In sum, the moral act is the achievement of self-integration within a community. It is an act of the responsible self in relation to other responsible selves. The polar 'ontological elements' most clearly involved in the moral act, says Tillich, are those of individualization and participation (ST,III,41; see ST,I,174-178).

The cultural act is one of self-creativity, by which Tillich means that it is marked by tension between the ontological elements of dynamics and form. While he takes form to be of the essence of culture, he also notes that the achievement of any new cultural 'form (e.g., a building, a poem, a law) is made possible only by breaking through the limits of the old form' (ST,III,60,50). So in devising the forms of cultural creation there is a dynamism which provides some contrast with the moral act. 'Self-integration constitutes the individual being in its centeredness; self-creation gives the dynamic impulse which drives life from one centered state to another under the principle of growth' (ST,III,51). The phrase 'the principle of growth' is especially significant in that Tillich connects it with the etymology of the word 'culture'. 'Culture, cultura, is that which takes care of something, keeps it alive, and makes it grow' (ST,III, 57). The contrast with the moral act is only a relative one, however, for every cultural act is the act of a centered self, and the moral act must find

cultural forms in which to manifest itself.
Moreover, the moral act is not one merely of static
self-integration, for self-integration incorporates
the two poles of self-identity and self-alteration.
The latter is a dynamic principle whereby the
centered self undergoes continual change as it takes
the risk of assimilating new content into itself,
despite the threat this poses to its already achieved
self-identity (ST,III,68,95,41-44).

Tillich divides culture into two basic functions
and then into a main trend of development he thinks
to be implied by each function. The two functions
are language and technology. Language is the
basic creation of culture, because, as we have seen,
without language man would not even have a
'world'. But the use of tools in technology implies
a liberation from bondage to the naturally given
conditions of existence (i.e., from the 'environment') which is akin to the world-fashioning role
of language. The function of language develops in
the direction of theoria, with its twin aims of truth
and authentic expression. The aim of truth is
pursued with cognitive concepts, such as those
employed in science and philosophy, while the aim
of authentic expression is sought with aesthetic
images, such as are to be found in the fine arts.
The technical function, with its calculation of means
and ends, develops into such activities of praxis as
economics, medicine, administration, law, and
education. All of these modes of culture exhibit a
dependence on the moral act, just as the moral act
depends on the creations of culture.

Some of these interrelations of morality and
culture can be briefly indicated. We have already
taken note of the fact that there can be no moral
acts without culture giving form to these acts by

supplying such things as 'the concrete ideals of
personality and community and the changing laws of
ethical wisdom' (ST,III,95). Morality also imparts
an explicit seriousness to culture by stressing a
depth of concern for the needs and rights of
persons which can keep cultural activities from
being carried on merely for their own sake, as if
they were disconnected from concrete human ends.
On the other hand, a morality pursued in indifference to the dynamics of everyday cultural life soon
becomes an empty form, devoid of specific content
and relevance (ST,III,160-161). In addition, there
are two common roots of morality and culture. The
first is man's possession of language. Neither self-
integration nor self-creation would be possible
without the universe of meaning language provides.
The second common root is the encounter of person
with person. Morality loses its meaning when a
person ceases to respond to other persons as
persons. And the basic cultural form, language,
becomes mere gibberish when one fails in his use
of it to be sensitive to the '"wall" of the listening
thou' (ST,III,58). So morality and culture depend
on one another at every turn.

2. RELIGION AS SELF-TRANSCENDENCE

Turning now to religion, Tillich associates it
especially with self-transcendence, although such
transcendence is also involved in both morality and
culture. In morality it is manifested as a kind of
circular process going from identity through altera-
tion and back to identity. And in cultural growth
it is evidenced by a horizontal development, whereby earlier cultural forms are being continually

transcended by later ones. But in neither of these two functions is there any transcendence of the finite itself. There is simply the substitution of one finite stage for another. The case is quite different with religion. 'It is striving in the vertical direction toward ultimate and infinite being. The vertical transcends both the circular line of center-edness and the horizontal line of growth'. Religious transcendence, then, 'is identical with the attitude of devotion toward that which is ultimate' (ST,III, 86,236).

Tillich interprets this religious drive to transcend the finite in terms of the polar ontological elements of freedom and destiny. These elements can be applied properly only to the human dimension, but he holds that there are analogies to them in the other dimensions of being. To say that man is free is to recognize his capacity to transcend 'any given situation, leaving the real for the sake of the possible. He is not bound to the situation in which he finds himself...' (ST,III,303). This means that man is not bound to the mechanisms of stimulus and response but can deliberate and decide in the light of reasons, reasons stemming from both the moral and the logical sides of his nature. It also means that he has the power of cultural self-creation through language, art, technology, theory, and consciously contrived social institutions. Man even has the freedom to be free from his freedom, that is, to surrender his own humanity (ST,II,31-32). But human freedom, though it has impressive scope, is not a total or infinite freedom. It is a finite freedom, which is to say that it exists in tension with what Tillich calls man's 'destiny'.

By man's destiny he means at least three things: the givenness of man's nature, the givenness of the concrete situations in which man must exercise his freedom, and the universality of man's experience of estrangement from his essential being.

Man's nature is that of a creature or a contingent being. For Tillich this means that he is prey to the threat of nonbeing, as is seen most clearly in the inevitability of his death, but also in the contingencies which pervade his existence and in his susceptibility to error. The presence of animal drives is also a part of man's creaturely nature, as is the sway exerted upon him by unconscious motivations stemming both from the peculiarities of his experience and from his social surroundings. All of these creaturely facts or contingencies of man's being help to define the finite context of human freedom.

Secondly, there are the specific conditions of each concrete situation in which human freedom is exercised. These conditions constitute, for one thing, the givenness of the centered self at any particular moment in which it acts. Such selfhood 'includes the communities to which I belong, the past unremembered and remembered, the environment which has shaped me, the world which has made an impact on me. It refers to all my former decisions. Destiny...is myself as given, formed by nature, history, and myself' (ST,I,185). And for another thing, these conditions refer to the particularities of the context surrounding the actions of the centered self, including the particular persons those actions will affect.

Thirdly, there is the experience of estrangement, which Tillich defines as man's being 'outside the divine center to which his own center essentially belongs' (ST,II,49). This experience does not reflect a structural necessity in the human situation, but it is still universal. It results from acts whereby each human being takes the risk of freedom, with its acceptance of responsibility and its possibility of lapsing into error and guilt. Responsibility can be achieved only through acts of freedom which constitute the self as a centered self. But with such acts there also comes the temptation, connected with the self's desire to assimilate everything to itself, to make itself the center of its own existence and of the world, and to subject everything around itself to an endless craving for self-gratification. These are the sins of hubris and concupiscence, respectively, bringing with them the guilt of estrangement from the power of being or divine center to which every finite thing essentially belongs. For Tillich maintains that it is only the ultimate or being-itself which can be the legitimate center of self and the world. To exalt one's finite self to the position of ultimacy, or any other finite thing to such a position, is to profane the holy, or that which alone is truly ultimate. The universality of tragic hubris and concupiscence, as well as of the awareness of having committed them and continuing to commit them, is part of the meaning of the destiny which underlies and conditions the exercise of human freedom.

It is important to Tillich, however, that destiny be seen not merely or even primarily as a limit upon the act of freedom. It ought also to be recognized as the very basis of freedom. 'In every act of existential self-realization, freedom and destiny are united. Existence is both fact and act' (ST,II,78). It is the givenness of man's nature which makes his freedom possible. And as for the second sense of 'destiny', it is 'the concreteness of our being which makes all our decisions our decisions' (ST,I,184), and it is from the concrete situation that these decisions derive their specific import. Even in the third sense, freedom and destiny are united. For he who seeks utterly to avoid the risk of estrangement would have to avoid being free, which would mean the avoidance of being human.

But what is the specific connection Tillich establishes between the polarity of freedom and destiny, on the one hand, and the religious impulse of self-transcendence in the direction of the ultimate, on the other? The connection is stated in the following passage (ST,I,210), which we will want to analyze:

Anxiety about meaninglessness is the characteristically human form of ontological anxiety. It is the form of anxiety which only a being can have in whose nature freedom and destiny are united. The threat of losing this unity drives man toward the question of an infinite, unthreatened ground of meaning; it drives him to the question of God.

Tillich thus associates the threat of losing the unity of freedom and destiny with the threat of meaninglessness. Let us first see why he does this, and then we can relate the threat of meaninglessness to religion as self-transcendence.

The anxiety about meaninglessness which stems from the polarity of freedom and destiny comes down to this: experience of a constant threat that one's freedom lose its essential connection with his destiny, in which case freedom ceases to be freedom and becomes mere contingency or arbitrariness; or that one's destiny lose its essential connection with one's freedom, in which case destiny ceases to be destiny and becomes mere necessity or compulsion. When the first side of this threat becomes actual, one succumbs to the illusion of an empty self, a self of pure subjectivity. And when the second side becomes actual, one succumbs to the illusion of the self as an object rather than a subject. In either case, the self loses its unity or centeredness and with that, the meaning of its life.

When the freedom of the self is pursued in obliviousness to the constraints imposed upon it by its destiny, it loses sight of its very nature and giveness as a finite self and is soon consumed by the evils of hubris and concupiscence. It can be so taken with its own greatness that it tries to make itself the center of everything, as though it were of infinite value and importance (hubris). It thereby confuses its finite truths with infinite truths; it attributes ultimate significance to its finite cultural creations; and it identifies its limited moral attainments with absolute goodness. But this image of the self is quickly brought to grief by the inescapable facts of human destiny: 'man's finitude, his weakness and his errors, his ignorance and his insecurity, his loneliness and his anxiety' (ST,II, 51). So this path leads only to frustration and disillusionment.

Another version of the evil of hubris, as Tillich interprets it, is the doctrine of certain existentialist philosophers, most notably the early Jean Paul Sartre, that the self is pure subjectivity, devoid of antecedent content or constraint (ST,I, 201). This is the doctrine of the empty self, which must create by sheer acts of the will, moment by moment, all that is true, good, or meaningful. But not only does this doctrine overlook the essential

nature of man, the concrete givenness of the self,
and those particular factors which figure in every
context of decision. It also portrays the self's
freedom as nothing but an empty contingency for
which 'no choice is objectively preferable to any
other; no commitment to a cause or person is meaningful; no dominant purpose can be established'
(ST,II,63). This is not a vision of purposive freedom but of a 'wilfulness without norms', i.e., of a
freedom which has degenerated into arbitrariness
(My Search for Absolutes 1969:112,hereafter MSFA).
It is a vision of an absurd and pointless freedom.
      Just as the route of hubris when unrelentingly
set out upon leads to meaninglessness, so does that
of concupiscence, which Tillich also identifies with
freedom detached from destiny. Concupiscence, the
illusion of an unbridled license to draw the whole of
reality into oneself for the sake of one's own gratification, can be manifested in the form of the
ceaseless sexual strivings of a Don Juan, the quest
for unlimited power of a Nero, or the search for
total knowledge of a Faust. But in every case it
is doomed to a tragic denouement, for the desire it
seeks to gratify is in its very nature unsatisfiable.
For it is an infinite desire, not limited to any
definite object and not restrained by any respect
for the dignity of persons. In the grip of such
compulsive and boundless craving, carried forward
in the name of unrestricted freedom, the self soon
comes to know the utter futility of its quest. Then
it experiences the drive to escape from its desperate
craving through its own death. So it oscillates
between its libidinous drives and its yearning for
self-extinction, just as Freud realized. Its situation
is one of acute anguish, if not complete despair
(ST,II,52-53).

In all the situations which we have so far described, situations in which freedom is torn away from destiny, the self fail to attain unity or center-edness and to find meaning for its life. It fails to attain this unity in the first version of hubris, because it lacks awareness of itself as finite, as but one perspective or center among many others. In trying to be the center of the universe, the self ignores its own inherent limitations, and without a realistic grasp of those limitations it cannot hope to achieve a centeredness appropriate to itself. The self also fails to attain centeredness in the second version of hubris, the illusion of a completely con-tingent freedom, because it has nothing to which it is responsible, no objective structure of value or purpose which can give it integration. The self fails to find centeredness in the situation of con-cupiscence as well, because particular drives eclipse its personal center, and because it is doomed never to experience the contentment that comes with the satisfaction of finite desires. It is thus driven relentlessly to the point of yearning for the elimina-tion of its freedom and for its own death. Were it more aware of the restraints upon the search for gratification implied by destiny, its experiences could be different.

But it is also possible to give an exaggerated and undue emphasis to destiny, i.e., to the role of factors in experience which limit the exercise of freedom. When this happens the result is again the disintegration of the self and a collapse into mean-inglessness. For those factors come to be seen only as limits and inhibitions of freedom, rather than being properly conceived as the conditions which underlie finite freedom and make it possible. So the sense of freedom itself is lost, and with that, the awareness of both self and world. Man ceases to understand himself as a finitely free being interacting with a world which is at least in part the outcome of his own creativity. He comes to view himself rather as an object manipulated by internal compulsions and mechanical forces of his environment. Tillich associates this view with the doctrine of causal determinism assumed by many biologists, psychologists, and social scientists, and he links it also with the technological mentality that has come to dominate the outlook of the Western world (ST,II,56;ST,III,74;CTB,138-189). With such a view, man and his world are swallowed up into the impersonal forces of the environment. He becomes just a thing, mechanically related to other things. He is no longer a centered self enjoying finite freedom but only an object whose moods and actions are shaped by forces entirely beyond any intentional control. Because these forces 'move against one another without a deciding center', the result is disintegration and meaninglessness (ST,II,63).

These are ways, then, in which the threat of losing the unity of freedom and destiny can expose man to the dissolution of his centered selfhood and the anxiety of meaninglessness. And it is just this anxiety, which, according to Tillich, propels man toward religion, which he conceives as the quest for 'an infinite, unthreatened ground of meaning', i.e., for God. In the religious act the self seeks to transcend itself as finite, and all things that are finite, in its search for an ultimate or divine power of being which can give it the courage to take its anxiety upon itself and to achieve the right balance of the polarity of freedom and destiny.

But why must human beings turn to religion for such courage? Could the anxiety not be dealt

with quite apart from religion, simply on the basis
of an intelligent appraisal of the situation, i.e., of
the need to keep freedom in balance with destiny?
Are not the resources of morality and culture,
wisely drawn upon, quite sufficient to resolve the
problem? Why, in other words, is there any need
to drive beyond the finite to the infinite? In order
to answer such questions from Tillich's point of
view we need to probe more deeply into his understanding of the nature of man and of finitude itself.

    As Tillich views the matter, the whole finite
universe, in each of its dimensions, is marked by a
quality of self-transcendence in the direction of the
ultimate: 'within itself, the finite world points beyond itself. In other words, it is self-transcendent
...The finitude of the finite points to the infinity
of the infinite' (ST,II,7-8). Elsewhere Tillich
states: 'The infinite is present in everything
finite, in the stone as well as the genius'. And he
speaks of self-transcendence as 'the rule of all life'
(ST,I,203;ST,III,247-248). But only in man does
this telos of everything in the universe toward the
infinite, a telos which includes man himself as a
finite being, become conscious.

    To see how man becomes conscious of his telos
toward the infinite and thus of his need for
religion, let us consider Tillich's account of the
relations of 'dreaming innocence', 'estrangement',
and 'reunion', terms which are central to his
conception of human nature and of the situation and
prospects of human beings in the world.

    Dreaming innocence was not an actual state of
mankind in its past history, nor is it a real stage
in the development of individual human beings.
Rather it is to be understood metaphorically as the
expression of a potentiality which lies behind the

states of estrangement and reunion and is needed
for the purpose of analytic contrast with them. The
characteristic of dreaming innocence is that in it
freedom and destiny are in harmony with one
another. But this is only because neither has been
actualized, so dreaming innocence cannot be seen as
a state of perfection. It is a potentiality only, one
which drives beyond itself to actuality. And the
mode of its transition to actuality is man's exercise
of his finite freedom. In freedom he steps out from
his essence (potentiality) into existence.

But he does so with anxiety, because he is
unsure as to how to reconcile his freedom with his
destiny.

He is embarrassed by the demand that he make
decisions implied in his freedom, because he
realizes that he lacks the complete cognitive
and active unity with his destiny which should be
the foundation of his decisions. And he is afraid
of accepting his destiny without reservations,
because he realizes that his decision will be
partial, that he will accept only a part of his
destiny, and that he will fall under a special
determination which is not identical with his real
destiny. So he tries to save his freedom by
arbitrariness, and then he is in danger of losing
both his freedom and his destiny. (ST,I,200)

In a word, man sees his destiny as something
'strange', as not quite a part of him, as a constraint or obstacle to the exercise of his freedom,
rather than as its familiar basis or condition. This
feeling of anxiety, embarrassment, or strangeness
is a sign of man's being in a state of estrangement
from his essential being. And he tends to cope

with it by estranged acts which move either in the direction of emphasizing his freedom at the expense of his destiny or of trying to escape from the demands of his freedom altogether.

This conflict between freedom and destiny in man's state of existential estrangement can readily be translated into a conflict between his sense and taste for the infinite and his awareness of his own finitude. His longing for the infinite is reflected from the side of freedom in the quest for infinite greatness which motivates tragic hubris. It can be seen in the self's claim to be the final arbiter of all value and truth in the illusion of freedom as sheer contingency. And it is manifested in the infinite craving of concupiscence. But when the quest for infinity is carried out in these ways, it is brought to grief, as we have already seen, by the inescapable fact of human finitude, encountered as destiny. So overpowering can this awareness of finitude become, in fact, that man is tempted to deny his capacity for significant freedom, and with it his capacity for self-transcendence. He then makes mockery of his hunger for the infinite and accepts a truncated, objectified view of himself as the helpless pawn of his destiny, now seen as necessity, the opposite of freedom.

But the mistake of these estranged acts is their failure to appreciate that the finite can neither be cut off from the infinite, nor can it be made into the infinite: 'whatever one knows about a finite thing one knows about God, because it is rooted in him as its ground; [and] anything one knows about a finite thing cannot be applied to God' (ST,II,9). This is the dialectic of the finite and the infinite, properly apprehended. The finite must be seen as incomplete in itself and as drawing its value and significance from its participation in the infinite ground of being to which it points.

This applies emphatically to man's exercise of freedom as bounded by destiny. 'The fact that man is never satisfied with any stage of his finite development, the fact that nothing finite can hold him, although finite is his destiny, indicates the indissoluable relation of everything finite to being itself' (ST,I,191). Man's estranged existence thus drives beyond itself in his quest for reunion with the ground of his being. This reunion, which Tillich also refers to as 'the New Being', is the ultimate aim and goal of human life. It is man's 'destiny' in a fourth sense of the term, a teleological sense. Resistance to self-transcendence toward this destiny 'produces the emptiness and meaning-lessness which characterizes the finite when cut off from the infinite' (ST,III,248). And it is out of his experience of this emptiness and meaninglessness that man comes to ask the fundamental religious question. 'Man must ask about the infinite from which he is estranged, although it belongs to him; he must ask about that which gives him the courage to take his anxiety upon himself' (ST,I,206).

Religion, therefore, is the outgrowth of man's awareness of his estranged stage and of his yearning to heal that estrangement through reunion with God, the root and ground of all finite being. Only from this source, the religious man believes, can come the courage he needs to deal with the anxiety generated by the demands and limits of his freedom.

We have now answered our earlier question as to why, according to Tillich's view of the matter, the finite resources of morality and culture do not suffice to enable man to deal with the anxiety which grows out of the polarity of freedom and destiny. But we need to look in more detail at some of the interrelations between religion, morality, and culture, as he conceives them. For this will help to give further clarity to our analysis of his theory of religion.

3.   RELIGION IN RELATION TO MORALITY

Let us look first at some ways in which morality needs religion, and then at religion's need for morality. This pattern can also be followed in our later discussion of the relations of religion and culture. Since we are interested in these relations only to the extent that they can help to illumine Tillich's theory of religion, we will touch only on some main points. We cannot hope to do justice here to the depth and penetration of his detailed inquiries into the interrelations of the three modes.

Tillich thinks that religion makes three necessary contributions to the moral life. 'Religion gives to morality the unconditioned character of the moral imperative, the ultimate moral aim, the reunion of the separated in agape, and the motivating power of grace' (ST,III,95). In My Search for Absolutes he refers to the first contribution as the provision of morality's negative criterion, and to the second one as the provision of morality's positive criterion. The negative criterion was stated by Kant in his famous categorical imperative, which prohibits us from treating a person merely as a thing. This prohibition lies at the core of the principle of justice, with its concern for giving to persons what they deserve or have earned, and for treating them as equal under the law. But the

positive criterion of agape goes much further.   It
seeks the enhancement of the other person instead
of being concerned merely with not violating his
dignity as a person.   It bids us to raise him to a
higher state and to give him more than his due.
Furthermore, the greatness of agape 'is that it
accepts and tolerates the other person even if he is
unacceptable to us and we can barely tolerate him.
Its aim is a union that is more than a union on the
basis of sympathy or friendship, a union in spite of
enmity' (MSFA,108).   But exactly how does religion
figure in here?   How is it implied or required in
either of these two criteria of the moral life?

        Religion is involved in the negative criterion of
morality because it is that which gives this criterion
its unconditional seriousness, that which makes its
demand categorical or absolute.   Tillich interprets
Kant's intuitions of sensibility and categories of
pure theoretical reason (in the Critique of Pure
Reason) as a doctrine of human finitude.   But he
sees Kant's doctrine of the categorical imperative
(as set forth in the Fundamental Principles of the
Metaphysic of Morals) as pointing to an unconditional element in the depth of practical reason which
bursts through the confines of finitude and exposes
the power and presence of the infinite (ST,I,82).
Whenever something ultimate, infinite, or unconditional is encountered in the dimension of the spirit,
there is religion.   For this is the direction in which
religion, as the self-transcendence of life, moves.
Or religion can be described as 'the dimension of
depth' which underlies and sustains both moral and
cultural activities.   In the case of morality this
dimension of depth, or the dimension of the holy,
as Tillich also terms it, is that which gives moral
values their value.   The holy is not itself a separate

type or system of values but the ground of all
values, including those implicit in moral action
(What is Religion? 1969:143,hereafter,WIR). The
categorical imperative gains its compelling power
from recognition of the infinite value of each human
person. And this recognition, in its turn, shows
awareness that each finite person in his essential
being participates in the holy itself, the infinite
ground of all being (ST,III,159).

If morality loses its sense of rootage in the
holy, as it will tend to do in a radically secular or
profane culture, then the categorical demand of its
negative criterion will also lose its force. And this
will mean a destruction of the awareness of moral
freedom as something purposive and meaningful,
because governed by a universal norm, and as a
capacity to transcend the mechanisms of impulse and
desire. 'Under the pressure of profanization the
moral imperative becomes conditional, dependent on
fears and hopes, a result of psychological and
sociological compulsion...' (ST,III,97). In contrast
to Kant, then, Tillich sees morality as leading
ineluctably from, as well as towards, religion. The
categorical imperative is not a purely self-contained
moral principle. Its unconditional character has its
source outside morality proper in the religious
vision of the participation of all things in the holy.
Thus Tillich joins with Otto in taking sharp issue
with Kant's reduction of religion to morality, arguing that the ethical elements in religious systems
are derivative from experience of the holy, and not
vice-versa. He deplores that moralization of the
holy which deprives it of 'its depth, its mystery,
its numinous character'. There is more to the
command to be holy than the command to be moral
(ST,I,216-217; see also Kegley and Bretall 1961:6).

In Tillich's view, Kant also failed to perceive
the inadequacy or incompleteness of a morality confined to such formal principles as the categorical
imperative (or to any abstract set of moral rules).
Ethics requires specific contents as well.   These
contents will vary, however, with the changing
requirements of the concrete situations of moral
choice.   For no two situations are ever exactly
alike, and the needs and potentialities of particular
individuals must be assessed and attended to in the
context of these situations.   The bridge between
the formal character of the moral imperative and the
demands of specific moral situations is the principle
of agape.   This principle 'unites the unconditional
character of the formalized categorical imperative
with the conditional character of the ethical content'
(ST,III,273).   Agape   includes   the   categorical
imperative and its associated principle of justice
even as it goes beyond it, in the direction of a
'creative' or 'transforming' justice that is attuned
to particular persons in concrete circumstances.
The negative and positive criteria of morality must
work in concert, for 'love without justice is a body
without a backbone', and morality without the
impetus of agape will soon degenerate into a witless
and insensitive legalism (MSFA,107; Theology of
Culture 1959:144-145,hereafter,TC).
      The criterion of agape has as its aim the union
of person with person (as well as the union of the
self with itself; something will be said about this
shortly).   But undergirding this criterion there is
something else: my recognition that the other
person 'is united with me in something that is above
him and me, the ultimate ground of the being of
each of us' (MSFA,108).   In other words, agape
carries   distinct   overtones   of   religion   as   self-

transcedence in the direction of the ultimate, as the longing of all things finite to find union with the infinite which is their ground. It is this aim, in the form of a quest for creative, transforming union with others, which constitutes the ultimate aim of morality, and which imparts to the moral life much of its sanctity and importance.

The third contribution of religion to morality is the motivating power of grace. Morality has need of this power in two main respects, each of which points in the direction of religion. The first is the need to cope with the burden of guilt which will inevitably be incurred when one accepts the risks of making moral decisions that are genuinely relevant to concrete situations. And the second is the need to overcome the state of estrangement, wherein the two criteria of morality are experienced as threat and command, rather than as a part of one's nature. The first need points to the experience of forgiveness of sins, or of 'accepting acceptance though being unacceptable'. And the second need points to the experience of regeneration, or of 'entering into the new being' which heals the split between what we are and what we ought to be. 'Every religion', Tillich insists, 'has a doctrine of salvation in which these two elements are present' (TC,142-143). Let us consider each of these needs in a little more detail.

As Kant rightly emphasized, the categorical imperative imposes an awesome duty upon man, which no one has a right to shirk. But Tillich points out that the demand of agape as the fulfillment of the moral imperative is far more stringent (ST,III,50). For it bids us attend to the creative nurture and enchancement of others in the concreteness of their being, and not just to accord them formal respect for their dignity as persons. In order to accomplish this end of agape, we must adapt existing moral codes and assumptions, representing the accumulated wisdom of our culture, to the unique requirements of new situations. But this exposes us to the risk of miscalculation and mistake, for we may have to wend our way through mutually exclusive choices, paying the price of losing the potential good of the others for the sake of realizing the apparent good of the one. And we may be called upon to violate the letter, if not the spirit, of accepted moral rules so as to accomplish the creative and transforming thing that the concrete situation seems to require. Here we are on our own. There is no way to be sure in advance that our assessment of the opportunities and needs of the situation is the correct one. If our assessment turns out to be in error, the consequences could be disastrous.

There is no true morality without such precarious risk taking, for it is required by agape. But such risk taking makes us vulnerable to the burden of guilt for wrong choices or for the uncertainty over whether we have made the best choices. This guilt, if unabated, can lead to radical self-condemnation and thus to the destruction of the moral agent's sense of his own unity and integrity as a person. In other words, by relentlessly pursuing the pole of participation, in the spirit of agape, we endanger the pole of detachment, or of the kind of self-acceptance or warranted self-love which is also an important matter of moral concern. If the self-disintegrating effects of guilt are to be avoided, what is needed is the religious experience of grace as forgiveness for our moral mistakes, as 'the power by which life accepts us in

spite of the violation of life we may have committed
by making a wrong decision' (MSFA,111).   This
power of grace Tillich describes elsewhere as the
power of being over nonbeing.   The nonbeing in
this instance is the finitude of our freedom, limited
by uncertainty and ignorance, and perhaps by
motives of which we ourselves are unconscious.
And the power of being is the courage to accept the
stringency of the demand of agape in the moral life
without succumbing to the scourge of self-condemnation and despair (CTB,52,166-167; Tillich
1954:40, Love, Power, and Justice).   This courage
is not something which can be created by mere
exertions of our wills, however dogged they might
be.   It comes to us, when it comes, as a gift of
grace.   Effective moral living requires this courage
but cannot itself create it.   The need for it, the
search for it, or the sense of its presence all lie
within the domain of religion, as Tillich understands
religion.   Without grace as forgiveness, or as the
acceptance of oneself despite the finite character of
one's moral decisions, one will shy away from the
risks of a morality deeply informed by agape.   And
he will therefore fail to be truly moral.   Grace as
forgiveness and the power of self-acceptance, then,
provides an important part of the motivation for the
moral life.   Viewed in this way, grace is but another
way of looking at the principle of agape, for the
love involved here is the love of oneself.
      Another important part of the motivation to be
moral is supplied by grace in its character of the
power for healing the state of estrangement.   Man
becomes painfully aware of his being in this state,
says Tillich, when he experiences the criteria of
morality as something external, as something set
over against him and demanded of him.   'In the

moral imperative we ourselves, in our essential being, are put against ourselves in our actual being' (TC,136). The principles of morality express man's essential being at the same time that they emphasize his estranged being, by reminding him of how far from the ideals of his essential being he falls short. This becomes especially apparent when it is realized that morality is fulfilled only when it is fulfilled in joy, its acts flowing spontaneously and naturally from a good will and a loving heart. But a good will and a loving heart cannot in their very nature be commanded. When they are experienced as command, and when one responds to them as command by resolutely willing to create them in himself, he is doomed to failure and frustration. Willing oneself to be moral in this deeper sense of morality is bound to be self-stultifying. Instead of solving the problem of alienation, it only exacerbates it. Because it commands the impossible, morality experienced merely as command leads to resistance and hatred of its own precepts. Tillich analyzes the basis of this frustration in one place under the rubric of the 'ambiquity of the good will': 'in order to will the good, the will itself must be good. Self-determination must make it good, which is to say that the good will must create the good will, and so on ad infinitum in an endless regression' (ST,III, 75). And in another place he states that agape is not a law but a present reality, if and when it is found in human life. 'It is not a matter of ought-to-be—even if expressed in imperative form—but a matter of being' (ST,III,272).

Tillich's remarks on the ambiguity of the good will can be taken as a criticism of Kant. We saw in the chapter on Kant's theory of religion that one of his answers to the question of how man can find

deliverance from his state of radical evil is to
choose a new disposition by making the moral law
the standard of all of his actions. As to how this
is possible, Kant could say only that since we are
obligated to do it, we can do it. Tillich sees this
answer as leading to the infinite regress referred to
above.

How, then, are the moral good will and a
loving heart to be brought into being, if not by
strenuous efforts of will, obedient to what is perceived as the moral demand that they be achieved?
Tillich's answer is that they come into being only
by grace, or specifically, by experience of the New
Being which is bestowed upon human beings as a
gift. And religion, not morality, 'is the sphere in
which the quest for the New Being appears over
against the split between essential and existential
being' (ST,II,80). Morality transcends itself in the
direction of religion by bringing us into a paradoxical situation.

It commands, which means that it stands against us.
But it commands something which can be done only if
it does not stand against us, if we are united with
what it commands. This is the point where the moral
imperative drives toward something which is not
command but reality. Only the 'good tree' brings
'good fruits'. (TC,142)

By the power of grace the reality of what the law
commands is achieved. 'It is the reality of...the
reunion with one's true being, and this means the
reunion with oneself, with others, and with the
ground of one's self and others' (ST,III,274).
Still, the power of grace does not preempt the
freedom which is part of man's essential nature. It

conquers the compulsions and the hostility to moral principles which belong to the condition of existential estrangement, freeing human beings to realize their essential nature by acts of good will and works of love (ST,II,79). The search for this liberating grace is a religious search that is of fundamental importance to morality.

Tillich does not devote as much attention to religion's need for morality as he does to morality's need for religion, so his view of the matter can be summarized quite briefly. There are two principal ways in which religion stands in need of morality. The first one is simply that there could be no transcendence of the finite self in the direction of the ultimate, and certainly no conscious inquiry into religious areas of the sort already described, without the establishment of the human self in the moral act (ST,III,95,159). And the second is that the principle of justice serves as a needed check upon idolatrous conceptions of the nature and demands of the holy. There is no true holiness or spiritual presence, Tillich insists, where there is no humanity or justice (ST,I,216; ST,III,144).

The fact of this mutuality of interaction between morality and religion should not be taken to imply any infringement on the autonomy of either. Tillich stipulates, however, that the autonomy of ethics pertains to the scholarly method with which ethical principles are analyzed, argued for, or criticized. It cannot take away from the religious import of moral principles which we have been discussing. Even though this import may not be recognized or focused upon, it is still there. Because of its possession of this religious significance Tillich stresses the 'theonomy' of morals, by way of contrast with the view that morals are simply

imposed upon man by some arbitrary, external
authority and do not express his own true nature
(the 'heteronomy' of morals), or with the view that
they are entirely self-contained and devoid of
inherent religious significance (the 'autonomy' of
morals, the term 'autonomy' now being used in a
much more restricted sense) (ST,III,251,267). As
for the autonomy of religion, we have already
spoken of Tillich's strong opposition to any attempt,
such as that made by Kant, to reduce religion to
morality.

4. RELIGION IN RELATION TO CULTURE

Tillich's view of the relation of religion to culture
can be approached through consideration of three
principles concerning this relation which he introduces in the last volume of the Systematic Theology
(ST,III,246-249). Since these principles bear both
on culture's need for religion and religion's need for
culture, we can discuss the two aspects together.
The first principle is 'the consecration of the
secular'. By this Tillich means that culture, properly understood, is open at any point or any time
to the impact of the religious ultimate, even without
the mediation of specific religious institutions or
traditions.

Everything secular is implicitly related to the
holy. It can become the bearer of the holy. The
divine can become manifest in it. Nothing is
essentially and inescapably secular. Everything has
the dimension of depth...Everything secular is potentially sacred, open to consecration. (ST,I,218)

The reason for this openness to the sacred in culture is that culture draws its life and, in particular, the creative dynamism which complements and criticizes its existing forms, from an inexhaustible source or ground which is the power of the unconditioned lying behind its conditional forms. Of course, culture cannot itself be identified with the holy. Because 'it is directed to the particular forms and their law', culture 'does not carry in itself the negativity of the unconditioned. against every form' (WIR,97). But like all things finite or conditioned, culture participates in the holy and points beyond itself to the holy as the power and presence by which it is sustained. Some examples which Tillich cites of the forms of secular culture becoming the bearers of the holy are a profound awakening of the social conscience; a fundamental contribution to man's self-understanding; or a breaking of his bondage to ecclesiastically sustained superstitions; each act being carried forward by individuals, groups, or movements within culture which may have little or nothing to do with religious institutions or may even be openly hostile to such institutions (ST,III,247; see also TC,130;ST,III,258; WIR,169). Organized religions stand to benefit greatly from such intrusions of the holy into the forms of secular culture, since they are thereby reminded that they do not exclusively represent the religious ultimate and that they also, as conditioned, stand under the judgment of the unconditioned.

The second principle is 'the convergence of the holy and the secular'. What Tillich means by this principle is that the secular drives toward the holy or toward union with the holy, even as the holy finds manifestation in cultural forms. The secular drives toward the holy because its forms derive their meaning, in the final analysis, from 'that which gives meaning to all things'. These forms 'are empty unless they are filled with the import of something unconditionally real which cannot be grasped either by any single form or by the totality of all forms' (WIR,150). Or as Tillich states the matter in another of his writings, there are 'absolutes' in cognitive, aesthetic, and communal forms of culture which lead beyond themselves to the final Absolute, an ultimate and inexhaustible source of meaning and value which is the object of religious concern (MSFA,passim). If culture be separated from this final Absolute which constitutes its religious 'substance', it is 'left with an increasingly empty form' (ST,III,97). Resistance to the religious dimension of life on the part of culture can produce only 'the emptiness and meaninglessness which characterizes the finite when cut off from the infinite' (ST,III,248). A similar fate awaits religious institutions which seek to insulate themselves against the forms of culture. For the only way in which they could accomplish this would be for them to lose their institutional character and to become completely 'silent and empty of all finite contents, thus ceasing to be a genuine possibility of a finite being' (ST,III,248). There are no forms of expression, religious or otherwise, except those provided by culture. So religion and culture converge toward one another, each having need of the other.

The third principle is not so much a different one from the other two as a summary version of them, or a statement of the fundamental principle in which they are both rooted. This is the principle of 'the essential belongingness of religion and culture to each other'. What this means is that

religion gives to culture its depth, substance, or
ultimate import, while culture gives to religion its
forms of self-expression. This principle overcomes
a dualistic separation of religion and culture even
as it guards against the usurpation of either function by the other. On the one hand the two are,
as we have seen, necessarily related. But on the
other hand, the cultural act 'prevents the finite
from being swallowed up by the infinite. It makes
the actualization of its potentialities possible' (ST,
III,248). Religion has no right or capacity to
encroach on this affirmation of the finite. The
theoretical and technical problems which are the
legitimate concern of culture cannot be settled by
appeal to the religious ultimate. This would be for
religion to exercise a heteronomous control over
culture. It would be a mistake, for example, to try
to resolve problems in logic, science, art, or social
organization on a directly religious basis (ST,III,
251-252; see also Tillich's Dynamics of Faith 1957,
Chap. V, hereafter DF). At the same time, religion
points to a reality by which cultural life is
nourished and the awareness of which is constantly
required if culture's finite accomplishments and
aspirations are to be kept in the right kind of
perspective. It is a reality which no cultural
forms, including those of organized religion itself,
can hope to encapsulate or contain, and whose
significance they can but partially convey. Finite
cultural forms transcend themselves in the direction
of the ultimate.

5. THE LARGER AND NARROWER SENSES OF RELIGION

The subject matter of this section has been anticipated in some of the earlier sections of this chapter, for there we have found it necessary at least to allude to two senses of 'religion', as the term is used by Tillich. The one sense is religion as a basic function of life under the dimension of the spirit, a function which differs from the other two functions of morality and culture and exists as an independent reality beside them. This is religion in the ordinary sense of the term, religion as one sort of social institution, with its own teachings, rites, and traditions. And it is this sense which Tillich designates as the 'narrower' sense of religion. But the other sense, which for him is clearly the more important of the two, is religion viewed as a quality of the other two functions of the spirit rather than as an independent function. It is the quality of self-transcendence in these two functions, whereby they point beyond themselves as finite modes of awareness and endeavor to the holy, or to the power of infinite being in which they are rooted and by which they are sustained. This is religion in the 'larger' sense of the term (ST,III, 96-97;MSFA,130-132). This distinction has a number of important implications which we need to trace out carefully if we are fully to understand Tillich's theory of religion.

One implication is that it is a serious mistake to identify religion merely with the foibles, limitations, and pretensions of particular religious institutions. This is to confuse religion in its innermost character, the self-transcendence of all life in the direction of the ultimate, with the

cultural forms which are intended to give explicit
expression to this self-transcendence but which
also, in the process, distort and profane it.
Religion is much more than 'a set of prescribed
activities to be performed, a set of stated doctrines
to be accepted, a social pressure group along with
others, a political power with all the implications of
power politics'. To see it merely as these things is
to be guilty of the 'institutional profanization' of
religion (ST,III,99). The whole history of religion
should show to the sensitive observer that religion
in the larger sense is locked in a continual struggle
with religion in this narrower institutional sense.
It is a struggle of religion against religion, for the
sake of the holy itself (ST,III,104). Religious
organizations, beliefs, and practices, like all finite
forms, exhibit the quality of self-transcendence,
pointing beyond themselves to the infinite reality by
which they are judged and found wanting.
    The institutional profanization of religion is
shown to be in error not only by the inner dynamics
of the history of religions just referred to, but also
by the very logic of the concept of religion as the
self-transcedence of all life in the direction of the
ultimate. Religion in this sense 'cannot become a
function of life beside others, because if it did it
would have to be itself transcended, and so on in
endless repetition. Life cannot genuinely transcend
itself in one of its own functions' (ST,III,96). The
narrower sense of religion is too restricted to tell
the whole story about the nature of religion. It
fails to do justice to religion's 'omnipresence', to
the fact that it is 'at home everywhere, namely,
in the depth of all functions of man's spiritual life'.
It is conceivable that religion in the narrower sense
could be absent from a human culture, but for

Tillich it can never be absent in this larger sense
(WIR,130,133;TC,7).

In an implied criticism of Otto, Tillich suggests
that it is incorrect to conceive of religion as being
rooted in a special faculty of the human spirit, a
religious a priori. For this is to set religion over
against the other faculties of the spirit, each with
its own a priori foundation (cf. Kant), and to see
it as existing alongside of them, instead of
recognizing it in the larger sense as the depth of
value and meaning which underlies and shines
through all of them. This comes close to being
another version of the institutional profanization of
religion. Its conception of religion is too tame, for
religion is not just one factor in a coordination of
human functions. As self-transcendence in the
direction of the ultimate, religion is 'a consuming
fire over against every autonomous function of the
human spirit. He who would seek a religious a
priori must be aware that all other a priori's
thereby sink into the abyss' (WIR,127).

We can also note two other criticisms Tillich
makes of Otto, since these two are related to this
first implication of Tillich's distinction between the
two senses of religion. A serious lack in Otto's
theory, by Tillich's reckoning, is its failure to
provide a systematic delineation of the relations
between religion and culture such as is provided by
Tillich's own conception of religion as being in its
larger sense the depth dimension in culture
(WIR,61). This second criticism is unfair to Otto,
whatever one may think of the first. The reader's
attention is called to the section in the chapter on
Otto above, where the aesthetic and philosophical
schematizations of the holy were discussed. Tillich
may not like Otto's analysis, and certainly it does

differ from his own, but he can hardly fault the theorist of Das Heilige with having failed to offer a systematic account of religion in its intimate relations to at least the cognitive and aesthetic facets of culture.

Tillich states the third criticism as follows: 'One cannot entirely avoid the impression that what Otto calls the rational is related to the irrational as something external. Otto himself feels this and considers it as an irrationality that is tied up with religion, but he does not indicate the essential relation that obtains between the mysterium and the rational form (quoted in Adams 1965:220, note 59).[1] That this criticism is also ill-founded is indicated by Otto's careful exploration of the interrelations of the nonrational and rational phases of the holy. But Tillich's notion that, for Otto, the rational and the nonrational exist in an 'external' relation to one another brings us back to his first criticism and what I think is his main point and concern about Otto's theory. Religion must be understood as a quality which lurks in the depths of rationality and in all acts of the human spirit. It is not just one special function among others. Tillich feels that Otto's emphasis on the religious a priori obscures this essential fact.

A second implication of Tillich's distinction between the two senses of religion is that it is as much a mistake to reduce religion to the moral function or to some aspect of the cultural function of life as it is to see it as a separate function. This is to fall into the error of the 'reductive profanization' of religion (ST,III,99). We have already noted Tillich's protest against the reduction of religion to morality, so we can go directly to his strictures against its reduction to some aspect of culture. For the sake of brevity, we will focus only on his discussion of the attempted reduction of religion to the cognitive aspect of culture, for this can serve to make the point. It will also enable us to make an important contrast between Tillich's theory of religion and that of Spinoza.

The following excerpt from Theology of Culture deals with the cognitive reduction of religion, which as Tillich sees it inevitably eventuates in the relegation of religion to something which does not really deserve the name of knowledge at all, but only stands at the threshold of scientific or philosophic knowledge.

History tells us the story of how religion goes from one spiritual function to the other to find a home, and is either rejected or swallowed by all of them...[Religion] is attracted by the cognitive function. Religion as a special way of knowledge, as mythological imagination or a mystical intuition—this seems to give a home to religion...religion is admitted, but as subordinate to pure knowledge, and only for a brief time. Pure knowledge, strengthened by the tremendous success of its scientific work, soon recants its half-hearted acceptance of religion and declares that religion has nothing whatsoever to do with knowledge. (TC,6)

Spinoza's views on religion clearly run in this vein. His mistake, as Tillich would see it, is to regard religion as merely ancillary to the cognitive work of philosophy and science, something needed only for those who cannot master the rigor of these disciplines and who require a substitute for them, however weak that substitute may be by comparison. This substitute, moreover, is heteronomous, imposed by authority from without. It does not well up from man's essential being or give expression to that essential being. Spinoza succumbed to this erroneous conception of the nature of religion, Tillich would say, because he failed to see that man's cognitive endeavors transcend themselves infinitely in the direction of a depth and mystery of being which they imply but cannot hope to encompass. The cognitive aspect of culture, like culture as a whole, is finite. And as such, it points beyond itself to the infinite. Awareness of the infinite is the meaning of religion in its larger sense, and it is this sense which Spinoza failed to take into account, concentrating only on religion of the institutional sort.

Tillich would perhaps want to say that the larger sense of religion is adumbrated in Spinoza's religion of reason (as we have termed it), with its putative demonstration of the infinite divine substance and of the dependence of all things upon this substance (Tillich would of course deny that being-itself is a substance). But even here, the view of religion is too intellectualized, too grounded in an unwarranted confidence in the powers of human reason, failing to grasp their finitude and limitation. There is a quality of ultimacy underlying and yet going beyond the bounds of human rationality which belies whatever pretensions it may acquire to completeness or adequacy within itself. In this way Tillich would make common cause with Otto in insisting on the nonrational part of religion as leading out from, and not simply going before, cognitive awareness. Each in his own way would challenge Spinoza's unqualified rationalism as implying too restricted an understanding of the nature of religion. (For samples of Tillich's attacks on the reduction of religion to the aesthetic or praxis aspects of culture see TC,6-7;ST,II,65;ST,III,100-101).

A third implication of the distinction between two senses of religion is that it explains the need for religion in its narrower sense and helps to put that sense of religion into its proper perspective. Religion in this sense is needed because it 'is the consequence of the estrangement of man from the ground of his being and of his attempts to return to it' (ST,III,403). A symptom of man's estranged state is that morality and culture are not experienced in their self-transcending, theonomous character. Man tends to live in the illusion of the self-sufficiency of the finite. In order to counteract this tendency there is need for the dogma and cultus of organized religion to open 'up the depth of man's spiritual life which is usually covered by the dust of our daily life and the noise of our secular work. It gives us the experience of the Holy, of something which is untouchable, awe-inspiring, an ultimate meaning, the source of ultimate courage' (TC,9). In fact, says Tillich, 'a specific religious culture must already have come into being before we can experience religious values in culture, ...or identify and label the religious elements' (WIR,175). Institutional religion is needed, then, to call explicit attention to the holy and to its pervasive presence in all human endeavors.

But this need must be kept in its proper perspective. Tillich insists that religion in its narrow institutional sense has only an 'emergency character' (TC,9). In a truly theonomous culture there would be no need for institutional religion. It would be superfluous because all of the finite

affairs of men would be conducted with a distinct
awareness of their self-transcending character.
The holy would be an intimate part of all of life.
Here religion would be 'what it is essentially, the
all-determining ground and substance of man's
spiritual life' (TC,8).   Tillich's vision of a completely theonomous culture which has no need for
institutional religion is quite similar to Kant's
vision of 'ecclesiastical faiths' serving as a transitory instrumentality for realization of the ideal of
an ethical commonwealth, with its quality of 'pure
religious faith'.

There is a danger, however, in religion seen
as a separate function of life. The danger is that
it tends to arrogate to itself the status and import
of the holy to which it can actually only bear
witness. In consequence, religious institutions are
tempted to stand in contempt of the secular realm
and to want to persecute those who do not bow
utterly to their own authority. They aspire toward
a completely heteronomous morality and culture. In
this way a wedge is driven between religion and
culture, between the sacred and the secular. The
holy is no longer recognized or borne witness to in
its essential character as permeating the whole of
human existence but becomes increasingly confined
to special beliefs and practices separated off from
other aspects of life. When this happens, religious
institutions will fail to perceive their finitude and
self-transcendence. This means that they will cease
to be sensitive to the power of the holy by which
they themselves are judged, a power which shines
through morality and culture and which can exert
from that direction a much needed corrective and
creative influence on their life. The concept of
religion in its larger sense, which can in no way be

thought of as the sole possession or prerogative of organized religious groups, exposes the mistake in this way of thinking. It keeps the claims of such groups within their proper bounds by reminding us of the dialectical relation of the two senses of religion that runs throughout religious history: 'religion as the self-transcendence of life needs the religions and needs to deny them' (ST,III,98).

A fourth and final implication of the distinction between the two meanings of religion is that it sheds light on what it would mean, according to Tillich's theory of religion, for a person to be nonreligious. A person is nonreligious who takes no interest in religion in the narrower sense of the term. He finds no place within his life for the explicit beliefs and practices of organized religion and he makes no conscious use of overt religious symbols in a quest for New Being. This kind of person can be called nonreligious because he lacks a religious intention. But while it is possible to be nonreligious in the narrower sense of religion, Tillich holds it to be impossible to be nonreligious in the term's larger sense. 'Every act of self-apprehension contains, as its foundation within reality, the relation to the Unconditional, but this relation is not in every case intended' (WIR,139; see also 59). Or as he states the point in another place, man is in his essential nature theonomous, however unaware of this fact he may be in his actual existence (ST,III,250). Or again, 'Nobody can escape the essential relation of the conditional spirit to something unconditional in the direction of which it is self-transcendent in unity with all life' (ST,III,130). So if we are speaking of religion with respect to what Tillich calls its 'substance', rather than with respect to the intent or conscious

attitude one may have toward it, it is impossible to
be nonreligious.   The substance of religion is the
self-transcendence of all finite things in the direction of the ultimate.   Every person's life, as finite,
is grounded in the ultimate, and it will contain
distinct signals and intimations of this grounding,
no matter how deliberately one may set out to
suppress or deny them.   Each in his own way will
have to come to terms with the lure of the ultimate
and his need for it, even if only along the abortive
lines of hubris or concupiscence, or of the attempt
to forego the responsibilities of his freedom.   And
in that way he will still be religious, in Tillich's
larger meaning of the term.

We will return to this question of the meaning
of nonreligion in the next section, when we are
discussing Tillich's conception of the personal side
of religion, which he takes to be the state of being
ultimately concerned.   Here again he states the case
that, while it is possible to lack a conscious religious concern and in that sense to be nonreligious,
it is impossible to be nonreligious in a larger sense.
For no person can be a person and not have some
ultimate concern.   But we need to approach this
claim in its context, so as to understand more
clearly why Tillich makes it and what he means by
it.

6.   THE PERSONAL SIDE OF RELIGION: FAITH AS
      ULTIMATE CONCERN

Tillich makes another important distinction in his
theory of religion, that between what we have
earlier referred to as the 'personal' and the 'cosmic'
sides of   religion (though   he does   not use these

terms). Religion on its personal side he calls 'faith', being influenced in this usage by the Bible.

The biblical word for religious existence is 'faith'. ...Faith is the state of being grasped by an ultimate concern. And, since only that which is the ground of our being and meaning should concern us ultimately, we can also say: Faith is the con- cern about our existence in its ultimate 'whence' and 'whither'. It is a concern of the whole person; it is the most personal concern and that which determines all others. It is not something that can be forced upon us; it is not something which we can produce by the will to believe, but that by which we are grasped. (Tillich, Biblical Religion and the Search for Ultimate Reality 1955:51-52, hereafter BRS)

There are a number of features of Tillich's understanding of faith which we will want to look at, and most of them are alluded to in this passage. The first feature is that faith is the state of being ultimately concerned, a state which contrasts with man's preliminary concerns and which 'deter- mines' all of his other concerns. Exactly what does this mean? For Tillich, to speak of a concern as 'ultimate' is automatically to relegate all other con- cerns to the status of 'preliminary' concerns, for he seems to assume out of hand and without argument that there can be only one ultimate concern. Also, a preliminary concern is one which focuses on things in their finite and immediate character and does not press beyond them to the power of infinite being which they presuppose and in which they rest (Adams 1965:225). In other words, a preliminary concern does not interest itself in the

self-transcendent character of finite things. An
ultimate concern, by contrast, is a concern with
the ground and meaning of all existence. And as
such, it is a total and all-encompassing kind of
concern: 'no part of ourselves or of our world is
excluded from it; there is no "place" to flee from it.
The total concern is infinite; no moment of relaxa-
tion and rest is possible in the face of a religious
concern which is ultimate, unconditional, total, and
infinite' (ST,I,12). In any conflict between an
ultimate concern and preliminary concerns, the
latter would have to give way, for they lack the
'unconditional, total, and infinite' character of the
ultimate concern. Since it will exercise primacy in
any hierarchy of personal preoccupations and
values, the ultimate concern 'determines' all other
concerns.

But we have to be careful here. For this way
of putting the matter might be taken to suggest
that Tillich sees as inevitable the exercise of
heteronomous control by religion over morality and
culture. However, as we have already seen, this
clearly is not his view. What is his view can be
clarified by having recourse again to the two senses
of religion. It is true that religion in the larger
sense of the term does take precedence over everything else in a person's life and that it does so of
necessity, by its very character of self-transcendence in the direction of that which is the root
and ground of all finite concerns. It probes, in
other words, to what is already most basic in them
all. But this does not mean that it is inevitable, to
say nothing of being desirable, that religion in the
narrower sense exercise such precedence. Religion
in the narrower sense is itself comprised of finite
cultural forms and therefore transcends itself in the

direction of the ultimate. So faith as ultimate
concern can and should exercise primacy, not only
over the finite activities of morality and culture,
but also over the finite teachings and practices of
established religious groups. Heteronomous religion
is religion that neglects the larger sense of religion.
It mistakes the finite for the infinite, forgetting the
self-transcending nature of all things finite. It
lords over some finite aspects of culture in the
name of other finite aspects. It treats the trap-
pings of institutional religion as though they were
identical with the infinite, giving to them, and
demanding for them, an allegiance that is infinite
and unconditional. What Tillich is saying, therefore, is that ultimate concern is appropriate only
to that which is truly ultimate. And no religious
dogma or cultus can qualify as being truly ultimate,
although it might be of distinct use in pointing
beyond itself to the ultimate. Religious faith viewed
as ultimate concern does not imply a heteronomous
relation between religion and culture, even though
the term 'ultimate concern' might be misconstrued in
this way.

A second feature of Tillich's understanding of
faith as the personal side of religion is that it is a
concern of the whole person, and that it is something by which he is 'grasped', not something which
can be brought into being by an act of his will.
Implicit in this feature is a contrast which Tillich
insists upon between faith, on the one hand, and
belief, volition, and feeling, on the other. Faith
is not to be identified with belief, because it is
something existential, while belief is something
theoretical. To believe something to be true is to
give it cognitive assent, and this can be done even
when there is not a great deal of evidence in its

favor.   Thus 'belief' is often contrasted with
'knowledge', as in the locution: 'I believe that it
is true, but I don't <u>know</u> it to be true'.   And
religious faith is frequently said to be a matter of
belief in this sense, meaning that it is giving
credence to doctrines which are not particularly
well supported or even supportable.

But to identify faith with an act of cognition,
whether well supported or not, is to misunderstand
its nature, according to Tillich.   An act of cognition
is a response only of part of the person, the
intellectual part.   And it is typically regarded as
being the more reliable the more the critical distance
that is maintained between the proclivities of the
knower and the properties of the known.   Religious
faith, by contrast, is existential, which means that
it is a response of the whole person and that it
expresses the fundamental orientation and commitment of his life, i.e., his perception of his life's
ultimate 'whence' and 'whither'.   Since this is the
case, it is not possible for a person to approach the
content of his ultimate concern with the techniques
of ordinary knowledge or in a spirit of detached
inquiry.   The content of faith is apprehended only
by faith, that is, with an intensity of passion and
involvement where the neat distinction between
knower and known cannot apply.   The committed
theologian, for example, is already what he seeks
better to clarify and understand.   And the person
of faith in general is already what he seeks more
fully to comprehend and become.   Each is involved
with his whole existence in the content of his
concern (DF,10-11;ST,I,22-23).

Tillich adds to this contrast between faith and
belief by calling attention to the difference between
existential certitude   and doubt,   on the one hand,

and theoretical certitude and doubt, on the other.
In the domain of ordinary cognition or theoretical
knowing, complete certainty is rarely possible, and
where it is, it has no reference to matters of fact.
We can be certain about the immediate data of our
sensory awareness, for example, but not about
whether the thing before us is in fact as we perceive it. And we can be certain about the elemental
logical and mathematical principles which enter into
all our theorizing, but this is a matter of form
merely, not of reality itself. All other cognitive
knowing is marked by degrees of probability, and
hence by degrees of theoretical doubt. Even our
most confident theoretical claims 'can be undercut at
any moment by criticism and new experience' (DF,
34). The certainty and doubt in cognitive acts pertain, however, to the status of particular claims,
not to our total life posture. In this respect they
differ from the certitude and doubt implicit in faith.

Existential certitude is implied in the very
concept of faith as ultimate concern, for this is
one's root concern, which gives meaning, value,
and purpose to all his other concerns. It is the
certitude of complete surrender and submission to
an object of ultimate concern. Still, there is an
ingredient of doubt in faith as well, an existential
doubt. This doubt is the awareness of the element
of risk and insecurity in any commitment to a concrete object of ultimate concern. It is not a doubt
about external claims, facts, or conclusions, but a
doubt as to whether one's life is centered on the
true ultimate, whether the content of one's concern
(a thing, a person, a group, etc.) does indeed
function as an adequate symbolization of the
ultimate, albeit in finite terms. This is the doubt
which accompanies the inevitable risk of faith, as

the act of a finite being and as given concretion in finite modes of manifestation and expression.

Tillich relates the certitude and doubt inherent in the act of faith to his theory of religious symbols and to Otto's analysis of the idea of the holy. He insists that the language of religion must be the language of symbol and myth, both because it expresses and depends on faith as an existential posture rather than stating cognitive claims which can be evaluated in an objective, literal manner, and also because it has only finite means at its disposal to focus on an ultimate which infinitely transcends all things finite. In stressing the symbolic character of religious language Tillich makes common cause with our other three theorists of religion, although he does not join with Spinoza in denying all cognitive significance to religious expression. There is a content to be believed in religious language, but it does not consist of 'true statements about objects in time and space'. Rather, it is the truth about the self-transcendence of our finite lives, a truth which requires existential response and participation in order to be understood (ST,III,132; Tillich 1973:249, 'The meaning and justification of religious language', hereafter MJRS).

The connection between religious symbols and the certitude and doubt of faith is brought out in two criteria Tillich offers for the 'truth' or adequacy of religious symbols. The first criterion is that such symbols should be 'alive', that is, have 'the power of expressing an ultimate concern in such a way that...creates reply, action, communication' (DF,96). In other words, religious symbols should elicit and convey the certitude of ultimate concern by providing powerful concrete images expressive of that concern (see DF,46). And the second criterion is that the symbols should imply an element of their own self-negation. 'That symbol is most adequate which expresses not only the ultimate but also its own lack of ultimacy' (DF,97). In other words, the symbols should give effective expression to the doubt which is a necessary structural accompaniment of any attempt to give finite expression to the meaning of the ultimate. This doubt keeps faith within its proper bounds, saving it from an idolatrous identification of the infinite with the finite, just as the certitude of faith keeps its doubt from collapsing into despair. Religious symbols should somehow capture this interpenetration of certitude and doubt in the act of faith.

Tillich also relates the certitude and doubt of faith to Otto's examination of the idea of the holy, by tying the certitude to the element of fascinans and the doubt to the element of tremendum. Through the reality of his ultimate concern, man becomes aware of his ability to 'transcend the flux of relative and transitory experiences of his ordinary life' and to find his fulfillment in the ultimate for which he yearns and to which he belongs. 'This is the reason for the ecstatic attraction and fascination of everything in which ultimacy is manifest' (DF,9,13). This sense of fulfillment, the 'restful affirmative confidence' which faith brings (DF,21), is its certitude. But at the same time, there is the inescapable fact of the 'infinite distance of the finite from the infinite and, consequently, the negative judgment over any finite attempts to reach the infinite' (DF,13). This fact is taken by Tillich to be the basis for experience of the infinite as 'wholly other', 'mysterious', 'separated', and 'terrifying'. It is the sense of being consumed in the presence of the divine. There is no way of avoiding this element of judgment and risk in the act of faith, even if one wanted to. It cannot be canceled out or annulled but can only be taken up into faith by way of courageous affirmation, which is also part of faith's legacy. The attraction and fascination of faith is laced with dark strands of doubt and dread. In this way Tillich seeks to exhibit an important continuity between his and Otto's ways of understanding the nature of religion.

So far we have been considering Tillich's rejection of an identification of faith, the personal side of religion, with belief or an act of cognition. We can note in passing that this implies from another direction a repudiation of Spinoza's religion of reason, made virtually synonomous with philosophical theoria. And just as faith cannot be identified with the cognitive act, so Tillich asserts that it cannot be made identical with the volitional act, i.e., with obedience to commands to believe certain things or to act in certain ways. This again would be to see faith as a limited response of a part of the person, rather than grasping its true nature as 'a total and centered act of the personal self' (DF,8). And it would be to overlook the fact that acts of will presupppose and give expression to the content of one's ultimate concern. They do not themselves create or constitute that concern. Faith is 'that by which we are grasped', not something which we will into being. In contending against an identification of faith with volitional acts of obedience, Tillich's theory clearly contrasts with Spinoza's technical view of religion as obedience to what are regarded as divine commands. Tillich readily concedes that there is an element of obedience in faith, but it 'is not the heteronomous subjection to a divine-human authority'. Rather, it is the posture of openness to the power of the ultimate by which one has been grasped, an 'obedience by participation and not by submission (as in love relations)' (ST,III,132). This kind of obedience is implied by what Tillich calls the certitude of faith.

Finally, Tillich denies that faith can be simply lumped with feelings and emotions. This third distortion of the meaning of faith, the emotionalistic distortion, must be rejected along with the intellectualistic and the voluntaristic distortions. 'Faith as the state of ultimate concern claims the whole man and cannot be restricted to the subjectivity of mere feeling' (DF,39). And yet, there is certainly emotion present in the act of faith, namely, the oscillation between the anxiety of one's finitude and estrangement and the courage which overcomes this anxiety through passionate surrender to an object of ultimate concern (ST,III,133). While faith cannot be restricted to any of the three acts we have been discussing—cognitive, volitional, or emotional—it is at the same time not devoid of any of them. It encompasses and yet transcends them all. Tillich spells this out for us in the following passage from Biblical Religion and the Search for Ultimate Reality (53):

Faith...is an act of self-surrender, of obedience, of assent. Each of these elements must be present. Emotional surrender without assent and obedience would by-pass the personal center. It would be a compulsion and not a decision. Intellectual assent without emotional participation distorts religious existence into a nonpersonal, cognitive act. Obedience of the will without assent and emotion leads into a depersonalizing slavery. Faith unites and transcends the special functions of the human mind; it is the most personal act of the person.

We came now to a third feature of Tillich's conception of faith, a feature which has been referred to earlier. This is his contention that it is impossible to be a person and not have some kind of faith, some sort of ultimate concern. The reason he holds this to be true is that he sees faith as the integrating factor in one's life, the focal point of orientation which pervades and gives a depth of meaning and value to one's other concerns. One's faith is one's 'spiritual center', apart from which the very meaning of his life would break down (DF, 20,17;CTB,46-51). As a centered act of the total personality and the most personal act of the person, faith is the key to one's whole personality structure. This being the case, personality and faith go hand in hand, and since faith is a religious act, one cannot be a person without being religious.

This analysis seems to conflict with Tillich's other contention, which we looked at earlier in this chapter, that the moral act is one of self-integration. For he seems now to be associating self-integration most closely with the religious act. He does not, as far as I can tell, try to resolve this conflict in interpretations. It could perhaps be resolved to some extent by saying that there are two crucial sources of self-integration, the moral one of a contrast between self and the world and the felt duty to respect others as persons, and the religious one of an ultimate source and focus of meaning. But this would preclude seeing self-integration as the essence of the moral act. Morality would belong to the genus of self-integration, but that would not be its differentia.

When Tillich argues that it is not possible to be a person and to be nonreligious, he is not using the term 'religious' in the narrower sense of giving explicit allegiance to a religious institution or to some set of overt religious symbols. He means 'religious' in the broader sense of having an ultimate concern, one which might well bring a person into conflict with organized religion. Scientists, artists, or moralists who set out to refute the teachings and practices of a given religious system are denying religion in the name of religion, in this interpretation. For they are pitting one ultimate concern, with its symbolic content, against another (DF,40). Or as Tillich states elsewhere: 'You cannot reject religion with ultimate seriousness, because ultimate seriousness, or the state of being ultimately concerned, is itself religion. Religion is the substance, the ground, and the depth of man's spiritual life. This is the religious aspect of the human spirit' (TC,8).

The fourth feature of Tillich's view of faith is a distinction he makes between the 'formal' and the 'material' conceptions of it. This ties in closely with the distinction made in Chapter 1 above between interpretive and normative theories of religion. Tillich says of the formal view of faith that it

is valid for every kind of faith in all religions and cultures. Faith, formally, or generally defined, is the state of being grasped by that toward which self-transcendence aspires, the ultimate in being and meaning... In this formal

sense of faith as ultimate concern, every human
being has faith. Nobody can escape the essential
relation of the conditional spirit to something
unconditional in the direction of which it is self-
transcendent in unity with all life. (ST,III,130)

The material view, by contrast, is one particular
religion's conception of what constitutes authentic
faith. For example, the Christian would say 'that
faith is the state of being grasped by the New
Being as it is manifest in Jesus as the Christ. In
this definition of faith, the formal and universal
concept of faith has become material and particular;
it is Christian'. And for the Christian, his particular definition of faith 'expresses the fulfillment
toward which all forms of faith are driven' (ST,III,
131).

When in his formal definition of faith, however,
Tillich states that 'nobody can escape the essential
relation of the conditional spirit to something
unconditional' and adds that this is the rule of all
life, he is offering us the perspective of a particular ontology and a particular doctrine of man.
This gives a distinct normative slant even to his
formal view of the nature of faith. Had he said
simply that faith is the state of being grasped by
something a person regards as ultimate, and not
gone on to insist that everyone must have such a
faith and that self-transcendence in the direction of
the ultimate is the characteristic of all finite things,
his theory of religion would have been freer of the
normative bias which colors it throughout. It would
then have been possible for someone to have an
outlook in which the finite is the final reality, and
who is therefore not conscious of, or concerned
with, any self-transcendent quality in his life. And

that person would be clearly nonreligious, in terms of this revised version of Tillich's theory of religion.

The normative character of Tillich's formal definition of faith also becomes apparent when we consider that, in the same passage from which the above quotations are taken, he immediately deduces from that definition a criterion for detection of faiths with 'unworthy contents'. Such faiths 'invest something preliminary, finite, and conditioned with the dignity of the ultimate, infinite, and unconditional' (ST,III,130). This simply states in another way the second criterion for the truth of the symbols of faith, namely, that they should contain an element of their own self-negation. Applying this criterion to his own religious tradition, Tillich is able to demonstrate, at least to his own satisfaction, 'the superiority of Protestant Christianity'. In fact, he thinks that a good name for this same criterion is 'the Protestant principle', and that this principle finds its most exquisite expression in the symbolism of the cross of Christ. 'Jesus could not have been the Christ without sacrificing himself as Jesus to himself as the Christ' (DF,98-99).

But it turns out that this claim about the superiority of Christianity is not meant by Tillich to apply to the ongoing institutional forms of the Christian religion. It is not these which are so clearly superior 'but the event by which Christianity is created and judged to the same extent as any other religion, both affirmatively and negatively' (ST,III,338). The symbol of the cross has captured in a uniquely apt way, Tillich believes, the meaning of religion in the larger sense as the self-transcendence of all finite things in the direction of the ultimate or the holy. And all religions in the

narrower sense are judged by this standard. Still,
the fact that Tillich is able to deduce such a
standard of judgment from his theory of religion
clearly shows its normative character. For the
theory has the effect of immediately branding as
idolatrous, and therefore grossly inferior, those
religions in which finite divine beings are worship-
ped and accorded supremacy, despite the fact of
their being finite. Tillich's formal analysis of the
nature of faith, regardless of what may have been
one's first impression, is not a pure example of an
interpretive theory of religion.

Tillich would probably not have been
particularly troubled by this observation. In an
early essay entitled 'On the idea of a theology of
culture', he contends that any universal philosophical concept, and especially a concept of religion, 'is
empty unless it is at the same time understood to be
a normative concept with a concrete basis'. It is,
'to a greater or lesser degree, a creative act of the
circle in which the individual moves' (WIR,158,156).
So this is a case, not so much of failure precisely
to apply our first criterion for interpretive theories
of religion, as a fundamental disagreement with that
criterion. It is a disagreement based on the conviction that it is impossible for the criterion to be
applied. And yet, as we have seen, a revised
version of Tillich's theory of religion would not be
all that difficult to come by, and such a version
would be much more purely interpretive in character
(Adams 1965:218-220 argues much to this same
effect).

7. THE COSMIC SIDE OF RELIGION: GOD AS THE SYMBOL FOR THE OBJECTIVE MEANING OF ULTIMATE CONCERN

Tillich complements his treatment of faith as the personal side of religion with an account of religion's cosmic side. This side he refers to variously as 'the ultimate', 'the infinite', 'the unconditional', 'the ground of all being and meaning', or 'being-itself', to cite some of the most frequently used terms. This is focused on and given expression in a particular set of religious symbols by a religious person or tradition. Tillich notes that the cosmic side of religion is contained implicitly in its personal side:

The unconditional concern which is faith is the concern about the unconditional. The infinite passion, as faith has been described, is the passion for the infinite. Or...the ultimate concern is concern about what is experienced as ultimate. In this way we have turned from the subjective meaning of faith as a centered act of the personality to its objective meaning, to what is meant in the act of faith. (DF,9-10)[2]

He prefers to speak of the 'objective meaning' of faith, as in this passage, rather than the 'object' of faith, because for him the latter term connotes one object among others in a universe of finite objects. And it suggests something which can be approached and handled in a detached, theoretical way, thus implying the intellectualistic distortion of the meaning of faith. It fails to do justice to the existential nature of faith as pointing 'to a participation which transcends both subjectivity and objectivity' (ST,I, 214,12).

Tillich thinks that Otto's theory of religion is deficient in that it does not bring the objective meaning of religious experience into sufficiently sharp focus. Otto was right to begin with the holy as a quality of experience and to subject that quality to extensive phenomenological analysis, but he failed to see the necessity for supplementing that analysis with an ontological approach, so as not to leave hanging the question of the status in reality of that which the phenomena make known. The ontological approach, as Tillich conceives it, does not restrict itself to the particular experience of the holy but seeks the objective meaning of religion in the character of being as such. It 'gives an analysis of the encountered world with respect to its finitude and finds through this analysis its self-transcending quality, its pointing beyond its finitude'. The referent or objective meaning of religion which this approach makes apparent is the power of infinite being by which all finite things are sustained and to which man looks for the courage to cope with the anxieties of his temporal existence (MJRS,249-250;ST,I,215-216,274). The last part of this sentence is particularly important, for it shows that the power of being or being-itself which Tillich has in mind as constituting the cosmic side of religion is no bloodless philosophical abstraction but 'the expression of the experience of being over against non-being' in the struggles and perplexities of man's everyday life. It is being-itself existentially encountered and understood (ST,II,11).

But there is need for the power of infinite being to be expressed symbolically, so as to give it concrete religious manifestation and appeal. And

the symbol Tillich generally uses for this purpose
is the symbol of 'God'. On the one hand, he uses
this term as the functional equivalent of any object.
of ultimate concern. In this sense, a religion like
early Buddhism can be said to have Nirvana as its
'God', although in the usual sense of that term it
is atheistic, having no belief in a God or gods.
And one who gives his ultimate allegiance to money,
success, truth, or nation can be said to have one
of these as his 'God', in this functional sense
(ST,I,211,220;DF,17-20). But on the other hand,
Tillich develops a doctrine of God as part of his
theological system. We shall be interested in the
latter, not for the sake of trying to assess its
theological significance or truth, but rather for the
light it can shed on his understanding of the objective meaning of religion, as generically conceived.
        Tillich repreatedly warns that the God of his
theology is not to be viewed as a literal personal
being but as a symbol for infinite being. This
symbol portrays God as personal, but not as a person, since an unconditional particular being would
be, he thinks, a contradiction in terms. Only
being-itself can be regarded as unconditional (ST,I,
207). Why not use some impersonal symbol for
being-itself, then, since it would be less misleading?
Tillich's answer is that an adequate symbol for
being-itself must encompass all the dimensions of
being, including the personal, even as it transcends
them all.

The God who is a being is transcended by the God who
is Being itself, the ground and abyss of every
being. And the God who is a person is transcended
by the God who is the Personal-Itself, the ground

and abyss of every person. In statements like these, religion and ontology meet. (BRS,82-83)

This plea for the symbol of God is in keeping with a third criterion for the truth or adequacy of religious symbols Tillich formulates in one of his writings, namely, that symbolic material ought to be taken from the human person, and not merely from trees, rocks, or animals, because 'only in man are all dimensions of the encountered world united' (MJRS,252). Thus the symbol God, as Tillich interprets it, points to being-itself in its twofold character of ground and abyss. It is the ground of all finite being, including the being of the human person. And it is also the abyss, that infinite depth of power and mystery which transcends all finite things. This is the generic referent of religion, the objective meaning which is meant or intended by the attitude of ultimate concern.

It is obvious that the religious ultimate conceived as ground and abyss will relate closely to the certitude and doubt of faith, as well as to the first two criteria for the adequacy of religious symbols. And it also ties in closely with Otto's analysis of the divine by means of such categories as fascinans and mysterium. In addition, Tillich sees the polarity of ground and abyss as a key to some of the similarities and differences among religious systems.

He states that 'every great religion has elements in its total structure which are subordinate in one religion and dominant in another' (ST,III, 141). And chief among these elements is the degree of emphasis given either to ground or abyss as aspects of the religious ultimate, an emphasis expressed in the degrees of concreteness or universality in each religion's characteristic forms of symbolization. Without some concreteness of expression, the ultimate could not even be encountered. It would have no significance for finite human beings. And the more concrete the mode of symbolization, the more intense and direct can be the concern it elicits. The most concrete manifestation of the ultimate is provided by polytheistic religions. But polytheism tends to lack the other pole of universality or all-inclusive transcendence of the concrete. Hence it borders on a demonic relativizing of the ultimate. 'Each of the polytheistic divine powers claims ultimacy in the concrete situation in which it appears. It disregards similar claims made by other divine powers in other situations. This leads to conflicting claims and threatens to disrupt the unity of self and world' (ST,I,222).

The fact that the religious ultimate, to be truly that, 'must transcend every preliminary finite and concrete concern' is given greatest stress by radical mysticism. It represents the extreme of universality in its form of religious expression, for it struggles constantly to negate and go beyond such forms, including even the form of the conscious experience of the meditating human self. But the price that mysticism pays for its resolute drive toward universality is vagueness, uncertainty, and abstractness in its symbolizations. Not only is this tension between the concrete and the universal a fundamental key to understanding the dynamics of the history of religions; Tillich also holds it to be the basic problem for every doctrine of God (ST,I, 211;WIR,93).

In between the extremes of polytheism and mysticism there are such religious outlooks as Zoroastrian and Manichean dualism, and priestly and prophetic monotheism. Tillich thinks that the Christian doctrine of the Trinity, which is adumbrated in such other religions as Judaism and Hinduism, is the most adequate symbolization of the needed balance between the concrete and the universal. It best preserves the tension between ground and abyss as traits of the religious ultimate (ST, I, 221, 228-230; ST, III, 283-284).[3]

This sketch of the cosmic side of religion, as conceived by Tillich's theory of religion, concludes my presentation of his theory. We can now turn to the problem of classifying it and critically appraising it in light of the criteria for interpretive theories of religion.

8.   CLASSIFICATION AND CRITICISM OF TILLICH'S THEORY

In classifying and criticizing Tillich's theory we will make use once again of our familiar three questions: (A) Can this theory properly be regarded as an interpretive theory of religion? (B) If it can, what type of interpretive theory can it be said to be? (C) What critical assessment of it can we make, in light of our criteria?

(A) We have seen that Tillich makes a distinction between 'formal' and 'material' conceptions of the nature of faith (or religion's personal side), a distinction closely related to our own distinction between interpretive and normative theories of religion. But we also saw that his way of presenting the formal conception of faith contains distinct normative implications, offering us the perspective of a particular ontology and a particular doctrine of man, involving a staunch defense of the superiority of Protestant Christianity (albeit its fundamental principle and symbol, not its institutional forms and practices), and branding as inferior polytheistic religions. His defense of the Christian doctrine of the Trinity, as over against other options like mysticism, ordinary monotheism, and dualism, again shows a normative thrust in his presentation of his theory, this time in explication of religion's cosmic side. Tillich's theory could also be said to have some explanatory force. His ontological portrayal of the participation of the finite in the infinite and of finite man's felt need for the infinite would explain the persistence of religion in human experience and human history.

But we also saw that it would not be all that difficult to separate out the normative element from Tillich's conception of faith. Such a revision of this conception would also have the effect of taking away much of the explanatory force of the theory, making it more purely interpretive in character. As for religion on its cosmic side, Tillich's theory could rather easily be steered away from the normative direction by using the notion of tension between concreteness and universality as a way of understanding some of the differences between religious systems, but without insisting on the norm of achieving a balance of these elements as part of the theory. Such a norm could then be employed as a separate move, consistent with the theory but not required by it, or not an integral part of it. Revisions like the ones that have been mentioned would bring Tillich's theory more nearly in line with his own distinction between formal and material conceptions of religion.

And he could still do all that he wants to do as a Christian theologian and religious philosopher without combining in one theory the normative and explanatory features of his treatment of religion with the interpretive features. Separating out the latter as a distinct phase in the study of religion would maintain the priority of the interpretive phase to the normative and explanatory phases that we have previously called attention to. Each phase is of course important in its own right. But it has been a persistent theme of this study that the interpretive phase is logically distinct from the other two, and that this distinction should be methodologically attended to and upheld.

Tillich's theory of religion is not a pure example of an interpretive theory of religion in its present form. But it contains strong interpretive aspects and makes substantial contributions to our understanding of the nature of religion. This fact, plus the fact that only slight revisions would be required to make it a more clear-cut instance of an interpretive theory, give us sufficient warrant for so considering it here.

(B) What type of interpretive theory could it be said to be? Looking at the theory from one angle, it would seem to be an example of an ontological theory of religion, in that it takes being-itself to be the common preoccupation of all religions. But from another angle it could be viewed as an example of a role-functional theory. The object of religious interest on its personal side has the role of being that concern which is ultimate, contrasting with all preliminary concerns. It 'determines' all other concerns, in the sense which we have specified. And it is that concern which focuses on the end and meaning of all existence, as compared with other types of concern in the outlook of the individual. And religious interest on its cosmic side is an interest in whatever it is that is thought to have ultimacy in the cosmos, that on which all else in the universe is thought to depend and to which all else is subordinate. In this functional interpretation of Tillich's theory of religion, being-itself would be one candidate for playing the role of the religious object on both its personal and its cosmic sides, but not the only candidate. A personal being, like the Jewish God, for example, could play this role, as could the gods of some polytheistic religions, taken collectively. In the role-functional form, the theory would contain no bias for or against the various candidates for filling the role specified by the theory. Tillich's ontological predilections and commitments have caused him to move rather strongly in the direction of an ontological type of theory, but the theory also admits of being construed as one of the role-functional type. This second interpretation has the advantage of freeing the theory from the bias of a particular ontology and allowing it to be truly generic in its scope.

(C) Enough has already been said to show that Tillich's theory of religion violates criterion (1). But it can be modified, as we have seen, to bring it into closer accord with this criterion. A way has been suggested to extract from the theory its explanatory force, so as to satisfy criterion (4). With respect to criterion (2), the category of ultimacy, with its related categories of existential certitude and doubt, on religion's personal side, and of ground and abyss on its cosmic side, does illuminate the nature of religious interest. And Tillich points to some interesting and important interrelations of these categories. We have found occasion to comment a number of times on the relations between Tillich's theory of religion and the theories of Spinoza, Otto, and Kant, showing the extent to which his theory complements and builds upon the insights of these previous theories (the third criterion).

That Tillich's theory amply satisfies the fifth criterion is shown by the subtle uses to which he puts it in exploring the logic of Christianity, and we have commented on the way in which his analysis of the cosmic side of religion through the polarity of concreteness and universality points up at least one important ground of similarity and difference among various religious systems (criterion (6)).

With respect to criterion (7), we can note that there is an unsettling ambiguity about the phrase 'ultimate concern', which Tillich is not always careful to resolve. It can mean the psychic stance of ultimate seriousness, or concern with that which is regarded as ultimate in the cosmos, or both. When Tillich speaks of ultimate concern as being of the essence of being religious he means for the phrase to be understood in both senses. For the sake of clarity he should always speak of 'ultimate concern <u>about</u> <u>the</u> <u>ultimate</u>', rather than just using the more misleading shorter phrase, 'ultimate concern'. For the latter tends to suggest a focus on the personal side of religion at the expense of its cosmic side, which would mean a violation of criterion (7). Statements such as the following (TC,8), which are fairly frequent in Tillich's writings, show this tendency to mislead:

You cannot reject religion with ultimate seriousness, because ultimate seriousness, or the state of being ultimately concerned, is itself religion.

But we have seen that Tillich's theory as a whole, despite such misleading statements, does give adequate attention to the cosmic and the personal sides of religion, so it does accord with the seventh criterion.

When Tillich argues that no statements in religious systems about a personal God or gods can be taken at face value, because being-itself, the putative common preoccupation of all religions, is not one being among others, he shows a lack of adequate generality in his theory (criterion (8)). This defect is on the other side of the coin from a similar defect in the theories of Spinoza, Kant, and Otto, all of whom tend to think of religion too much in theistic terms. What are needed, clearly, are theories which do not tilt the scales in either direction but leave it an open question as to whether the religious object be viewed as a personal being or beings or in impersonal terms. The theory should not exclude in advance or give weight in advance to any relevant option against the others, and the options cited here are certainly relevant, since they figure prominently in the history of religions.

Tillich's extensive analysis of the interrelations of morality and the various cultural interests with religion shows commendable sensitivity to the second part of the ninth criterion. And he takes pains, as we have seen, to try to safeguard the autonomy of religion, as well as the autonomy of morality and the cultual interests. I do not think that he quite succeeds, however, in upholding the autonomy of morality, for he seems to be saying that both its positive and its negative criteria flow from a religious source. If this is true, in what could the autonomy of morality consist, given the fact that all of its other claims and principles can presumably be

brought down to these two criteria? Of course,
Tillich is talking here about the rootage of moral
principles in religion in the larger, not the narrower
sense of the term. So he would be plainly unsym-
pathetic to the notion that any particular religious
system or institution is in any position to settle
moral questions on overtly religious grounds, or to
impose its answers to moral questions in some
external or authoritaran manner upon moral agents.
But the precise relation between religion in the
larger sense of the term and morality is left obscure
in Tillich's theory. And this obscurity is deepened
when we consider that self-integration, which was
supposed to be the peculiar province of morality, is
also said by Tillich to be the unique contribution of
religious faith.

If religious interest is taken to be something
that is deliberate and intentional, then there is no
problem with Tillich's theory so far as criterion
(10) is concerned. For we have seen what it would
mean for a person to be nonreligious in the
narrower sense of religion, which is its deliberate
and intentional sense. I have suggested a way in
which his theory could be brought into line with
the tenth criterion, even with respect to religion's
larger sense. This revision would have the effect
of removing altogether one of the most widely
criticized features of Tillich's theory, namely, the
extent to which it makes it impossible for one to be
nonreligious. It is notable, though, that the
criticism itself has been seriously marred by an
almost universal failure to take into account the two
senses of religion pointed up by the theory, and
thus to meet the theory on its own ground.

Despite the additional level of complexity that
it introduces into the task of trying to understand

the nature of religion, I consider Tillich's distinction
between the two senses of religion to be the most
suggestive and useful single contribution of his
theory of religion.   It reminds us that religious
interest need not find expression only in the
commitments and practices of explicitly religious
institutions, and that criticism of such institutions
may well stem from religious, and not merely from
antireligious or nonreligious motives.   It makes us
more sensitive to the possibility that what seem to
be scientific or philosophic claims, for example, are
sometimes religious claims in disguise, since religious claims are not always made in a familiar
religious parlance or in some obviously religious
context.   This distinction in Tillich's theory also
suggests the possibility of much more intricate and
subtle connections between religion and culture than
would be allowed by too facile an identification of
religion with a certain kind of cultural form.   And
he traces out a number of these kinds of connections with admirable and clarifying skill.   Finally,
the distinction makes apparent the possibility that
even the most radically 'secular' kind of culture
may raise and seek to cope with problems of profound religious import, and that it may arrive at
significant religious insights in the process.   So
religion, for Tillich, is emphatically not the exclusive preserve of people or groups which are religious in the narrower sense of the term.   All of
this makes it just that much harder to say with
confidence exactly what the religious dimension of
life is, but it alerts us just that much more to its
pervasive influence.

   This completes my survey of the four theories
of religion I have selected for intensive study and
criticism.   Hopefully, this survey has put into

useful historical perspective the task of trying to
arrive at an adequate interpretive theory of
religion.   The third and final part of this book I
label 'Constructive', because in it I will be constructing an interpretive theory of my own and
discussing some of the similarities and differences
between it and the other four theories.

Part Three

Constructive

A New Theory of Religion

As I have indicated earlier, the theory of religion which I shall construct in this chapter is of the role-functional type. It consists of a set of categories whose conceptual interplay and tensions are intended to clarify the nature of religious interest and to suggest some of the lines of possible development and difference within and among religious traditions. In addition to explaining and illustrating each of the categories, I will explore some of their interconnections and mutual tensions, pointing up in an illustrative way the significance of this sort of exploration for analysis of the logic of religious systems.[1]

The categories of this theory and their structure of relations are designed to interpret the role which an object of interest has when it is the object of religious interest for an individual or a group. These categories should not be construed as attributes shared by objects of religious interest in different religious systems, for those objects of interest and their attributes differ widely from one such system to another. And whether a given object is fit to play the role, or best fit to play it in comparison with other claimants to that role, depends on the specific attributes it possesses or is thought to possess. But inquiry into this question is not part of the task of an interpretive theory of religion, as we have already seen. For it would take us beyond a theory with interpretive force to one with normative force. The structure of categories assigns a common function or role to all religious objects, then, but not a common set of attributes. An interest is religious when it is an interest in something accorded the role specified by the theory, regardless of what that something is or is believed to be in itself—an entity, a set of entities, a state, a process, a power, a principle, or whatever. And in order to qualify as an object of religious interest, an object must be accorded the entire role specified by the theory, and not just some part of that role. This means that it must exhibit each of the six categories and exhibit them on both the personal and the cosmic sides. For the reader's convenience, the theory is presented in summary form in an appendix.

The categories are six in number: uniqueness, primacy, pervasiveness, rightness, permanence, and hiddenness. Let us examine each category in turn.

1.   UNIQUENESS

The first way in which a religious object can be distinguished from other objects of interest is that it is held in awe as something radically separate or set apart, something in a class by itself. It is contrasted with all else in one's personal life, outlook, or experience, and it is claimed to have a singular and unparalleled place in or in relation to the cosmos. In the case of polytheistic religions, it is a set of entities (i.e., the gods) which is unique, and not any single member of the set, although certain gods may hold unique sway over

parts of the cosmos.   The following typical religious
locutions can help to make this category clear.

(1.1)   There   is   no   other   like   Thee—how   then   a
        greater?   Even in the three worlds, O Thou
        Lord   of   matchless   greatness!   (said   of
        Krishna by Arjuna in the Bhagavadgita, see
        1963:115)

(1.2)   No one is good but God alone.   (Luke 18:19,
        RSV)

(1.3)   I am the World-honored, Who cannot be
        equaled.   (The Eternal Buddha in Saddharma-
        pundarika, in Hamilton 1952:123)

(1.4)   ...there is no god but He, the living, the
        Everlasting...there   is   no   god   but   He,   the
        Creator of everything.   (Koran 2:255,6:103,
        in Williams 1963:27,29)

(1.5)   Nirvana is spoken of as 'the unconditioned
        state', and as 'happiness of the kind for
        which there is no parallel anywhere in the
        universe'.   (Bu 1956:45)

(1.6)   There is none holy like the Lord, there is
        none besides thee, there is no rock like our
        God.   (I Samuel 2:2, RSV)

(1.7)   Rama is termed 'the eternal, the unborn, the
        one   without   a   second'.   (M.   K.   Gandhi,
        Ramanama, the Infallible Remedy,   in   Renou
        1963:209)

(1.8)   Christ   is   called   'the   only-begotten   Son   of
        God, ...begotten, not made... .   (Nicaeno-
        Constantinopolitan Creed, in Bettenson 1943:
        36-37)

(1.9)   God...is not His own creature, and not a
part of his creation or an attribute of it.
He is the Praised and Exalted, set apart in
His holy Existence, aloof in His glorious
selfhood from all things He has created
... .   (Ibn Taymiya, quoted in Williams
1963:195-196)[2]

(1.10) As the being of each thing consists in
manifoldness and the One cannot be manifoldness, the One must differ from being.
(Plotinus 1950:140 [Ennead VI, ix])

(1.11) Tao cannot be heard; if heard, it is not
Tao. Tao cannot be seen; if seen, it is not
Tao. Tao cannot be spoken, if spoken, it is
not Tao. (The Chuang Tzu, in Chai and Chai
1961:96)

(1.12) ...what is beautiful is to be loved, and the
Absolutely Beautiful is the One, who has no
equal; the Unique, who has no opposite... .
(Al-Ghazali, Ihya 'Ulum al-Din, in Williams
1963:187)

As these passages suggest, religious objects
can be unique in different ways. For example, a
religious object may be said to possess a radical
purity or goodness that contrasts with the evil
tendencies and actions of men, or it may be claimed
to have a beauty which admits of no comparison
(1.2, 1.12). Its uniqueness may consist, at least
in part, in its special origin (1.8), in its not having had an origin (1.7), or in its being the origin
or source of all else (1.4, 1.9). Its serene unity
may set it off from the teeming multiplicity of beings (1.10), or its unconditioned character may
sharply distinguish it from karma-laden existence,

conditioned by ignorance (1.5). Its elusiveness or nonsubstantial character may demarcate it from those things which can be percceived by the senses and categorized with names (1.11). The term 'holy' in 1.6 is a translation of the Hebrew <u>qadosh</u>, which itself suggests the uniqueness of the religious object by its root meaning of 'separate' or 'withdrawn'. Some applications of this category on the personal side are implied by parts of 1.5, 1.6, and 1.12. The religious object provides a happiness that nothing else can, and it is to be depended upon and loved as nothing else. Attributes like 'absolute', 'supernatural', 'infinite', 'noncontingent', 'unconditioned', 'transcendent', and 'wholly other' also express this uniqueness in the discourse of religions.

2. PRIMACY

Not only does the religious object contrast radically with all else, it also takes precedence over all else. On the personal side it is that object of loyalty 'to which final priority is assigned in the inevitable conflict of loyalties' (Greene 1957:94). And on the cosmic side it is regarded as the final reality, the root principle or power on which everything else depends and from which (or in comparison with which) everything else derives its relative status and significance. The following religious utterances exemplify this second category.

(2.1) Hail to thee! On thee 'tis meet and right
       That mortals everywhere should call.... .
       For thee this whole vast cosmos, wheeling
         round

The earth obeys, and where thou leadest
It follows, ruled willingly by thee.
(Cleanthes, 'Hymn to Zeus' in Grant 1953:152-153)

(2.2)   On Me fix thy mind; to Me be devoted;
worship Me; revere Me; thus having disciplined thyself, with Me as thy goal, to Me
shalt thou come. (Krishna to Arjuna in the
Bhagavadgita, in Radhakrishnan and Moore
1957:134)

(2.3)   ...I count everything as loss because of the
surpassing worth of knowing Christ my Lord.
(Philippians 3:8, RSV)

(2.4)   Better than absolute sovereignty on earth,
better than going to heaven, better than
lordship over all the worlds is the reward of
reaching the stream (the attainment of the
first step in sanctification). (The
Dhammapada, in Radhakrishnan and Moore
1957:306)

(2.5)   One All is lord of what is fixed and moving,
that walks, that flies, this multiform creation. (Addressed to Visvadevas, i.e., all
the gods, in the Rigveda III, 54, in Radhakrishnan and Moore 1957:22)

(2.6)   Man follows the laws of earth;
Earth follows the laws of heaven;
Heaven follows the laws of Tao;
Tao follows the laws of its intrinsic
   nature.
(Tao-Te Ching, in Ballou 1944:547)

(2.7)   Like a bird tied with a string, every
creature is dependent on God and none else.

No one can be his own ordainer. (The Mahabharata, in Renou 1963:125)

(2.8)   For Thou, O Lord, art most high over all the earth; thou art exalted above all gods. (Psalm 97:9, RSV)

(2.9)   He is before all things and in him all things hold together. (Colossians 1:17, RSV)

(2.10)   ...all beings have root in me, I am not rooted in them... . Under me as supervisor nature sends forth the moving and unmoving; because of this, the universe revolves. (Krishna to Arjuna in the Bhagavadgita, in Ballou 1944:65)

(2.11)   He is the Supreme Monarch, subject to no one, with no superior over Him who can permit, or command, or chide, or forbid, or prescribe what He shall do and fix bounds for Him. (Al-Ashari, Kitab al-Luma', in Williams 1963:179)

(2.12)   The supreme God is a Being eternal, infinite, absolutely perfect; but a being, however perfect, without dominion cannot be said to be Lord God... . It is the dominion of a spiritual being which constitutes a God... . (Issac Newton, The Mathematical Principles of Natural Philosophy, II, 311ff., quoted in Burtt 1954:294)

2.1 brings out especially well the tie between personal and cosmic primacy in the religious object, in this case Zeus. Implicit in 2.4 is the Buddhist worldview, wherein primacy is assigned to the first step toward a state or principle (and thus, by implication, to the state or principle itself, i.e., to nirvana or dharma) rather than to a distinct being. This state or principle is regarded not only as the supreme aim of life (personal primary) but also as the final reality (cosmic primacy). 2.2 and 2.3 lay stress on personal primacy, while 2.5 through 2.11 focus on the role of cosmic primary in the religious object. The close connection between the uniqueness and primacy of the religious object has already been suggested by 1.1. But 2.12 reminds us that, no matter how unique an object of interest may be, if it lacks primacy it cannot properly be termed the religious object.

Two examples might help to elucidate this last point. One is the dispute about the relation between the Father and the Son in the early history of Christianity. Arius viewed the Son as being unique in that he was begotten before time and was a perfect creature, not to be compared with the rest of creation. But he reserved primacy for the Father, who alone was self-existent. The clear implication, readily admitted by Arius, was that the Son was 'not God truly, but by participation in grace... . He too is called God in name only'. (Athanasius, C. Ar., I, 5, quoted in Kelly 1958:229; see also Kelly's discussion, 227-229). One option was to make Christ a member of a class of gods, and thus to grant him a share in a kind of collective primacy with the Father (cf. 2.5, where collective primacy is ascribed to the Vedic deities). But Jewish monotheism, the seedbed of Christianity, tended to foreclose this option. In fact, it was in staunch defense of monotheism that Arius refused to attribute equality of status to the Son in relation to the Father. However, the problem with Arian theology, so far as the majority of fourth-century Christians was concerned, was the fact that Christ already had for them the role of personal primacy (i.e., nothing was more important than Christ in their lives, not even God the Father), and this created strong pressure to accord him cosmic primacy as well. The doctrine of the Trinity was the outcome, and its paradoxicality can be at least partly explained as the result of conflict between this pressure and that exerted by traditional Jewish monotheism.

The second example comes from Buddhism. The Buddhists, as Edward Conze points out, have adopted an attitude of agnosticism to the question of a personal Creator, but 'they have not hesitated to stress the superiority of the Buddha over Brahma, the God who, according to Brahminic theology, created the Universe' (Conze 1959:39). The point is that the Creator of the Universe, while he must certainly be recognized as unique, would not have primacy for Buddhists, even if his existence were admitted, because the supreme aim of life is not worship and service of a god or the gods but release from the suffering which plagues all sentient existence. Lacking such primacy, Brahma could not qualify as the object of religious interest for Buddhists.

The converse point to the above also holds, i.e., an object of interest might be primary but lack uniqueness, and hence would not qualify as a religious object. For example, a mere incremental primacy—being first or highest in a gradually ascending order of like things—would not be suffi-cient, because the object's contrast with whatever is next lowest in the scale of value or importance would not be radical enough for it to fulfill the role illustrated and supported by the religious utterances cited in connection with the first category.

But a tension between uniqueness and primacy is also suggested just at this point, namely, that primacy implies relevance to those other factors and concerns which gain their degrees of importance in reference to it, while uniqueness, if extreme enough, would make such relevance impossible. An example of this tension is provided by Conze's discussion (1959:111-112) of the Unconditioned (or Absolute) in Buddhist thought:

By its very definition, the Absolute has no relation to anything. At the same time the idea of salvation implies that there is some kind of contact or fusion between the Unconditioned and the Conditioned. This idea is logically untenable, and when they thought about it, the Buddhists discovered a great number of paradoxes and contradictions... .

Awareness of this tension can be useful, for example, in trying to come to terms with such elusive concepts in the history of Buddhism as the concept of 'emptiness'. For given the fact that the Unconditioned is by definition totally unlike any conditioned thing (uniqueness), it follows that it would be

impossible for a person to enter into any kind of relation with it, much less to possess or gain it. Further, one could never know that one had attained Nirvana. Emptiness has no properties, no marks, it has nothing by which it could be recognized, and so we can never know whether we have it or not. (Conze 1959:135)

And yet, paradoxically, one is expected to aspire toward it as the supreme end of life and final reality (primacy).

The tension between uniqueness and primacy should not be over-stressed, however, for there is also a mutual connection between the two categories. It is partly the sui generis character of the religious object which entitles it to the role of unqualified primacy in the life of the person and in his vision of the world. And similarly, since the primacy of the religious object is not merely over this or that aspect of experience or the world but over all things taken together, a contrast with all else is implied. The relation of the two categories is therefore a complex one, posing various possibilities for stress and development within and among the doctrinal schemes of the various religions. The situation becomes even more subtle and complex, of course, when we consider the interconnections and tensions of all of the categories of the theory of religion here being proposed.

A problem posed by the category of primacy for a general theory of cultural interests is that of preserving the autonomy of other cultural interests vis-à-vis the religious one. A theory of religion should avoid, as has been stressed already, the implication that such basic interests as the scientific, aesthetic, moral, or philosophic are in some way methodologically dependent on the religious perception of primacy. A way out of this problem is to say that while nothing will be as valued or as important in the life of the religious person as the object of his religious concern, lesser concerns are not thereby eclipsed or usurped. In fact they can be, and commonly are, recognized as having intrinsic and not merely derivative importance, although

they do not have the final priority commanded by
the religious object. And it is also possible to be
nonreligious, in which case perhaps no value or
loyalty would have primacy in one's life, or else
what is of ultimate importance would lack other
aspects of the distinctive role played by an object
of religious interest.

In sum, then, the category of primacy puts us
in mind of the fact that the religious object is held
to be superior to each and every (other) thing in
the universe and to all (other) things taken together (it may or may not itself be considered a
thing). The mere aggregate of all things would not
have such primacy, but an organic whole, not
simply the sum of its parts, might (cf. Nature as
the religious object for the Stoics and Spinoza).
Attributes which suggest this category are ones like
'supreme', 'highest', 'lord', 'almighty', etc.

3.   PERVASIVENESS

A third feature of the role of the religious object is
that, on the personal side, it relates, or is expected to relate, crucially and intimately to every
aspect of life, bringing the diverse elements of life
into a focused and integrated pattern. But not
only is it viewed as the ordering principle of personal existence, probing the very depths of man's
inner being; it is also seen as somehow suffusing or
integrating the cosmos as a whole. The bond which
is thereby established between the deepest levels of
the self and the pervading core of reality gives to
the religious person a unified conception of the
world and of his own place within it (see McDermott
1970:395-396). This concept may stem (as, for

example, in theistic religions) from the conviction that the religious object is the sustaining power of the universe, the ground of cosmic order and value to which man as creature is called to dedicate his life. But even in those religions (such as Buddhism) where the reality and value of worldly existence, or even of the self as such, may be denied, the very act of denial affords a way of focusing upon the world as a whole and contrasting the sum total of its seductions with man's true destiny, a destiny which is also reality's final word. The religious object's permeation of life and of the cosmos, and the unified concept of self and world it affords I subsume under the category of pervasiveness. Following are some locutions which can help to suggest the variety of ways in which this category finds expression in the discourse of religions:

(3.1) (O man), follow not that whereof thou has no knowledge. Lo! the hearing and the sight and the heart—of each of these it will be asked. (Koran 17:36b, in Pickthall 1953:206)

(3.2) And on that day there shall be inscribed on the bells of the horses, 'Holy to the Lord'. And the pots in the house of the Lord shall be as the bowls before the altar. (Zechariah 14:20, RSV)

(3.3) Rama's name, to be efficacious, must absorb your entire being during its recitation and express itself in your whole life. (M. K. Gandhi, Ramanama, the Infallible Remedy, in Renou 1963:209)

(3.4)   ...what is the Noble Truth of the Path that
leads to the cessation of suffering?—It is
just the Noble Eightfold Path, consisting of
right outlook, right resolves, right speech,
right acts, right livelihood, right endeavor,
right mindfulness and right rapture of concentration. (Majjhima-nikaya, in Radhakrishnan and Moore 1957:275)

(3.5)   So, whether you eat or drink, or whatever
you do, do all to the glory of God. (I
Corinthians 10:31, RSV)

(3.6)   While the fulness of spiritual being
transcends our categories, we are certain
that its nature is akin to the highest kind
of being we are aware of in ourselves
... . There is in the self of man, at the
very centre of his being, something deeper
than the intellect, which is akin to the
Supreme. (S. Radhakrishnan, An Idealist
View of Life, excerpted in Radhakrishnan
and Moore 1957:625-626)

(3.7)   It [Tao] pervades everywhere and never
becomes exhausted. (Tao-Te Ching, in
Ballou 1944:547)

(3.8)   It is far, and It is near. It is within all
this, and It is outside all this. (Reference
to Brahman in Isa Upanishad, in Renou 1963:
67)

(3.9)   Gradually, as his soul was enriched with
spiritual knowledge, he saw the whole world
forming one vast symmetrical expression of
God's power and love. Life became a divine
gift for every moment and sensation of
which, were it even the sight of a single

leaf hanging on the twig of a tree, his soul should praise and thank the Giver. (Joyce 1964:149-150)

(3.10) He who, dwelling in all things, yet is other than all things, whom all things do not know, whose body all things are, who controls all things from within—He is your Self, the Inner Controller, the Immortal ... . (Brhadaranyaka Upanishad, III 7.15, in Radhakrishnan and Moore 1957:84)

(3.11) . . . the whole earth is full of his glory. (Isaiah 6:36, RSV)

(3.12) Everywhere he goes, he remains pure, undefined, his light penetrates the ten quarters, and the ten thousand things are of one Suchness. (Rinzai Gigen, Rinzai Roku, in Fromm et al. 1970:34)[3]

(3.13) There is a reality, a truth of all existence which is greater and more abiding than all its formations and manifestations; to find that truth and reality and to live in it, achieve the most perfect manifestation and formation possible of it, must be the secret of perfection whether of individual or communal being. This reality is there within each thing and gives to each of its formations its power of being and value of being. (Sri Aurobindo, The Life Divine, excerpted in Radhakrishnan and Moore 1957:608)

3.1 through 3.5 emphasize the religious object's suffusion of personal life, the idea that in principle, if not yet in fact, every part of life comes within its orbit and belongs under its sway.

3.2 is especially interesting. In stating that in the day of the Lord no common thing will be left untouched by the holy, it suggests a meaning of 'holiness' (qadosh) which goes beyond and runs somewhat counter to its etymological meaning, already alluded to in connection with the first category. As Mary Douglas has noted: 'Granted that its root means separateness, the next idea that emerges is of the Holy as wholeness and completeness' (Douglas 1970:64).[4] These two meanings of 'holy' can be reconciled to some extent when we reflect that the holy confers completeness on life by insuring that different classes of things shall not be confused, thereby giving 'correct definition, descrimination and order' to them. This means, among other things, separation of the course of personal or community life from whatever is seen as impure or defiled, i.e., lacking in wholeness or completeness (Douglas 1970:67 and chap. 3, passim). But even if we grant this connection, there is a tension between the two meanings which is left unresolved and which can be interpreted as a form of tension between pervasiveness and uniqueness. For instance, how can that which is radically distinct from all else pervade everything? And how can anything be said to be impure or incomplete at any time, and thus to contrast with the holy, if all things are pervaded by it? The second question also implies a tension, as we shall see, between pervasiveness and the category of rightness.

3.6 and 3.13 focus on the kinship between the depths of personal experience and the core of reality that is disclosed and furthered by preoccupation with the religious object. But 3.6 also states the conviction that no matter how intimate this kinship is or may become, the religious object still transcends human categories and outreaches human understanding. It is still in some sense still 'wholly other'. A tension between pervasiveness and uniqueness is thus again implied.

3.6, 3.8 and 3.10 through 3.12 stress primarily the cosmic pervasiveness of the religious object. But 3.8, 3.10 and 3.12 suggest a tension once more between pervasiveness and uniqueness. For the religous object is at once 'within all this' (or 'in all things') and 'outside all this' (or 'other than all things'), and it 'remains pure, undefined', despite its purported presence in all things. 3.9 brings out vividly the perception of the world as a unity or totality fostered by religious awareness.

One religious reason for the sort of tension we find expressed in 3.8 has been elaborated by Ninian Smart. He notes that in Vedantic Hinduism it is both the case that the finite world, viewed as a single composite entity, contains the divine mystery and that it conceals that mystery. The sublime and awe-inspiring features of the world call attention to the divine, but not to themselves as divine. Rather they point to a holy something which lies beneath or beyond them, and of which they are only signs or traces. Accordingly, the world contains and manifests the divine in one sense (pervasiveness) but conceals and veils it in another (cf. the sixth category: hiddenness). Smart explains the latter fact by saying that 'to be an adequate target for worship, the divine must be unobvious and impervious to full exploration' (1958:42). In terms of our analysis, it can also be explained on the ground of the religious object's uniqueness, the fact that it cannot be identified with or even compared with anything else in the world.

A relation of mutual implication between primacy and pervasiveness is implicit in 2.9 of the previous section, namely, that the being, power, or principle which has primacy ('is before all things') thereby provides the focus of unity and cohesion for those things subordinate to it ('in him all things hold together'). This relation is also given expression by Isidore Epstein's observation that for Judaism 'God is Schechinah ("The Indwelling"), immanent and omnipresent, not necessarily in the sense that God is coextensive with creation, but that His providence extends over all creation' (Epstein 1959:137, my italics). A corollary point is suggested by 3.10: whatever lies nearest to the root and source of all things can be expected to rule them most effectively, i.e., not merely externally but 'from within'.

It would seem, therefore, that primacy and pervasiveness go most naturally together, while there is more of a marked tension between these two categories, on the one hand, and the category of uniqueness, on the other. Still, it can be argued that one important indication of the uniqueness of the religious object is that, unlike anything else in experience or the world, it underlies and permeates all things. Also, its very diffuseness makes it difficult to characterize or comprehend in ordinary ways. Attributes suggesting the category of pervasiveness are ones like 'omnipresent', 'immanent', 'indwelling', and 'all-encompassing'.

4.   RIGHTNESS

The category of rightness makes explicit a function of the religious object already alluded to in our discussion of the foregoing three categories. This is its valuative role, the fact that it is held to be incomparable in goodness and beauty (cf. uniqueness), to determine the relative status and importance of all else (cf. primacy), and to be the source of unity, harmony, or completeness for man's life and for the world (cf. pervasiveness). To put the matter more precisely, we are reminded by the category of rightness that interest in a religious object is an interest in a goodness or power of goodness which is supreme and inviolable, which orders the believer's life pursuits and defines his destiny, and which affords him the promise and hope of capacity to fulfill that destiny as so defined against all odds. The statements which follow suggest this fourth category in various ways.

(4.1)   ...I have not heard of Heaven praying to the emperor for blessing. I therefore know that Heaven gives the standard to the emperor. (The Mo Tzu, in Chan 1963:219)

(4.2)   ...the one Inner Soul of all things is not sullied by the evil in the world, being external to it. (Katha Upanishad, in Renou 1963:69)

(4.3)   Whenever we speak of good and evil, good always precedes evil. (I-shu, in Chan 1963: 570)

(4.4)   What issues from the Way is good. (Book of Changes, quoted in Chan 1963:528)

(4.5)   Thy righteousness is like the mountains of
        God,
        thy judgments are like the great deep;
        Man and beast thou savest, O Lord. (Psalm
        36:6, RSV)

(4.6)   The cosmic order [of which T'ien is the
        source and sustainer] also includes an order
        for human society and human conduct. (Kim
        1972:155)

(4.7)   The attainment of Nirvana, without clinging
        to the world, is the Supreme Good.
        (Milindapanha, II, i. 5, quoted in Smart
        1958:58)

(4.8)   I am a mass of sin;
           Thou are all purity;
        Yet thou must take me as I am
           And bear my load for me.
        (Tukaram (a Maharashtrian poet) in Renou
        1963:187. The 'thou' is Visnu.)

(4.9)   When I call Him Lord, I call Him Judge.
        (Theophilus, ad. Autol. 2, 36-38, cited in
        Kelly 1958:467)

(4.10) Sincerity is not just a state of mind, but an
        active force that is always transforming
        things and completing things, and drawing
        Man and Heaven together in the same cur-
        rent. (Chan 1963:96)

(4.11) The Great Whole is the goal of life which is
        to be fulfilled through the investigation of
        things, the fulfillment of one's nature, and
        serving Heaven. When this is done, one will
        reach the highest sphere of life, that of
        'forming one body with all things', which is

the sphere of 'great jen (humanity)'.   (Chan 1963:752)[5]

(4.12) I appear in the world
Like unto this great cloud,
to pour enrichment on all
Parched living beings,
To free them from their misery,
To attain the joy of peace,
Joy of the present world,
And joy of nirvana.
(Saddharmapundarika, in Hamilton 1952:123. The speaker is the Eternal Buddha.)

(4.13) How is virtue to be attained? It is to be attained through Tao. (Wang Pi, Commentary on the Lao Tzu, in Chan 1963:321)

(4.14) ...God shows his love for us in that while we were yet sinners Christ died for us. (Romans 5:8, RSV)

(4.15) Eternal Law [Rta] hath varied food that strengthens; thought of Eternal Law removes transgressions. (Rigveda, in Radhakrishnan and Moore 1957:25)

(4.16) ...the Wise Creator desires (only what is good; his will is wholly good, and his creative activity is in accordance with his will ...so long as evil is not annihilated, he whose will is good has not perfectly fulfilled what he wills. (Mardan-Farrukh, Shikand Gumani Vazar, in Zaehner 1956:62)

4.1 through 4.6 portray the religious object in its role as the embodiment of a goodness which reigns supreme over evil and which is the ultimate source and standard of all that is fitting and right

within the world.   4.7 through 4.11 show how this
cosmic rightness defines human destiny and calls
into judgment every person's life to the extent that
it runs counter to or falls short of that destiny.
4.12 through 4.16 give assurance of a path or
means whereby men can find deliverance from the
evil forces or illusions which plague their lives and
attain at last to their true goal.   This last cluster
of passages makes it plain that interest in a religious object is not interest in mere clarity of·under-
standing, but in the secret of salvation.   This
means that the fundamental goal of religion is active
or practical, rather than contemplative or theoretical.   For while religious systems do seek to give a
comprehensive view of the world and to shed light
on the facts of human existence, they do so for an
ulterior end, that of pointing the way to the transformation of life.   In the words of Rudolf Otto, 'To
speak of a "religion of redemption" is...to be guilty
of a redundancy, at any rate if we are considering
the more highly developed forms of religion' (Otto
1958:166).
        Some interconnections between the category of
rightness and the preceding three categories which
are implicit in the quotations above (and which have
been alluded to in the opening paragraph of this
section) can   be briefly   noted.   4.2   ascribes   a
rightness to the religious object on the cosmic level
which also implies its cosmic uniqueness, i.e., its
radical contrast with a world in which evil dwells
(cf. 1.2).   4.8 suggests a similar relation between
these two categories on the personal level.   4.1 and
4.3 link the rightness of the religious object to its
primacy on the cosmic side, while 4.7 and 4.9
correlate these two categories on the personal side.
4.2 ('the one Inner Soul of all things'), 4.10, and

4.11 (see also 3.13) tie together rightness and pervasiveness, in both their cosmic and their personal aspects. 4.6 and 4.15 also imply a confluence of these two categories, since T'ien and Ṛta are names for an ultimate principle of law or rightness which is also the cohesive force underlying and sustaining the cosmos. Tao, Logos, and, to some extent, Dharma have a similar dual connotation in other religious traditions.

An important correlation between rightness and pervasiveness is suggested in an article by Joel Kupperman on Confucian ethics. What marks Confucian ethics as religious, and not merely social or philosophical in character, according to Kupperman, is that it encompasses 'all of the passions and appetites which may be involved in valuing something or thinking it valuable', and not just those directly involved in moral choice. What matters most in religious ethics, in other words, is not specific moral decisions or overt moral behavior, which affect only a relatively small part of day-to-day life, but an all-pervading harmony of appetites and passions in the inner man, so that one's inner dispositions are wholly attuned to and informed by the cosmic good (Kupperman 1971:190-192). The concept of 'sincerity' (Ch'eng) which figures so prominently in The Doctrine of the Mean (and which is referred to in 4.10) attests to the deep affinity between rightness and pervasiveness in Confucian religious thought.

Despite interconnections of this sort, however, there are also potential strains or tensions in the interplay of rightness and the preceding categories which need to be considered. On the one hand, as we have seen, the radical bliss, purity, or goodness associated with the religious object underscores its uniqueness. But from another standpoint, its uniqueness, if given strong enough stress, can preclude any meaningful comparison between the religious object and ordinary standards or conceptions of rightness. The religious object will then be seen as elevated not only above evil (as in 4.2) but also above goodness, or at least above goodness which can be comprehended as such by man. One classical expression of this tension is the Book of Job, where God's response to Job's bitter complaints is a detailed reminder of the radical distinction between himself and man. But this reminder does not resolve the problem of Job's undeserved ill treatment at the hands of God. It enhances the sense of God's uniqueness, but at the price of a clear sense of his rightness.

There is also grist for conflict between the categories of rightness and primacy. If, on the one hand, the rightness of the religious object is given great emphasis, this might threaten at least its cosmic primacy. 4.16, for example, portrays a God (Ohrmazd) whose rightness is never in question, but whose primacy is, since he is locked in a struggle with evil forces over which he does not exercise immediate full control. Strong stress on the rightness of the religious object could also threaten its primacy in the sense of making it subservient to standards of value higher than itself.

If, on the other hand, the emphasis is given to the primacy of the religious object, this might tend to threaten its rightness. This conflict becomes quite pronounced in the history of Islam, where we find the Mu'tazilite group contending for the subordination of Allah's sovereignty to his justice, and the Ash'arite and Maturidite groups arguing for the view that no course of action, however right it might seem, is <u>incumbent</u> upon Allah (see section 19 of the creedal statement of al-Maturidi, in Williams 1963:170), for all his actions are the outcome of the radical freedom of his will. This latter emphasis on the cosmic primacy of Allah threatens the sense of his justice and equity in dealing with his creatures, since it leads to belief in double predestination, and it also, by the same token, erodes the confidence of believers in the surety of their salvation. Thus the role of rightness is called into question on two scores. This kind of stress on the cosmic primacy of the religious object can also become a threat to its personal primacy, because morally sensitive men must now question whether such a God can command sufficient respect to be the focal point of their lives (on this point see Tillich, CTB, 184-185).

Finally, tension can also arise between the categories of rightness and pervasiveness. We have already had occasion (in section 3) to raise the question of how anything can be said to be impure or incomplete if all things are pervaded by the holy. One way of answering this question would be to insist that the distinction between good and evil is only relative; that, viewed from a larger perspective, both are necessary in the scheme of things and both emanate from the religious ultimate as their root. Thus Chuang Tzu, emphasizing the omnipresence and dialectical working of the Tao, states: 'Because of the right, there is the wrong, and because of the wrong, there is the right'. And the Neo-Confucianist Ch'eng Hao asserts: 'Good and evil in the world are both the Principle of Nature' (Chan 1963:183,529). This type of answer preserves the pervasiveness (and the

primacy) of the religious object, but at the expense
of a clear conception of its rightness. And it runs
the risk of seeming to advocate too tolerant or
indifferent an attitude toward evil.

Observations of this kind are intended to be
purely analytical in character, of course. My purpose in making them is not to criticize any religious
system as such or to appraise its success in dealing
with its conceptual problems, but only to suggest
the extent to which the problems and tensions of
specific religious systems can be related to the
generic role played by the object of religious interest itself, as that role is delineated by this theory.

Attributes which imply the category of
rightness are ones like 'all-good', 'just', 'holy', (as
a moral quality), 'loving', 'saving', 'blissful', and
'worshipful' (in its etymological sense of 'worthful').

5.   PERMANENCE

The fifth category, permanence, calls attention to
yet another aspect of the generic role played by an
object of religious interest. Whatever this object
may be for a given religious system or a given
religious individual, it is regarded as something
immune to the ravages of time. The implication of
this on the cosmic level is that the religious object
is seen as being either (a) timeless, i.e., transcending time, standing outside the temporal process altogether; or (b) everlasting, i.e., enduring
through time but not threatened with extinction by
time's unfolding. And on the personal level the
implication of this fifth category is that the religious object is thought to provide a definitive way of
coping with the changeable and precarious character

of human existence, a way of satisfying man's deep longing 'for some ultimate integrity and serenity beyond the reach of such crises as birth and death and the inevitable transitoriness of life' (Hamilton 1952:xxviii). The following quotations can help toward an elucidation of the category of permanence.

(5.1) Nirvana, first of all, is not a kind of Ens,
It would then have decay and death.
There altogether is no Ens
Which is not subject to decay and death.
(Vimalakirti-Nirdesa Sutra, in Hamilton 1952:152)

(5.2) He [Ohrmazd] is the first born out of the Boundless Time (Zrvana), but not limited by time and he has existed from eternity in Boundless Time. (Masani 1968:37, commenting on the Gathas)

(5.3) It [Tao] is prior to Heaven and Earth, yet has no duration. (The Chuang Tzu, in Chai and Chai 1961:95)

(5.4) 'Across what then, pray, is space woven, warp and woof?' He said: 'That, O Gargi, brahmins call the Imperishable....(Brhadaranyaka Upanishad, Radhakrishnan and Moore 1957: 85)

(5.5) The Lord is king for ever and ever; the nations shall perish from his land. (Psalm 10:16, RSV)

(5.6) Truly, truly, I say to you, before Abraham was, I am. (John 8:58, RSV)

(5.7) By meditation some perceive the Self in the self by the self; others by the path of knowledge and still others by the path of works. Yet others, ignorant of this [these paths of yoga], hearing from others, worship; and they too cross beyond death by their devotion to what they have heard. (<u>Bhagavadgita</u>, Radhakrishnan and Moore 1957:147)

(5.8)   <u>Prajna</u> is the experience a man has when he feels in its most fundamental sense the infinite totality of things, that is, psychologically speaking, when the finite ego, breaking its hard crust, refers itself to the infinite which envelops everything that is finite and limited and therefore transitory. We may take this experience as being somewhat akin to a totalistic intuition of something that transcends all our particularized, specified experiences. (Fromm et al. 1970:74)

(5.9)   Those who trust in the Lord are like Mount Zion, which cannot be moved, but abides forever. (Psalm 125:1, RSV)

(5.10) But when in these noble truths my threefold knowledge and insight duly with its twelve divisions was well purified, then, O monks, in the world... . I had attained the highest complete enlightenment. Thus I knew. Knowledge arose in me; insight arose that the release of my mind is unshakable; this is my last existence; now there is no rebirth. (<u>Samyutta-nikaya</u>, in Radhakrishnan and Moore 1957:275)

(5.11) To him, who is Thy true friend in spirit and in actions, O Mazda Ahura,

To him Thou shalt give Healthful Weal and
   Immortality;
To him Thou shalt give perpetual communion
   with Truth and the Kingdom of Heaven,
And to him Thou shalt give the sustaining
   strength of the Good Mind.
(D. J. Irani, The Divine Songs of
Zarathushtra, quoted in Masani 1968:77).

(5.12) ...love towards a thing eternal and infinite
feeds the mind wholly with joy, and is itself
unmingled with any sadness, wherefore it is
greatly to be desired and sought for with all
our strength. (Spinoza, On the Improvement of
the Understanding, in Spinoza 1951, II:5)

5.1 through 5.6 show how religious objects
exemplify the category of permanence on the cosmic
level. 5.3 and 5.4 (cf. also 5.8) describe religious
objects which are timeless, while 5.2 and 5.5 refer
to ones which can be interpreted as everlasting.
5.7 through 5.11 suggest some of the ways in which
religious objects manifest the category of permanence on the personal level. And 5.12 typifies the
yearning of the religious spirit for some eternal
ultimate which can counterbalance the corrosive
effects of time and give man ground for hope in the
face of the shocks and deprivations of his
ephemeral life.
    Belief in personal immortality is one way in
which religious traditions provide such hope. 5.11
is a Zoroastrian affirmation of this belief, which is
also adhered to in Christianity, Islam, and later
Judaism. The author of 5.9, by contrast, was perhaps expressing confidence in collective rather than
individual immortality. Those who serve the Lord

and die do not serve in vain, because their contributions live on in the nation Israel, anointed by God to be the instrument of his holy purpose in the world. 5.7 cites four routes within Hinduism by which one can come to what is seen as the culmination of the religious life, a crossing beyond death. 5.8 sets forth a Zen Buddhist perspective on the problem of time, the conviction that eternity (and the serenity which accompanies it) can be discovered in the here and now, at the absolute present, through a radical shift in the way in which one perceives the nature of things. And 5.10 testifies to the glorious realization of the Buddha himself that he was no longer the captive of time, that he had at last achieved the goal of release from the wearisome cycle of birth and rebirth.

Some of the conceptual connections between the category of permanence and the preceding categories can be briefly spoken of. Then we can go on to consider some of the tensions inherent in its relations to the other categories. 5.1 brings out quite clearly a connection between permanence and uniqueness. The religious object, as permanent, contrasts sharply with a world subject to decay and death. A connection between permanence and primacy is suggested by 5.12, where Spinoza states that a thing eternal 'is to be desired and sought for with all our strength', i.e., all else is to be subordinated to it as the supreme aim of life. Or to put the matter another way, a basic reason the religious object is accorded primacy is that the ephemeral and contingent is judged to be inferior to the enduring and lasting.

5.4 and 5.8 imply connections between permanence and pervasiveness. Space is 'woven, warp and woof' across the Imperishable (Brahman), according to 5.4. And the 'infinite' of which D. T. Suzuki speaks in 5.8 is said to 'envelop' everything which, in contrast to itself (cf. uniqueness) is finite and limited, and therefore transitory. It is characteristic of religions to view the permanent as underlying and suffusing the impermanent things of this world. Suzuki also speaks in this passage of a 'totalistic intuition' of the infinite, linking this with a perception of the 'infinite totality of things'. This language brings to mind another nuance of meaning earlier associated with the category of pervasiveness, namely, the unified perspective on self and the world brought about by preoccupation with an object of religious interest.

Permanence and rightness are closely entwined, since the path to the permanent is regarded as the path of human destiny, requiring adherence to some specified pattern of right thought and behavior. 5.10 and 5.11 bring out this connection especially well. Furthermore, a large part of what salvation means in the religious traditions is being able effectively to cope with such threats of time as the accumulation of evil deeds, the bondage of birth and rebirth, the terrors of death, the disintegration of things of value, and the anxieties of an uncertain future. Still another connection between permanence and rightness stems from the conviction that the rightness embodied in or exemplified by the religious object is a rightness for all time; hence it is a permanent rightness.

But there is also the possibility of conceptual conflict between the category of permanence and the other categories already discussed. If the religious object is viewed as everlasting (in the sense of the term specified above), then its involvement in time might be taken as detracting from its uniqueness, i.e., as not allowing for sufficient contrast between it and the spatiotemporal world. And this interpretation of the permanence of the religious object might also constitute a threat to its primacy. For example, one consequence of the Zoroastrian God's involvement in time is that he must win his way through to complete cosmic primacy through his skill and powers of persuasion. And in so doing, he takes the risk of failure, since the outcome of his conflict with Ahriman depends crucially on what transpires in the course of world history and that, in turn, depends on the actions of men, who have the ability to thwart the divine purpose. Another way in which Ohrmazd's involvement in time threatens his primacy is implicit in the teaching that both he and Ahriman spring from Boundless Time (see 5.2). For this teaching contains the seed of the conviction that Time rather than Ohrmazd is ultimate, a belief which is in fact adhered to in the Zervanite heresy.

If, on the other hand, the religious object is believed to be timeless, a tension is created between permanence, thus construed, and the two categories of pervasiveness and rightness. An example of the tension with pervasiveness is the struggle of the Hindu philosopher Sankara to resolve the problem of how Brahman can be 'the basis of this world with its changes, and so on, while in its true and real nature it at the same time remains unchanged, lifted above the phenomenal universe' (The Vedanta Sutras with the Commentary by Sankarakarya, in Radhakrishnan and Moore 1957:532). Here the permanence ('remains unchanged') and the uniqueness ('lifted above the phenomenal universe') of the religious object are

closely related, but the problem is posed of how
that which is unchanging can be said to be the
basis of a world of change, i.e., how it can be the
underlying power or principle on which the phenomenal world rests (cf. pervasiveness). The
solution to this problem Sankara proposes is that
plurality and change are ultimately only appearance
or illusion, the products of ignorance. But this
creates the new difficulty of explaining why this
ignorance itself should exist on such a wide scale.
No finally satisfying logical solution to this difficulty is given by Sankara. He attributes the great
power of maya to Brahman and sees its actualization
as the work of the Creator Isvara, in whom are
name and form, the figments of ignorance. But he
leaves us with the paradox that this name and form
'are not to be defined either as being (i.e.,
Brahman), nor as different from it...' (ibid, in
Radhakrishnan and Moore 1957:530,534).

The conflict between permanence (seen as
timelessness) and rightness could be elucidated in
many ways, but I have selected only two, both of
which have to do with theistic religions. The first
is implicit in the following statement:

For centuries theologians have seen the traditional
scriptural accounts of creation, of covenant, of
historical deliverance, of incarnation and atonement
as confirming a doctrine of God who is best understood as absolute and unchanging, while not realizing the anomaly of this doctrine with God's activity
witnessed in each scriptural account. (Henry 1973:4)

The point is that it is difficult to see how an
absolute and unchanging (i.e., timeless) deity could
perform those acts in historical time upon which, in

the view of religions like Judaism and Christianity, man's deliverance (i.e., rightness on the personal side) is dependent.

A second way in which the conflict between permanence and rightness comes out in theistic religions is as follows. If God is timeless, then nothing that transpires in time can make any difference to him. He must already embody all the goodness or value it is possible for him to embody, since he cannot change. This could be taken as a confirmation of God's inviolable goodness, i.e., of rightness exemplified on the cosmic side. But on the personal side the conception of God as timeless has the consequence that he has no need of man's work. And if he has no need of it, why does he ask it, and why should man perform it (Britton 1969:34-35)? Why indeed did God create man in the first place, or the world itself, for that matter? And what sort of meaning can be given to man's life by a religion if its teaching is that his struggles and accomplishments in time can make no difference whatever to God? In other words, rightness in the theistic context seems to require a mutual responsiveness between man and God which the doctrine of God as timeless would appear to make impossible.

Of course, one can go the route of recent 'dipolar' theists like Charles Hartshorne and argue that God's existence is eternal and necessary, but at the same time that there is mutability and contingency in God. The first allegation has to do with God's necessary essence, says Hartshorne, while the second has to do with his accidental properties (1973:106, see also Hartshorne's many other writings on this theme). But the fact that serious questions can be raised about the coherence of this interpretation again emphasizes the tension between the categories of permanence and rightness (Vaught 1972:18-34).

Attributes which suggest the category of permanence are ones like 'imperishable', 'immortal', 'unchanging', 'everlasting', 'everliving', 'eternal', and 'timeless'.

6.   HIDDENNESS

The last category needed to interpret the role of an object of religious interest is hiddenness. On the personal side this category recalls the oft-stated inability of religious man to find resources within his thought or speech adequate to capture the depth and richness of his experience of the religious object's presence, or to depict its dreadful majesty and power. And on the cosmic side this category relates to the apprehension of the religious object as something inexhaustibly mysterious in and of itself, something which man can only hope to see darkly, as through a thick cover or veil. Following are some passages from religious literature which can help to give specific content to this category.

(6.1)   God Most High...is not an attribute, nor a body, nor an essence, nor a thing formed, nor a thing bounded, nor a thing numbered, nor a thing divided, nor a thing compound-ed, nor a thing limited. He is not described by mahiya (what-ness), nor by kaifiyyah (how-ness), and He does not exist in place or time. There is nothing that resembles Him.... (Al-Nasafi, 'Aqa'id, cited in Cragg 1969:14)

(6.2)   Now Tao by its very nature cannot be defined. Speech by its very nature cannot express the absolute. (The Chuang Tzu, in Dye and Forthman 1967:274)

(6.3)   Your real form transcends speech and intelligence. You are ineffable and infinite, called ever by the Vedas: 'Not this! Not this!' (Tulsidas, Ramacaritmanas, in Renou 1963:196. The statement is made about Rama.)

(6.4)   God is clothed with terrible majesty,
        The Almighty—we cannot find him... . (Job 37:22b-23a, RSV)

(6.5)   What is meant by the soul as suchness is the oneness of the totality of things, the great all-including whole... . For the essential nature of the soul is uncreate and eternal. There all things in their fundamental nature are not nameable or explicable ...the immortal (i.e., suchness) and the mortal (i.e., birth-and-death) coincide with each other. Though they are not identical, they are not a duality. (Asvaghosha, Discourse on the Awakening of Faith in the Mahayana, in Ballou 1944:152)

(6.6)   There is no difference at all
        Between Nirvana and Samsara.
        (Nagarjuna, Madhyamika Sastra, in Hamilton 1952:154)

(6.7)   O the depth of the riches and wisdom and knowledge of God! How unsearachable are his judgments and how inscrutable his ways! (Romans 11:33, RSV)

(6.8) The deeper and more intimate a spiritual experience, the more readily does it dispense with signs and symbols. Deep intuition is utterly silent. Through silence we 'confess without confession' that the glory of the spiritual life is inexplicable and beyond the reach of speech and mind. It is the great unfathomable mystery and words are treacherous. (S. Radhakrishnan, An Idealist View of Life, in Radhakrishnan and Moore 1957:624)

(6.9) The soul neither sees, hears nor under-stands while she is united to God. (St. Teresa, El Castillo Interior, chap. I, quoted in Smart 1958:70)

(6.10) Behold, I go forward, but he is not there:
And backward, but I cannot perceive him;
On the left hand I seek him, but I cannot
behold him;
I turn to the right hand, but I cannot see
him. (Job 23:8-9, RSV)

6.1 through 6.7 exhibit the application of the category of hiddenness to the religious object on the cosmic side, while 6.8 through 6.10 make ex-plicit its application on the personal side. Also implicit in these passages are some of the important interconnections between hiddenness and the other categories.

6.1 through 6.3 bring out an obvious tie between hiddenness and uniqueness. The repeated negations in each passage connect man's extreme difficulty in trying to comprehend or characterize the religious object in worldly terms with the radi-cal distinction between that object and the finite world. 6.4 and 6.7 suggest a link between hiddenness and primacy. The transcendent majesty and supreme wisdom of God spoken of in these passages prevents man from fathoming God's nature or fully understanding his ways, but these same attributes also establish God's claim upon human life as the ultimate claim. G. van der Leeuw assists us further in understanding this link by his elaboration upon the statement that 'the ultimate meaning is at the same time the limit of meaning' (1963, II:680):

The religious significance of things is that on which no wider nor deeper meaning whatever can follow. It is the meaning of the whole; it is the last word. But this meaning is never understood, this last word is never spoken; always they remain superior, the ultimate meaning being a secret which reveals itself repeatedly, only nevertheless to remain eternally concealed. It implies an advance to the farthest boundary, where only one sole fact is understood:—that all comprehension is 'beyond'... .

What this means is that inherent in the very notion of ultimate meaning (or primacy) is a capacity in the religious object to bring man sharply up against the limits of his understanding, to point his attention beyond those limits to a limitless realm of mystery, and convince him that it holds the key to that realm of mystery. And because it must encompass the unknown as well as the known, the religious object itself will be shrouded in secrecy, so that with every revelation of ultimate meaning there will be the correlate of bafflement and concealment.

6.5 and 6.6 suggest a sense in which hiddenness and pervasiveness (in combination with uniqueness) are mutually related. The fact that the religious object is seen as pervading and integrating the cosmos and the diverse aspects of human life means that it must somehow raise into a higher unity all entities, powers, or domains which from another point of view are strongly opposed. But this reconciliation of opposites cannot be understood in a purely rational way, as is evidenced by the deliberately paradoxical character of both passages. The essential point would seem to be that stated in the last sentence of 6.5, namely, that while the religious object and the world are not identical, they are also not to be understood simply as a duality. Louis Dupré makes this same point when he says, 'The transcendence of the sacred over the profane, its fundamental negation, does not relegate the two to different universes. The sacred is in the profane' (Dupré 1972:164-165). And he goes on to remind us that religious symbols (and presumably, paradoxes functioning as symbols) can sustain the delicate balance between sheer opposition, on the one hand, and simple identity, on the other, in a way which rational analysis and literal expressions cannot. But they can do so only because the negative element, present in all symbols, is predominant in religious ones (ibid). The fact that religious symbols are in the final analysis more important for what they deny than for what they affirm, and that they are indispensable in religious discourse, is itself highly relevant for understanding the category of hiddenness. But the point being emphasized here is that one principal thing the symbols of the various religions do deny is the possibility of finally figuring out the mystery of the religious object as transcendent-immanent (unique and yet pervasive). This mystery is an essential part of the religious object's hiddenness.

6.8 and 6.9 suggest a correlation between hiddenness and rightness. Both point to an intense and direct experience of the religious object which is seen as saving, or as being man's highest good. And they imply that the closer one approaches to the kind of experience being spoken of, the less confident he will be about the adequacy of signs or even symbols to express the bliss of his spiritual life or the profound reorientation and renewal it effects within him. From this perspective, words and concepts are either seen as superfluous, or as dangerous, in that they threaten to disrupt the unreflective unity of the self and the religious object. This correlation between hiddenness and rightness pertains specifically to mystical religions (or mystical movements within theistic religions). But there is something akin to it in theistic conceptions of the religious object as well. This is the insistence that the drive toward conceptual clarity and verbal exactness, when pushed too far, becomes blasphemous or idolatrous, because it tends to reduce God to an object or to the status of a finite being. Not only does this tendency threaten the uniqueness of God, it is also viewed as being highly detrimental to a saving knowledge of God, wherein man encounters him not as finite object, but as infinite subject. It is essential to both the mystical and the theistic interpretations of rightness, therefore, that the hiddenness of the religious object be carefully maintained.

In addition to these points I should also mention the paradoxes generated by the notion that God, Brahman, Tao, etc., are in some sense the ultimate sources of evil as well as good. The difficulty of reconciling this notion with the claim to unqualified rightness in the religious object testifies again to its hiddenness. Something like this difficulty lies behind 6.5 and 6.6. It is also implicit in 6.10, where Job comes up against the strangeness and mystery of God through his experience of calamitous and inexplicable suffering.

Lastly, I will briefly note two interconnections between hiddenness and permanence. The first relates to the allegation in 6.1 that Allah does not exist in place or time. Given the fact that man's schemes of interpretation must all be derived from his temporal experience, it follows that these interpretations will always be inappropriate to Allah's real nature. The permanence of Allah thus implies his hiddenness. The second correlation centers on the notion that man's life in time can function as a springboard to the eternal. This is quite enigmatic, if the religious object is viewed as being outside time, because it leaves unexplained how there could be any such interaction between the temporal and the timeless realms. The paradoxicality of this is also strongly suggested in 6.6. There is something undeniably strange about the belief that samsara can be man's point of departure toward nirvana, because there is again a blending of opposites, a crossing of types which in other contexts are diametrically opposed. The Buddhist would be the first to admit that this defies understanding, but he would remind us that what is crucial in Buddhism is not the ability to solve such conundrums (which have the positive value of exposing the limits of our understanding and declaring the hiddenness of nirvana), but sticking resolutely to the path.

More could of course be said about the
tensions between hiddenness and the other categories.   Suffice it to say here, though, that the
hiddenness we have been speaking of cannot be
total in any religious system.   For if it were, there
would be no system.   To insist that speech is
inadequate as applied to the religious object or to
the depths of religious experience is not the same
thing as saying that it can be entirely dispensed
with, or that all speech is equally inadequate.   The
exhibition of the other categories of this theory by
the various religions shows clearly that there are
important things which can be known and spoken of
concerning the religious object in those traditions.
And to the extent that this is true, there is a
tension between the other categories and the category of hiddenness.   This tension is most pronounced, perhaps, in the relation between hiddenness and rightness.   For at least enough must be
known about the religious object and what it requires for life for man to find his salvation in terms
of it.   But here, as elsewhere, the revealing and
the concealing go hand in hand.   Attributes which
suggest the category of hiddenness are ones like
'ineffable', 'unsearchable', 'unnameable', 'mysterious', and 'empty'.

The theory of religion sketched in this chapter
can make no claim to final adequacy.   The nature of
religious interest is a large and elusive topic, and
(as was indicated in Chapter 1) there is room for
many different theories, each approaching the topic
in its own way and making its own kind of contribution to our understanding of it.   In the next
chapter we can consider some of the relations of
this theory to the other four theories presented
previously.   I will also state there some advantages

that I think this theory has over those theories. But whatever advantages it does have are due in no small measure to the fact that I have been able to build upon the insights of these and other theories of religion, and to profit from their mistakes.

The New Theory in Relation to the Other Theories

In this last chapter I will first attempt to show how the categories of the theory of religion presented in the preceding chapter are implicit in some aspects of the other four theories. This will exhibit the extent to which this new theory is continuous with the other four theories. Then I will discuss the application of the ten criteria for interpretive theories of religion to the new theory, seeking thereby to bring out some of its advantages over certain features of the other theories.

1.   SUGGESTIONS OF THE SIX CATEGORIES AND
      THEIR INTERRELATIONS IN THE OTHER
      THEORIES

(A)   The uniqueness of the religious object on its cosmic side is implicit in Kant's contention that God alone conforms perfectly and absolutely to the moral law, in contrast with the conditioned character of even the most resolute human responses to that law. This cosmic uniqueness is also implied by Otto's designation of the holy as inherently wholly other, meaning that its 'kind and character are incommensurable with our own', that it 'has no place in our scheme of reality but belongs to an absolutely different one', and that it lies 'quite beyond the sphere of the usual, the intelligible,

and the familiar' (H,29,28,26). We saw also that
the absolute attributes used for philosophical schematizations of the holy have the function of calling
our attention to the complete uniqueness of the
divine when compared with all that is merely creaturely and mundane. And Otto's distinct contrast
between the numinous and the natural moments of
consciousness (H,27) suggests the uniqueness of
the religious object on its personal side. For this
means that religious experience is like nothing else
in the individual's experience. It contrasts not
only with other types of experience taken singly
(e.g., with the moral or the aesthetic types), as
would be implied simply by its autonomous character, but with all the other types taken together.
For all of them except the religious type belong to
the natural moments of consciousness.

Something similar to Otto's sense of the unique
role played by the object of religion in the total
context of one's experiences is conveyed by
Tillich's statement that 'faith...is the existential
acceptance of something transcending ordinary
experience' (CTB,172-173). The cosmic uniqueness
of the religious object is also given stress by
Tillich. In a statement that is again reminiscent of
Otto, he notes that 'substantial holiness...is
attributed to no finite thing' (WIR,104). In the
same vein, he remarks that 'if man and his world
are described as finite, God is infinite in contrast
to them' (ST,I,252). And in another passage he
suggests that it is the uniqueness of God which is
threatened when he is viewed as a distinct being,
and that primacy and rightness in such a being
would not be enough to compensate for this lack of
uniqueness: 'If God is a being, he is subject to
the categories of finitude, especially to space and

substance. Even if he is called the "highest
being," in the sense of the "most perfect" and the
"most powerful" being, this situation is not
changed' (ST,I,235).[1]

Of course, Kant, Otto, and Tillich are not so
much calling attention to the category of uniqueness
per se as they are giving emphasis to particular
kinds of uniqueness in the religious object. And
the spirit of the last quotation from Tillich is more
normative than interpretive. For he is saying that
a God who is one being among others, albeit the
highest and most perfect of beings, could not be
truly God. Still, some suggestion of the need for
uniqueness as a generic functional category applying to the religious object in all religions is present
in the three theories. And this is all that I intend
to show.

(B) Spinoza's comments on the first and the
fourth of his 'dogmas of universal faith' imply the
religious object's primacy on the cosmic and the
personal levels. And they also state a line of
connection between the two levels. As we saw
earlier, he asserts that the imagery of the oneness
of God (and hence, of his superiority over all else)
and of God's exercising supreme right and dominion
over all things, is necessary to elicit man's entire
devotion, admiration, and love, and thus to motivate
him to a life of unstinted obedience.[2]

The cosmic and personal primacy of the
religious object in Kant's theory of religion is tied
so inextricably to its rightness as to be inseparable
from it, so I will discuss it later under that head-
ing. As for Otto, the cosmic primacy of the religious object is implied by his category of overpoweringness or majestas, for this draws attention to 'a
consciousness of the absolute superiority or

supremacy of a power other than myself' (H,21).
And corresponding to this on the personal side is
the category of creature-consciousness or creature-
feeling, i.e., 'the emotion of a creature, submerged
and overwhelmed by its own nothingness in contrast
to that which is supreme over all creatures' (H,10).
This suggests that all other pursuits and interests
pale so completely in significance before the religious concern as to be utterly subordinate to it.

Primacy on the cosmic side is implicit in
Tillich's conception of God as 'the power of being,
resisting and conquering nonbeing' (ST,I,272), for
he goes on to say that the nature and significance
of this divine power is aptly expressed by the
symbol of omnipotence. And he ties this symbol to
primacy on the personal side in the following way:

Only the almighty God can be man's ultimate concern.
A very mighty God may claim to be of ultimate concern; but he is not, and his claim comes to naught,
because he cannot resist nonbeing and therefore he
cannot supply the ultimate courage which conquers
anxiety... . The symbol of omnipotence gives the
first and basic answer to the question implied in
finitude. (ST,I,273)

The very phrase 'ultimate concern' of course implies
the primacy of the religious object on the personal
side, for as we have already seen, there is an
important sense in which it 'determines' and makes
'preliminary' all other concerns in the life of the
person of faith. And since this concern is about
that which is regarded as ultimate in the cosmos,
the phrase also implies the cosmic primacy of the
religious object.

(C) Spinoza's third dogma of universal faith, that God is omnipresent, suggests the cosmic pervasiveness of the religious object, and his explanation of its indispensability for faith makes a connection between cosmic pervasiveness and cosmic rightness. If things could happen unnoticed to God, because of his not being present to notice them, says Spinoza, then doubt would be cast on the equity of his judgment as directing all things, and men might fail to obey him on that account.

The personal pervasiveness of the religious object is implied by Kant's assertion that respect for the moral law and fear of God as its complete embodiment lays a radical claim upon the human heart which admits of no evasion or escape, not even in the most fleeting moments of human life. Man has the duty to attain a radical purity in his inner disposition, a duty which touches necessarily on every aspect of his being. Complementary to this basic theme in Kant's theory of religion is his claim that it would be impossible for human beings to cherish morally pure dispositions did they not believe that their dispositions are known in complete detail by a God to whom they are like an open book. And as Spinoza observed, God could not be all-knowing were he not also all-present. So there is a suggestion of the religious object's cosmic, as well as personal, pervasiveness in Kant's theory.

Otto   directs   our   attention,   in   his   own characteristic manner, to the personal and cosmic pervasiveness of the religious object. There is a definite tension, he reminds us, between the concept of the numinous or divine as a personal being who transcends the self and the world, on the one hand, and experience of it as 'fundus animae, the "bottom" or "ground" of the soul', on the other

(H,112). It is true that this latter is given more stress in mystical religions than in those of the theistic type, but it is not entirely lacking in any religion.

On the contrary, one may venture to assert that all gods are more than mere (personal) gods, and that all the greater representations of the diety show from time to time features which reveal their ancient character as 'numina' and burst the bounds of the personal and theistic. This is obviously the case where the experienced relation of the worshipper to his god does not exclusively take the form of contact with a 'beyond' and transcendent being, but comes somehow as the experience of seizure and possession by the god, as being filled by him, an experience in which the god wholly or partially enters the believer and dwells in him, or assimilates him to his own divine nature, commingling with his spirit and becoming very part of him; or, again, where the god becomes the sphere in which 'we live and move and have our being'. And what god has not in some sense this character?   (H,199)

And it is but a step from the sense of the Numen's possession and pervasion of the soul to the conception of it as a kind of presence or Self which pervades the universe, a conception given classical expression in Vedantic Hinduism (see H,199).

    Otto links the pervasiveness of the religious object with its character as mysterium, i.e., with its hiddenness. He tells us that the sense of the religious object as pervasive and radically impersonal reflects the nonrational element in religious experience, while personal, theistic conceptions of it reflect the rational element in that experience.

Taoism gives such preponderant emphasis to the former, for example, as to be perhaps the least rational of the great religions. It is that religion in which the sense of mystery seems to loom most large (H,201, note 2). But since the motif of pervasiveness is not lacking in theistic religions either, there is a 'mysterious overplus' in their conceptions of the religious object as well. This is born out by the strictures against crude anthropomorphism in those religions and by their frequent recourse to impersonal modes of discourse in speaking of God (H,193-203).

When Tillich states that faith is a centered act of the total personality, encompassing and integrating intellect, will, and emotion, he is in effect referring to the religious object's pervasiveness on the personal level. And when he speaks of God as the ground of being, this can be taken as an allusion to its role of cosmic pervasiveness. In fact, Tillich's entire analysis of the relations of morality and culture to religion rests on the cosmic pervasiveness of that which is the focus of religious interest, as does his conception of the larger sense of religion. As we saw earlier, the ultimate aim of morality is a creative, transforming union with others, the quest for which exemplifies the longing of all finite things to find reunion with the infinite which is their ground. Culture owes the dynamism and self-criticism of its ongoing life to the inexhaustible divine import which underlies and sustains it. And nobody can avoid being religious in the larger sense of the term, because nobody can escape the participation of the conditioned human spirit in the unconditioned power of the divine.

(D) The category of rightness in its cosmic application is adumbrated by Spinoza's first dogma of universal faith, which presents God as the exemplar of true life and as the merciful and just judge of mankind. The fifth dogma gives explicit emphasis to the personal application of this category by stating the manner of life laid down by religion for mankind, a life of justice and charity which emulates the character of God. The sixth dogma also implies rightness on the personal level with its insistence that all and only those who obey God will find salvation, as does Spinoza's explanation of the need for the seventh dogma: without it, men would despair of being saved. The seventh dogma itself calls attention again to the divine mercy.

The role of cosmic rightness (as well as cosmic primacy and uniqueness) is suggested by God's complete embodiment and exemplification of the moral law in Kant's theory. The mandate placed upon human beings by this law, as embodied in God, to persevere in a course of life which makes steady progress toward holiness, implies rightness at the personal level. Primacy at this level is also implied here, in that persistence in this course of life is clearly intended by Kant to be understood as man's highest responsibility. God's role as benevolent ruler and preserver of the human race, and especially his providing human beings with the ethical commonwealth as the means to their attainment of holiness, points to rightness on the cosmic and the personal levels, as does his role as righteous judge, both in this life and in the life to come.

Cosmic and personal rightness are also combined in the category of fascinans in Otto's theory of religion. This category refers on the one hand, as we saw, to the objective or inherent value of the holy, i.e., to its 'supremest right to make the highest claim to service', and to receive unqualified 'praise because it is in an absolute sense worthy to be praised' (H,52). The term Otto uses to designate this cosmic rightness of the religious object is 'august'. On the other hand, the category of <u>fascinans</u> focuses on the subjective value of the holy, i.e., on its character as 'saving'. It brings the promise and bliss of redemption through healing intimacy with itself, and this despite the awesome and distancing dread it also inspires.

Tillich's conception of the holy or the infinite as the ground of all value and the goal of every finite thing implies cosmic rightness, as well as a close connection between that and the cosmic pervasiveness of the religious object. Rightness on the personal side figures in his affirmation that religion is the outgrowth of man's awareness of his estranged state and of his yearning for New Being. It is also implicit in his analysis of morality's need for the motivating power of divine grace, with its promise of forgiveness and regeneration—two elements he takes to be prominent in every religion. We also noted that Tillich associates the certitude of faith with Otto's <u>fascinans</u>, referring thereby to the ecstatic lure of the ultimate and to the serene confidence and sense of utter fulfillment that faith bestows. This again suggests the category of rightness in its personal application.

(E) There is very little in Spinoza's theory, at least as he himself presents it, of the category of <u>permanence</u>. The eternality of God, and hence permanence on the cosmic side, is perhaps implicit in the other traits of God as portrayed in the seven dogmas, but it is not spelled out as such. 5.12 in the previous chapter shows a connection between cosmic permanence and personal primacy brought out by Spinoza in his book On the Improvement of the Understanding (1677; published right after Spinoza's death in that same year). But this connection is not referred to in the theory of religion developed in the Tractatus. Permanence on the personal side is perhaps suggested by the sixth dogma of universal faith, that all and only those who obey God are saved, but this is only the barest suggestion. The dogma does not state that such salvation is eternal, or that it bears in any way on the threats and contingencies of man's life in time. Spinoza hastens to declare, in fact, that the character of such salvation, i.e., whether it be 'natural' or 'supernatural', is a matter unimportant to faith. This is a question of truth which lies wholly within the domain of philosophy.

Kant does give recognition, in his own way, to the category of permanence by the stress he gives to an afterlife, as required for man's unending improvement in the moral life (and hence, for his moral happiness), and also for the conjoining of worthiness to be happy with actual happiness. Since God must preside over such an afterlife as righteous judge, personal and cosmic permanence are brought together in Kant's theory.

What Otto calls the 'subjective' meaning of fascinans, namely, the beatitude or salvation brought or vouchsafed to human beings by their experience of the holy, contains the seed of the category of permanence on the personal side. Otto notes that in a religion like Islam, salvation means 'the entering upon the "Allah" state of mind here and now', but also the expectation of a paradise to come. And the Christian gospel proclaims a salvation which is both to be experienced here and now and fulfilled by God hereafter. Salvation in religions like Hinduism and Buddhism means primarily the promise of ultimate unity with Brahman or entry into the state of bliss of Nirvana (H,166-167). But though there are such occasional allusions in Otto's thoughts on the nature of religion to the hope of living forever with the deity or entering into a state of being which lies beyond the bounds of time, he seems to take all of this more or less for granted and does not give it any particular prominence in the development of his theory. It is especially surprising that he gives so little explicit attention to the category of permanence on its cosmic side, i.e., that he scarcely relates it to the 'objective' meanings of the holy.[3]

Tillich alludes to the category of permanence on the cosmic level in his approach to the eternality of the divine. He asserts that this eternality is neither timelessness, nor the endlessness of time. Instead, it 'includes past and future without absorbing their special character as modes of time' (ST,I,276). Or again, 'The divine life includes temporality, but it is not subject to it. The divine eternity includes time and transcends it' (ST,I,257). By these statements Tillich means to say that God or being-itself occupies an eternal present which moves from past to future, but without ceasing to be present. In this way it can recreate the past by creating the future, since 'the past becomes something different through everything new which happens' (ST,I,276). Thus the moments of time which are 'dissected' in finite existence are united in the eternality of the infinite. And this leads, in turn, to the category of permanence on the personal level:

Faith in the eternal God is the basis for a courage which conquers the negativities of the temporal process. Neither the anxiety of the past nor that of the future remains. The anxiety of the past is conquered by the freedom of God toward the past and its potentialities. The anxiety of the future is conquered by the dependence of the new on the unity of the divine life. (ST,I,276)

It is apparent from the above that Tillich has tried to find a middle position between the two alternative meanings of permanence set forth in my theory of religion: timelessness or everlastingness. The divine eternity, in his view, 'includes' time while yet 'transcending' time. This suggests an interrelation of the categories of pervasiveness and permanence.

He also quite explicitly relates primacy to permanence by claiming that the divine omnipotence is eternity with respect to time, just as it is omnipresence with respect to space (a link between primacy and pervasiveness is thus also suggested). Were God not eternal, 'it would mean his subjection to a superior power, namely, to the structure of dissected temporality'. A God unable to anticipate every possible future, he goes on to say, would be 'dependent on an absolute accident'. Hence, he could not 'be the foundation of an ultimate courage. This God would himself be subject to the anxiety of the unknown. He would not be being-itself' (ST,I,274-275).

(F) The uncompromising rationalism of both Spinoza and Kant is strikingly reflected in the entire neglect of the category of hiddenness in their respective theories of religion. Otto, on the other hand, gives considerable emphasis to this category, at least by implication, through insisting on the equal importance of the nonrational meanings of encounter with the holy to its rational meanings. The holy is <u>mysterium</u> <u>tremendum</u>, 'aweful mystery'. And encounter with it strikes the mind with 'stupor', 'blank wonder', and 'astonishment' (H, 25-26). Thus does Otto conjoin cosmic with personal hiddenness.

A link drawn by Otto between the pervasiveness of the religious object and its character as <u>mysterium</u> has already been discussed. And a connection between hiddenness and uniqueness is implicit in the close association he makes between the mysteriousness of the holy and its being something inherently 'wholly other'. Otto also calls attention, as I did in the presentation of my theory, to a tension between hiddenness and rightness. For were the holy so utterly mysterious as to be completely unintelligible and incomprehensible, it could have no saving significance for mankind:

The mysterious obscurity of the numen is by no means tantamount to unknowableness. Assuredly the '<u>deus</u> <u>absconditus</u> <u>et</u> <u>incomprehensibilis</u>' was for Luther no '<u>deus</u> <u>ignotus</u>'. And so, too, St. Paul 'knows' the peace, which yet 'passeth understanding' (H,135).

The fact that rational schematizations of the holy are possible also shows that, despite its mystery, it is at least partially susceptible to human understanding and appropriation. So a tension between hiddenness and rightness is suggested from this direction as well.

Cosmic hiddenness is implied by Tillich's characterization of God as abyss, as the inexhaustible power and depth of meaning which resists comprehension in finite forms even as it 'gives to every particular meaning its reality, significance, and essentiality' (WIR,58). This suggested relation between hiddenness and pervasiveness is made more explicit by Tillich's statement that it is impossible to draw God 'into the context of the ego-world and the subject-object correlation', and thus to make him a clear-cut object of knowledge, because 'he himself is the ground and meaning of this correlation, not an element within it' (ST,I,272; see also WIR,138). So God's very nature as the ground of all being makes him forever elusive and mysterious. Hiddenness on the personal side is implied by Tillich's contention that existential doubt is a necessary structural accompaniment of all attempts to respond to the ultimate and to give expression to its meaning for human life. This doubt is made inevitable by the fact of the infinite distance between the finite and the infinite, and it is reflected in one of the criteria for the truth of religious symbols, that they imply an element of their own self-negation. In this way Tillich seeks to do justice to man's experience of the holy as something 'wholly other', 'mysterious', 'separated', and 'terrifying'.

In this section I have tried to exhibit some of the affinities between the new theory of religion proposed in this book and the theories of Spinoza, Kant, Otto, and Tillich, by indicating ways in which the categories of the new theory can be said to be implicit in aspects of the other theories. I have also mentioned some of the interconnections of these categories which, at least by implication, the other theorists have commented upon. What this section has amounted to, therefore, is a discussion of the extent to which the new theory satisfies a part of the third criterion for interpretive theories of religion, i.e., the extent to which it encompasses important theories of the past by bringing some of their main insights and contributions into the unity of its own perspective. As for the rest of the third criterion, to what extent this new theory builds upon and complements the earlier theories, that remains to be seen. This question will be explored in the next section through utilization of the other criteria.

2.   SOME STRENGTHS OF THE NEW THEORY

We have noted that all of the other theories of religion, in one way or another, contain or apply norms of religious judgment, in violation of the first criterion for interpretive theories of religion. A strength of my theory is that it does not contain such norms, nor does it make any attempt to rank one religious system over another or to assess the value of religion itself. It might be thought that the better religion would be the one which achieves the most precise balance among the six categories, avoiding as far as possible tensions among them. But the maintenance of such tensions might be important in religion, or at least in some religions, in order to do justice to the paradoxicality of the religious object as conceptualized or experienced. There is nothing in the theory itself which suggests that this would be in any way inappropriate or inadvisable, or, for that matter, that it would be any _more_ appropriate or advisable than the quest for as complete a consistency among the categories as they themselves will allow. Furthermore, no greater weight is given or implied by the theory to one or more of the six categories over the rest. While it is true that the theory articulates normative possibilities by allowing for such weighting in various religious systems, it does not itself actualize any of these possibilities.

But suppose, to take but one of the categories at random, that a system of thought were found not to contain any element of hiddenness, as that category is described by the theory. Would it not then be a bad religous system? Not at all. In that event, it would not even qualify as a religious system, assuming that the theory is right in its portrayal of the distinctive common role of objects of religious interest. It is one thing to interpret what is and what is not a religious system, and quite another to determine which is the better or best religious system. My theory has the virtue of keeping these two questions separate. If a system of thought should turn out not to be a religious system, as viewed by the theory, this simply means that its claims fall into a different province of reflection and inquiry than the religious one. It does not mean that these claims are any less (or more) significant or valuable in their own right.

In addition to its avoidance of normative implications, the new theory has the advantage of containing no explanation of why man is religious (the fourth criterion). It therefore carries out more exactly the task of an interpretive theory of religion than do the theories of Otto and Tillich, both of which fail to make a clear enough distinction between the interpretive and the explanatory elements they contain. The new theory also has the advantage over the theories of Spinoza and Kant of exploring some grounds of difference, and not merely of similarity, among religious systems (the sixth criterion). This is an advantage it shares with the other two theories.

Furthermore, the new theory adheres more closely to the eighth criterion than any of the other theories. Spinoza, Kant, and Otto, as we noted, tend to give too much of a theistic slant to their theories, while Tillich's theory is slanted too much in the other direction, in that it denies out of hand the possibility of straightforward theism in religion. Of course, Spinoza's theory does deny cognitive status to theism, but that is because it denies cognitive status to religion altogether. The focus of religious interest in his theory, however, is exclusively on the symbolism or imagery of the theistic God, which makes the theory provincial in its scope. The new theory has a more adequate generality than any of the other theories of religion, since it is slanted neither in a theistic nor a nontheistic direction.

Another advantage of the new theory is that it does not suffer from the reductive character of either Spinoza's or Kant's theory, thus abiding by the first part of criterion (9). But the second part of this criterion exposes an incompleteness in the presentation of my theory, namely, that I have not probed in any depth the interrelations of religion, as characterized by the theory, and such other cultural interests as philosophy, morality, science, or art. The new theory is thus at something of a disadvantage when compared with the theories of Otto and Tillich, both of which explore such interrelations in rich detail. It does not satisfy the second part of the ninth criterion as well as these two theories do. I am not saying that this kind of analysis could not be done in terms of the new theory; I am simply pointing out that it has not been done here.

However, I can make some brief suggestions about how the role of religion in relation to the other cultural interests might be understood in terms of my theory. One suggestion about a difference between morality and religion has already been made, in connection with the category of pervasiveness (see Chapter 7, section 4, and Kupperman 1971). My other suggestions will have to do with the relation of religion to the other cultural interests taken as a group, rather than singly. Something like Tillich's notion that religion provides the 'dimension of depth' or 'ground of meaning' by which other cultural endeavors are nourished, is implied by the conjunction of the categories of primacy, pervasiveness, and rightness in the new theory of religion. As we have seen, these categories mean that religion gives to a person or a group an object of final loyalty (primacy), a unified concept of the human self and its world (pervasiveness), and a sense of man's ultimate purpose and destiny (rightness). In other words, religion provides an overall structure of value and meaning within which the specific commitments of the other types of cultural activity can find their place, and from which they can draw significance, while still retaining their methodological autonomy and intrinsic importance.

Implicit in the category of permanence is another contribution religion can make to the various nonreligious cultural interests. No thoughtful person can escape the disturbing awareness that even the best results of his pursuit of cultural ideals, whether in art, philosophy, science, or morality, will suffer corrosion, if not extinction, by the relentless passage of time. This sense of being at the mercy of time might prove extremely debilitating for cultural life, were it not for the religious intuition of a power of permanence or preservation lying at the heart of things. And finally, the category of hiddenness implies a safeguard against cultural hubris or overweening confidence in the competence of the human mind and spirit to fathom or control the immensities of the world. The quotation from G. van der Leeuw in Chapter 7, Section 6 above is highly pertinent in this regard, as are Tillich's comments on finite cultural expressions as pointing beyond themselves to an infinite depth of meaning which they can at best only hint at, never exhaustively convey.

Of course, satisfaction of the second part of the ninth criterion would require more than such bare suggestions. And more specifically, it would require that the relation of religion to each of the cultural interests, considered individually, be elucidated. In order for me to do this properly, I would have to offer well-developed theories of the nature of each of the cultural interests, something I am unfortunately not prepared to do at present. The theory of religion I have presented in these pages is a step in the direction of a general theory of cultural interests and their interrelations, which remains to be worked out.

The new theory is quite explicit about what it would mean not to be religious, all or part of the time, and it can help us in deciding problematic cases (criterion (10)). This means that it has an advantage at least over Tillich's theory, so far as the first part of this criterion is concerned. For Tillich has trouble satisfying this part of the criterion with his 'larger' sense of religion. To be nonreligious in terms of the new theory would mean that a person, group, or system of thought has no focus of interest which exhibits all of the categories of the theory, on both the cosmic and the personal sides.

As for the second part of the tenth criterion, a problematic case like humanism (to cite one example) might be decided through use of the theory in the following way. Should humanism fail to exhibit the category of pervasiveness on the cosmic side, for instance, it would not be a religion in the full sense of the term. And it seems unlikely that the humanist would want to maintain that his focus of interest, mankind, is cosmically pervasive, though it might well be personally pervasive. He might also be reluctant to argue for the cosmic uniqueness of mankind, given the continuity of the development of all living things in modern evolutionary theory or the distinct possibility of intelligent but nonhuman forms of life on other planets. Also, the ephemeral character of the human species, as viewed by modern cosmology, might make the humanist unwilling to contend for mankind's cosmic permanence (or primacy). These are some suggestions of ways in which the new theory could structure an investigation of whether the particular problematic case of humanism is or is not a religion. Other cases could be approached in similar fashion. And it is worth noting that the new theory's precision and usefulness in this regard are not purchased cheaply by sacrificing the breadth called for in the eighth criterion. Since all of the other theories suffer from lack of an adequate generality, their satisfaction of this tenth criterion is to an extent bought at that price. The point has already been made in the case of Spinoza (see Chapter 3,

Section 6). So the new theory has the advantage over the other theories of satisfying both criteria equally well.

I do not think that the new theory of religion has any outstanding advantages over the other theories in terms of the remaining criteria. But it should be made clear that it does satisfy those criteria. It adheres to criterion (2) in its provision of a set of categories whose relevance to the nature of religion is exhibited by their central role in a variety of religious systems, as well as by their ability to bring into unified perspective some of the most basic features of the other four theories of religion. And the interconnections and tensions of these categories have been examined in some detail by reference to various religious systems. This examination has also helped to bring into perspective some aspects of the logic of particular religious systems (the fifth criterion). And obviously, more could be done in this regard through utilization of the categories of the theory. What I have said on this topic is programmatic and illustrative only. Finally, a balanced interpretation of the cosmic and the personal sides of religion has been given by the new theory's stress on both sides in the case of its categories, and by its insistence that both sides must clearly be present for an object of interest to function as an object of religious interest. The theory thus satisfies criterion (7).

In this section I have cited some strengths of my theory of religion, as compared with the other theories studied in this book. Others might want to assess my theory differently, and perhaps more severely. But when viewed in the context of the methodological discussion of the first two chapters and of the religions of the world, as well as against the background of the other four theories of religion, I am satisfied that the new theory does build upon and complement those theories, and that it makes a distinctive contribution of its own toward our understanding of religion in its generic character, as the expression of a basic kind of human interest. But even if this book (and especially its constructive part) has done nothing more than increase our appreciation of the importance, the difficulty, and the fascination of trying to comprehend the nature of religion, it has amply fulfilled its primary purpose.

Appendix: Some Criteria for Interpretive Theories of Religion

(1) An interpretive theory of religion should not contain norms of religous judgment.

(2) It should provide us with a structure of categories whose conceptual interplay, tensions, and connections can illuminate the nature of religous interests.

(3) It should encompass, build upon, or complement previous theories which have value and importance for clarifying the nature of religion or significant aspects of religion.

(4) It should not give a causal explanation of why man is religious.

(5) It should prove heuristically fruitful for investigating the logic of single religious systems.

(6) It should prove effective for helping to bring into perspective some of the grounds of difference and similarity among various religious systems.

(7) It should give equal stress to the personal and the cosmic sides of religion.

(8) It should be adequately general, not provincial, in its scope.

(9) It should enable us to distinguish religious interest from other basic types of human interest, and yet do justice to the interdependence of religious and other interests.

(10) It should tell us what it means not to be religious, all or part of the time, and aid us in deciding problematic cases.

	PERSONAL	COSMIC
UNIQUENESS	Contrasted with all else in one's life; held in awe as something radically separate or set apart in one's outlook or experience.	Claimed to have a singular and unparalleled place in, or in relation to, the cosmos as a whole.
PRIMACY	That object of loyalty 'to which final priority is assigned in the inevitable conflict of loyalties' (T. M. Greene).	Seen as the final reality, the root principle or power on which everything else depends and from which (or in comparison with which) everything else derives its relative status and significance.
PERVASIVE-NESS	Relates, or is expected to relate, crucially and intimately to every aspect of	Believed to suffuse and integrate the cosmos as a whole; affording a unified

	PERSONAL	COSMIC
PERVASIVE-NESS	life, bringing the diverse elements of life into a focused and integrated pattern.	conception of the world and of one's place within it.
RIGHTNESS	Defines human destiny and calls into judgment every person's life to the extent that it runs counter to or falls short of this destiny; gives assurance of a path or means for coping with the powers of evil and attaining life's true goal.	Regarded as a goodness, or a power of goodness, which lies at the heart of the world, and which is inviolable and saving.
PERMANENCE	Provides a definitive way of coping with the changeable and precarious character of human existence, and of coming to	Viewed either as timeless, i.e., transcending time, standing outside the temporal process altogether; or as everlasting, i.e.,

	PERSONAL	COSMIC
PERMANENCE	terms with the threat of death.	enduring through time but not threatened with extinction by time's passage.
HIDDENNESS	A depth and richness of experience which cannot be captured in words and which eludes conceptual understanding.	Seen as inexhaustibly mysterious and strange in and of itself; encompassing the unknown as well as the known.

Notes

NOTES TO CHAPTER 1:   THE TASK OF AN INTERPRETIVE
THEORY OF RELIGION

1. This characterization of analytical philosophy
    of religion will do for our purposes, but it is
    actually too narrow. The task of analytical
    philosophy of religion also includes assessment
    of the meaning and relations of the kinds of
    religious utterances which do not even pose
    questions of truth or falsity. Such utterances
    may either not be statements at all, or they
    may not be presented as proposals for belief.
    Examples would be utterances which express,
    declare, or seek to evoke emotions, attitudes,
    or intentions; or those which enjoin certain
    courses of action.
2. Findlay's critique is of Stace's _Mysticism_ and
    Philosophy, published in 1961. There are
    other aspects of this book he views quite
    favorably.
3. Freud, 1970 can also be found in _The Standard_
    Edition _of_ _the_ _Complete_ Psychological _Works of_
    Sigmund _Freud_, trans. James Strachey, Vol.
    IX (London: Hogarth, 1959), pp. 117-127.
4. In discussing the nature of religion in light
    of its alleged causes one would have to take
    care to avoid the genetic fallacy, which would
    uncritically identify later stages in the

development of religion with its earliest stage
of emergence, or which would confuse the causes
of a phenomenon with the nature of the phenomenon itself. Freud's analysis of religion's
nature tends to fall prey to this fallacy.
5. For what follows on the relation of the logic
of relgous inquiry to the logic of religious
discourse I am indebted to William Christian.
See his Meaning and Truth in Religion (Princeton, N.J.: Princeton University Press, 1964),
especially chapters V and VI.
6. The degree of cohesiveness may vary from
system to system, of course.

NOTES TO CHAPTER 2: SOME THEORETICAL OPTIONS

1. On the assumption that religion is a cultural
institution, Spiro (1966:98) offers a formal
definition of it as 'an institution consisting
of culturally patterned interaction with
culturally postulated superhuman beings'.
2. Classical goalfunctional analyses of religion
are contained in Durkheim 1915; Malinowski,
1948; and Radcliffe-Brown, 1939. See also
Kluckhohn, 1967 (copyrighted 1944).
3. The explanatory import of the goal-functional
method itself has been called into serious
question. A thoroughgoing and systematic
critique of functionalism as a method of explanation has been presented by Carl G.
Hempel, 1968. Some telling criticisms are also
contained in Melford Spiro's previously cited
article, 'Religion: Problems of definition and
explanation', and a useful brief overview of

criticisms and relevant literature is given in
Hans H. Penner, 1971.

4.   On basic claims see the brief discussion in
Chapter 1, section 7, above. An extensive
treatment of these, under the rubric of 'basic
proposals', can be found in Christian (1964),
Meaning and Truth in Religion, passim.

5.   Braithwaite states some other differences
between religious and moral assertions, but
none of them differentiates religion from
morality in any really crucial respect. For
example, one difference he states is that 'in
the higher religions, at least, the conduct
preached by the religion concerns not only
external but also internal behavior'. Thus, in
religion, there is 'intention to feel in a
certain way...'. But resolutions to feel in
certain ways gain their importance from the
fact that they are 'powerful reinforcements of
resolutions to act'. So the subservience of
religion to morality is again underscored. See
Braithwaite 1955:21-22.

6.   For a brief review of some of the criticisms
that have been leveled against Braithwaite's
theory see Frederick Ferré, 1961:124-129. A
more sustained criticism can be found in
Christian, 1964:136-142. The phrase 'distinctively religious valuations' is Christian's.
See the examples he gives on p. 141.

7.   Arnett argues throughout his book for the
autonomy of the religious mode of judgment
and attempts to counter in a number of places
views of religion which would subsume it under
some other mode. For his account of the
relations between religion and philosophy, and
religion and science, see esp. pp. 42-43 and

61-64. Chapters three and four of his book are devoted to the relations between religion and morality and religion and art, respectively.

NOTES TO CHAPTER 3: SPINOZA: RELIGION AS OBEDIENCE TO GOD

1. In the Preface to his Tractatus Theologico-Politicus Spinoza speaks of this point as 'the chief conclusion I seek to establish in this treatise...'.
2. Harry Austryn Wolfson notes that Spinoza here takes explicit issue with Moses Maimonides, who had taught that the scriptural law has two distinct objects, right thinking and right living. Spinoza eliminates the first from the scope of the faith that is taught by the Bible. See Wolfson, 1958, II, 328; and Maimonides, 1963, bk. III, chap. 27.
3. This statement contrasts again with the thinking of Maimonides, who held that the class of true prophets consists of those whose rational as well as imaginative faculties have reached a high state of perfection. See Maimonides, 1963, bk. II, chaps. 36-40. Maimonides' conception of the role of the faculty of imagination in prophecy, working through visions and dreams, reflects the theory of prophecy set forth by the Muslim philosopher al-Farabi. Spinoza presents much this same theory of the workings of imagination in prophecy, but in contrast both to al-Farabi and Maimonides, he discounts entirely any role for the rational faculty. See Ibrahim Madkour's

chapter on al-Färäbi in Sharif, 1963, I, 450-468, 463-466.

4. I have modified Elwes' translation somewhat in light of my own reading of the Latin text.

5. The notion of a philosophical elite who could attain to the essential hidden meanings of Scripture through reason and philosophical reflection, and thus who did not need to rely on Scripture's pictorial and sensuous language, as the masses must, was defended by such Muslim philosophers as Ibn Ṭufail and Ibn Rushd. See Majid Fakhry, 1970:301-302,315. Maimonides made a similar distinction between the religion of the masses and the religion of a wise elite. And as Leo Strauss states, he even went so far as to assert 'that the knowledge of God of which the general run of men is capable, and which is sufficient for them, has no cognitive significance whatever'. The reason for this conclusion is that, according to Maimonides, God has no positive attributes. See Strauss, 1965 (first published in German in 1930):170-171; and Maimonides, 1963, bk. I, chaps. 35,60; bk. III, chap. 28.

6. The technical meaning of 'obedience', it will be recalled, is quite heteronomous, external, or authoritarian, i.e., it 'consists in acting at the bidding of external authority'.

7. A version of this line of argument was suggested to me by William Christian, but I do not want to hold him to what I have done with it here. Some of Spinoza's arguments in defense of the second premise, which is the crucial one, can be found in E,II, 70-74 (propositions XXXIII-XXXVI). The words in quotes, both in the argument itself and in the

following paragraph, were quoted earlier, in
the last paragraph of section 3 of this
chapter.

NOTES TO CHAPTER 4: KANT: THE ROUTE FROM MORALITY TO RELIGION

1. A slightly enlarged second edition of this work
    appeared in 1794. It has been translated under
    the title of Religion Within the Limits of
    Reason Alone by Theodore M. Green and Hoyt H.
    Hudson, with Introductions by Greene and John
    R. Silber (New York: Harper and Row, Harper
    Torchbooks, 1960). I shall speak hereafter of
    this work as the Religion.
2. This book is based on the notebooks of three of
    Kant's students. He was in the habit of giving
    these lectures on ethics in the years 1775 to
    1781. Macmurray's Introduction can be con-
    sulted for further details.
3. Kant's concept of 'moral happiness', as set
    forth in the Religion, makes very questionable
    T. M. Greene's claim that 'Kant never refers
    to happiness save in phenomenal terms—as
    essentially associated with man's psycho-
    physical nature and his capacity for pleasure',
    or that 'there is in Kant no significant hint'
    of 'a doctrine of happiness or beatitude which
    the immortal part of us can enjoy'. The joy of
    continued improvement in the moral life, simply
    for its own sake, would seem to qualify for
    such a doctrine of happiness or beatitude.
    See Greene, 1975:55.
4. James Collins' comments (1967:142) in this
    connection are clarifying:

Kant found it necessary to give his own meaning to the widespread eighteenth-century search for the minimum of theology. Hume and the deists understood it to mean the quest for an irreducible set of doctrines on God and man's relations with him, which recommends itself to natural reason, and which constitues the philosopher's religion. Although he accepted the ideal of some irreducible theistic doctrines, Kant did not simply identify the acceptance of them with religion. This would make religion a highly theoretical and abstruse affair, in which only those of a philosophical cast of mind could genuinely participate. Even after a critical purification of doctrines, religion is a matter of the mind's disposition and the heart's practical response, bound up closely with the moral concerns which all men can appreciate and act upon. Kant repudiated the Humean split between popular and philosophical religion, since Rousseau taught him that religious reform can be carried on at the heart of every man's religious life, without segregating the religious position of the philosopher from that given in everyday belief.

Not only does this state very well Kant's position with regard to the natural theology of the time, it also sums up (in the last sentence) an important difference between Kant and Spinoza. I should add that I have found Collins' book very helpful in its discussion of Kant's views on religion.

NOTES TO CHAPTER 5: OTTO: RELIGION AS EXPERIENCE OF THE HOLY

1. The term Gefühl has a somewhat more extended sense than the English word 'feeling' for Otto, meaning something like a mode of awareness, a recognition, or a sense of something. I will continue to use the translation, 'feeling', but with the intention that it be understood in this more extended way.
2. This distinction is not explicitly made by Otto, but it is sometimes implied. He is not completely clear on the subject, but a possible interpretation is that he holds numinous ideograms to be a certain kind of schemata, in which case we would speak of 'nonrational' and 'rational' schemata, the distinction being more one of degree than of absolute difference in kind. In this interpretation, no religious experience is completely unschematized (which would be more in keeping with the Kantian notion of schematization), but some schemata (nonrational schemata or numinous ideograms) tend to call attention to the experience itself, as a relatively uninterpreted given. Others (rational schemata) serve to give a rational interpretation of the experience. If one agrees with this interpretation and prefers to do so, he can substitute 'rational schemata' where I have simply spoken of 'schemata'.
3. Other schematic concepts of a philosophical nature mentioned by Otto in Das Heilige, but not developed, are 'completion', 'necessity', and 'substantiality'. See H,112.
4. For more detail on Otto's defense of his claim that Christianity is the superior religion the

reader is referred especially to Chapters X and XI of Das Heilige.

5. For examples of notions which do 'fall to pieces' and are 'cut out' as the development of religion proceeds see H, 26-27,64, 122-124. The first two of these have already been mentioned parenthetically in the discussion of merely contingent modes of rationalization above. The third is rationalization by means of 'disgust', a rationalization which gradually gives way to more exalted conceptions of the holy. See also in this regard H,134, item (e).

6. Otto occupied posts in systematic theology at Göttingen, Breslau, and Marburg. Paul Tillich was for a time a colleague of his at Marburg.

NOTES TO CHAPTER 6:   TILLICH: RELIGION AS SELF-TRANSCENDENCE   IN   THE   DIRECTION   OF   THE   ULTIMATE

1. Adams quotes from 'Die Kategorie des "Heiligen" bei Rudolf Otto', Theologische Blätter 2 (1923), 11-12.

2. This passage, like many others in Tillich's writings, vitiates Frederick Ferré's complaint that Tillich's theory of religion as ultimate concern is incomplete and needs to be complemented with a category ('comprehensiveness') which can do justice to the referential character of religious concern. See Ferré 1970: 10-11.

3. In ST,III,283 Tillich notes two other roots of trinitarian thinking in the history of religions, in addition to the tension between concrete and universal symbolizations of the religious ultimate. These are: 'the symbolic

application of the concept of life to the divine ground of being' and the threefold manifestation of the ultimate 'as creative power, as saving love, and as ecstatic transformation'.

NOTES TO CHAPTER 7:   A NEW THEORY OF RELIGION

1.   The systems I have mainly in mind are those commonly identified as the 'great world religions', i.e., Buddhism, Christianity, Hinduism, Islam, Judaism, Taoism, and the like. I intend for these systems to be used as the principal measuring rods for gauging the adequacy of my theory. For with the theory I have sought to interpret the type of human interest which is of pivotal importance in these systems, as they exist in the present and as they have existed in the past. But what of the future? Is it possible that the character of religious interest might change in some fundamental respects as the future unfolds? I allow that this is possible; I do not presume to state what religion will be or must be for all time. The more limited task I have taken on here has required presumption enough.

2.   The original reference is Ibn Taymiya, _Majmu' al-Rasa'il wa al-Masa 'il_, Vol. I, Cairo, 1922.

3.   Suzuki points out that Rinzai is speaking here of the Man or Person or Self, i.e., the real Self which constrasts with the psychological self belonging to the finite world of reality. See p. 32.

4. Cf. also the Latin term <u>sacer</u> (English:
    'sacred'), whose root meaning is 'whole',
    'intact'.
5. Chan is here commenting upon and quoting
    from Fung Yu-lan's <u>Hsin</u> <u>li-hsueh</u>.

NOTES TO CHAPTER 8:   THE NEW THEORY IN RELATION TO
THE OTHER THEORIES

1. This statement can be compared with that of
    Plotinus, quoted as 1.10 in Chapter 7 above.
    See also the point about 'a mere incremental
    primacy' in Chapter 7, section 2.
2. It should be borne in mind, of course, that
    there is an important sense in which no cosmic
    role is accorded to the object of religion in
    Spinoza's theory.   See the discussion of
    Spinoza's theory in light of criterion (7), in
    Chapter 3, section 6.
3. Another example of this merely allusive or <u>en</u>
    <u>passant</u> way of referring to the category of
    permanence is H,228:   'The meaning of the
    Christian knowledge that is by faith lies in
    this, that Christ Himself, who really died was
    brought again by God to real life and perfected
    unto the glory of the eternal life of God; and
    that we live in expectation of the same with
    Him'.   This passage nicely conjoins cosmic and
    personal permanence.

References

Adams, James Luther (1965). Paul Tillich's Philosophy of Culture, Science and Religion. New York: Harper and Row.

Arnett, Willard E. (1966). Religion and Judgment: An Essay on the Method and Meaning of Religion. New York: Appleton-Century-Crofts.

Ballou, Robert O. (ed.) (1944). The Portable World Bible. New York: Viking.

Bellah, Robert (1958). 'The place of religion in human action'. Review of Religion 22, 137-154.

Bettenson, Henry (ed.) (1943). Documents of the Christian Church. London: Oxford University Press.

Bleeker, C. J. (1963). The Sacred Bridge: Researches into the Nature and Structure of Religion. Leiden: E. J. Brill.

Braithwaite, R. B. (1955). An Empiricist's View of the Nature of Religious Belief. Cambridge: Cambridge University Press.

Britton, Karl (1969). Philosophy and the Meaning of Life. Cambridge: Cambridge University Press.

Brown, Robert (1963). Explanation in the Social Sciences. Chicago: Aldine.

Bu, U Mya (1956). 'Major concepts of Buddhism', Orient Review and Literary Digest, Buddha Jayanti Number (3), 37-46.

Burtt, E. A. (1954). The Metaphysical Foundations of Modern Science. Garden City, New York: Doubleday, A Doubleday Anchor Book.

Campbell, Colin (1972). Toward a Sociology of Irreligion. New York: Herder and Herder.

Chai, Ch'u and Chai, Winberg (eds.) (1961). The Story of Chinese Philosophy. New York: Washington Square Press.

Chan, Wing-Tsit (ed.) (1963). A Sourcebook in Chinese Philosophy. Princeton, N. J.: Princeton University Press.

Christian, William A. (1941). 'A definition of religion', Review of Religion 5, 412-429.
_____ (1957). 'Three kinds of philosophy of religion', The Journal of Religion 37, 31-36.
_____ (1964). Meaning and Truth in Religion. Princeton, N. J.:Princeton University Press.
_____ (1965). 'Spinoza on theology and truth', In Robert E. Cushman and Egil Grislis (eds.), The Heritage of Christian Thought, 89-107, New York: Harper and Row.

Collins, James (1967). The Emergence of Philosophy of Religion. New Haven: Yale University Press.

Conze, Edward (1959). Buddhism: Its Essence and Development. New York: Harper and Row, Harper Torchbooks.

Cragg, Kenneth (1969). The House of Islam. Belmont, Calif.: Dickenson.

Douglas, Mary (1970). Purity and Danger: An Analysis of Concepts of Pollution and Taboo. Harmonsworth: Penquin.

Dupré, Louis (1972). The Other Dimension: A Search for the Meaning of Religious Attitudes. Garden City, N. Y.: Doubleday.

Durkheim, Emile (1915). The Elementary Forms of the Religious Life, trans. Joseph W. Swain. London: George Allen and Unwin.

Dye, James W. and Forthman, William H. (eds.) (1967). Religions of the World: Selected Readings. New York: Appleton-Century-Crofts.

Epstein, Isidore (1959). Judaism. Harmondsworth: Penquin.

Fakhry, Majid (1970). A History of Islamic Philosophy. New York: Columbia University Press.

Ferré, Frederick (1961). Language, Logic and God. New York: Harper and Brothers.

_____ (1970). 'The definition of religion', Journal of the American Academy of Religion 38 (March), 3-16.

Findlay, John (1966). 'The logic of mysticism', Religious Studies 2, 145-162.

Freud, Sigmund (1957). The Future of an Illusion. New York: Doubleday, Doubleday Anchor Books.

_____ (1970). 'Obsessive actions and religious practices', In Personality and Religion. William Sadler, Jr. (ed). New York: Harper and Row, Harper Forum Books.

Fromm, Erich, Suzuki, D. T., and de Martino, Richard (1970). Zen Buddhism and Psychoanalysis. New York: Harper and Row, Harper Colophon Books.

Gilkey, Langdon (1970). Religion and the Scientific Future: Reflections on Myth, Science and Theology. New York: Harper and Row.

Grant, Frederick C. (ed.) (1953). Hellenistic Religions. New York: Liberal Arts Press.

Greene, T. M. (1957). Moral, Aesthetic, and Religious Insight. New Brunswick, N. J.: Rutgers University Press.

Hamilton, Clarence H. (ed.) (1952). Buddhism: A Religion of Infinite Compassion. New York: Liberal Arts Press.

Hartshorne, Charles (1973). 'Analysis and cultural lag in philosophy', Southern Journal of Philosophy 11, (1-2), 105-112.

Hempel, Carl (1968). 'The logic of functional analysis', in Readings in the Philosophy of the Social Sciences, May Brodbeck (ed.), 179-210. New York: Macmillan.

_____ (1966). Philosophy of Natural Science. Englewood Cliffs, N. J.: Prentice-Hall.

Henry, Granville C. (1973). 'Nonstandard mathematics and a doctrine of God', Process Studies 3 (1), 3-14.

Holy Bible: Revised Standard Version (1952). New York: Thomas Nelson and Sons.

Horton, Robin (1964). 'Ritual man in Africa', Africa 34, 85-103.

Joyce, James (1964). Portrait of the Artist as a Young Man. New York: Viking.

Kant, Immanuel (1929). Critique of Pure Reason, trans. Norman Kemp Smith. London: Macmillan.

_____ (1930). Lectures on Ethics, trans. Louis Infield, with an Introduction by J. Macmurray. London: Methuen.

_____ (1956). Critique of Practical Reason, trans. Lewis W. Beck. Indianapolis and New York: Bobbs-Merrill, A Liberal Arts Press Book.

_____ (1960). Religion Within the Limits of Reason Alone, trans. Theodore M. Greene and Hoyt H. Hudson, with Introductions by Greene and John R. Silber. New York: Harper and Row, Harper Torchbooks.

Kegley, Charles W. and Bretall, Robert W. (eds) (1961). The Theology of Paul Tillich. New York: Macmillan.

Kelly, J. N. D. (1958). Early Christian Doctrines. New York: Harper and Brothers.

Kim, Ha Tai (1972). 'Transcendence without and within: The concept of T'ien in Confucianism', International Journal for Philosophy of Religion 3 (3), 146-159.

Kluckhohn, Clyde (1967). Navaho Witchcraft. Boston: Beacon.

Kupperman, Joel J. (1971). 'Confucius on the nature of religious ethics', Philosophy East and West 21 (2), 189-194.

Leeuw, G. van der (1963). Religion in Essence and Manifestation. 2 vols. New York: Harper and Row, Harper Torchbooks.

McDermott, Robert (1970). 'The religion game', Journal of the American Academy of Religion 38 (4), 390-400.

Maimonides, Moses (1963). The Guide of the Perplexed, trans. S. Pines. Chicago: University of Chicago Press.

Malinowski, Branislaw (1948). Magic, Science, and Religion and Other Essays. Garden City, N. Y.: Doubleday, Doubleday Anchor Books.

Masani, Rustom (1968). Zoroastrianism: The Religion of the Good Life. New York: Macmillan.

Otto, Rudolf (1958). The Idea of the Holy, trans.
    John W. Harvey. New York: Oxford University
    Press, A Galaxy Book.
Penner, Hans H. (1971). 'The Poverty of
    Functionalism', History of Religions 11, 91-97.
Pfleiderer, Otto (1886). The Philosophy of Religion
    on the Basis of Its History, trans. Alexander
    Steward and Allen Menzies. 2 vols. London and
    Edinburgh: Williams and Norgate.
Pickthall, Mohammed Marmaduke (1953). The Meaning
    of the Glorious Koran. New York: New American
    Library, A Mentor Book.
Plato (1961). Republic, trans. Paul Shorey, in
    Edith Hamilton and Huntington Cairns (eds.).
    The Collected Dialogues of Plato. Princeton:
    Princeton University Press.
Plotinus (1950). The Philosophy of Plotinus:
    Representative Books from the Enneads, Joseph
    Katz (ed.). New York: Appleton Century-
    Crofts.
Pollock, Frederick (1899). Spinoza: His Life and
    Philosophy. London: Duckworth.
Puligandla, R. (1971). 'Could there be an essential
    unity of religions?' International Journal for
    Philosophy of Religion. 2, 14-27.
Radcliffe-Brown, A. R. (1939). Taboo. Cambridge:
    Cambridge University Press.
Radhakrishnan, Sarvepalli and Moore, Charles A.
    (eds.) (1957). A Sourcebook in Indian
    Philosophy. Princeton, N. J.: Princeton
    University Press.
Renou, Louis (ed.) (1963). Hinduism. New York:
    Washington Square Press.
Schleiermacher, Friedrich D. E. (1928). The
    Christian Faith, H. R. Macintosh and J. S.
    Stewart (eds.). Edinburgh: T. and T. Clark.

Sharif, M. M. (ed.) (1963). A History of Muslim Philosophy. 2 vols. Weisbaden: Otto Harrassowitz.

Smart, Ninian (1958). Reasons and Faiths. London: Routledge and Kegan Paul.

_____ (1970). The Philosophy of Religion. New York: Random House.

Spinoza, Benedict (1951). The Chief Works of Benedict de Spinoza, trans. R. H. M. Elwes. 2 vols. New York: Dover.

Spiro, Melford E. (1966). 'Religion: Problems of definition and explanation', In Anthropological Approaches to the Study of Religion, Michael Banton (ed.), 85-126. London: Tavistock.

Strauss, Leo (1965). Spinoza's Critique of Religion. New York: Schocken; first published in German in 1930.

Swanson, J. W. (1967). 'Religious discourse and rational preference ranking', American Philosophical Quarterly 4, 245-250.

Tillich, Paul (1951-1963). Systematic Theology. 3 vols. Chicago: University of Chicago Press.

_____ (1952). The Courage to Be. New Haven: Yale University Press.

_____ (1954). Love, Power and Justice. London and New York: Oxford University Press.

_____ (1955). Biblical Religion and the Search for Ultimate Reality. Chicago: University of Chicago Press.

_____ (1957). Dynamics of Faith. New York: Harper and Row, Harper Torchbooks.

_____ (1959). Theology of Culture. New York: Oxford University Press.

_____ (1969a). My Search for Absolutes. New York: Simon and Schuster; paperback edition, 1969.

_____ (1969b). What Is Religion?, trans. James Luther Adams. New York: Harper and Row, Harper Torchbooks.

_____ (1973). 'The meaning and justification of religious language', In God, Man, and Religion, Keith E. Yandell (ed.), New York: McGraw-Hill. First published 1961 in Religious Experience and Truth, Sidney Hook (ed.). New York: New York University Press.

Turner, Victor (1962). Chihamba: the White Spirit Manchester University Press.

Vaught, Carl G. (1972). 'Hartshorne's ontological argument: An instance of misplaced concreteness', International Journal for Philosophy of Religion 3 (1), 18-34.

Wallace, Anthony F. C. (1956). 'Revitalization movements', American Anthropologist 58, 264-281.

_____ (1966). Religion: An Anthropological View. New York: Random House.

Whitehead, Alfred North (1957). Process and Reality. New York: Harper and Brothers.

Williams, John A. (ed.) (1963). Islam. New York: Washington Square Press.

Wolfson, Harry A. (1958). The Philosophy of Spinoza. 2 vols. in one. New York: Meridian; first published in 1934.

Zaehner, R. C. (1956). The Teachings of the Magi. New York: Macmillan.

Index of Names

Subject Index